RELIGION AND CULTURE IN THE MIDDLE AGES

*The Towneley Cycle*

Series Editors
Denis Renevey (University of Lausanne)
Diane Watt (University of Wales, Aberystwyth)


Editorial Board
Miri Rubin (Queen Mary, University of London)
Jean-Claude Schmitt (École des Hautes Études en Sciences Sociales, Paris)
Fiona Somerset (Duke University)
Christiania Whitehead (University of Warwick)

RELIGION AND CULTURE IN THE MIDDLE AGES

# The Towneley Cycle

## Unity and Diversity

PETER HAPPÉ

UNIVERSITY OF WALES PRESS
CARDIFF
2007

British Library Cataloguing-in-Publication Data
A catalogue record for this book is available from the British Library.

ISBN 978-0-7083-2048-8

Typeset by Florence Production Ltd, Stoodleigh, Devon
Printed in Great Britain by Antony Rowe Ltd, Wiltshire

For reson wyll that ther be thre –
A man, a madyn, and a tre.
Man for man, tre for tre,
Madyn for madyn; thus shal it be.
                    (*Annunciation*, 10/31–4)

I warne you, both man and wyfe,
That I am rysyng and I am life;
And whoso truly trowys in me,
That I was euer and ay shall be,
Oone thyng I shall hym gif:
Though he be dede, yit shall he lif.
                    (*Lazarus*, 31/51–6)

'There is nothing scholars love more than a giant, contradictory codex in which nothing adds up', Alfred Hickling on *The New Annotated Sherlock Holmes*.
                    (*The Guardian*, 4 December 2004)

End of *Harrowing* (25) and start of *Resurrection* (26), from Huntington MS HMI, fol. 101ʳ.

# CONTENTS

# SERIES EDITORS' PREFACE

Religion and culture in the Middle Ages aims to explore the interface between medieval religion and culture, with as broad an understanding of those terms as possible. It puts to the forefront studies which engage with works that significantly contributed to the shaping of medieval culture. However, it also gives attention to studies dealing with works that reflect and highlight aspects of medieval culture that have been neglected in the past by scholars of the medieval disciplines. For example, devotional works and the practice they infer illuminate our understanding of the medieval subject and its culture in remarkable ways, while studies of the material space designed and inhabited by medieval subjects yield new evidence on the period and the people who shaped it and lived in it. In the larger field of religion and culture, we also want to explore further the roles played by women as authors, readers and owners of books, thereby defining them more precisely as actors in the cultural field. The series as a whole investigates the European Middle Ages, from *c.*500 to *c.*1500. Our aim is to explore medieval religion and culture with the tools belonging to such disciplines as, among others, art history, philosophy, theology, history, musicology, the history of medicine, and literature. In particular, we would like to promote interdisciplinary studies, as we believe strongly that our modern understanding of the term applies fascinatingly well to a cultural period marked by a less tight confinement and categorization of its disciplines than the modern period. However, our only criterion is academic excellence, with the belief that the use of a large diversity of critical tools and theoretical approaches enables a deeper understanding of medieval culture. We want the series to reflect this diversity, as we believe that, as a collection of outstanding contributions, it offers a more subtle representation of a period that is marked by paradoxes and contradictions and which necessarily reflects diversity and difference, however difficult it may sometimes have proved for medieval culture to accept those notions.

# ACKNOWLEDGEMENTS

A work such as this incurs unquantifiable debts to many others who have worked in this field, and the Bibliography is an indication of how much I owe to those in whose footsteps I have followed. On a more personal note, I am very pleased to thank all those who have given me valued help, information and advice as I have worked on this project, particularly Richard Beadle, Garrett P. J. Epp, David Freemantle, Alexandra Johnston, Barbara Palmer and Elsa Strietman.

The frontispiece is reproduced by kind permission of the Huntington Library, San Marino, California.

# ABBREVIATIONS

| | |
|---|---|
| Beadle, *York* | *The York Plays*, ed. Richard Beadle (London: Edward Arnold, 1982) |
| Cawley, *Wakefield* | *The Wakefield Pageants in the Towneley Cycle*, ed. A. C. Cawley (Manchester: Manchester University Press, 1958) |
| Cawley and Stevens, *MS* | A. C. Cawley and M. Stevens (eds), *The Towneley Cycle: A Facsimile of Huntington MS HM1* (Leeds: University of Leeds, 1976) |
| *CD* | *Comparative Drama* |
| *EDAMR* | *Early Drama, Art and Music Review* |
| *ELH* | *English Literary History* |
| *EMD* | *European Medieval Drama* |
| *ET* | *Early Theatre* |
| *FCS* | *Fifteenth Century Studies* |
| *HLQ* | *Huntington Library Quarterly* |
| *JEGP* | *Journal of English and German Philology* |
| *JMEMS* | *Journal of Medieval and Early Modern Studies* |
| *LSE* | *Leeds Studies in English* |
| *MÆ* | *Medium Ævum* |
| *MED* | *Middle English Dictionary*, ed. Hans Kurath (Ann Arbor, MI: University of Michigan Press, 1954–) |
| *METh* | *Medieval English Theatre* |
| *MLN* | *Modern Language Notes* |
| *MLR* | *Modern Language Review* |
| *MLQ* | *Modern Language Quarterly* |
| *MP* | *Modern Philology* |
| *N&Q* | *Notes and Queries* |
| *PBSA* | *Publications of the Bibliographical Society of America* |
| *PMLA* | *Publications of the Modern Language Association* |

| | |
|---|---|
| *PQ* | *Philological Quarterly* |
| REED | Records of Early English Drama |
| *RORD* | *Research Opportunities in Renaissance Drama* |
| *SP* | *Studies in Philology* |
| Stevens and Cawley, *Plays* | *The Towneley Plays*, ed. Martin Stevens and A. C. Cawley, 2 vols, EETS, s.s. 13 (Oxford: Oxford University Press, 1994) |
| Tilley | M. P. Tilley, *A Dictionary of the Proverbs in English* (Ann Arbor, MI: University of Michigan Press, 1950) |

# Introduction:
# The Problem of Unity

To expect unity in a work as large as the Towneley Cycle raises a number of questions, and these questions may refer to a complexity of contexts, both in regard to the time of the cycle's inception and for the modern interpreter responding from a new and changing critical environment. Nor is it possible to answer many of these definitively even if the notion of 'unity' can be adequately described. Yet the object of this enquiry is to explore a range of different aspects of this work to see whether we can find it to be coherent, and in what ways, and also, in contrast, to establish discontinuities and inconsistencies which may not make for unity and which are nevertheless manifestly there. It is hoped that the idea of unity can be used here as a means of describing and perhaps reconciling a number of different approaches to the cycle. During the twentieth century the reputation of the Towneley Cycle grew immensely in spite of the discontinuities which are a substantial part of this discussion, and parts of it, at least, have provided intense intellectual stimulus, religious experience and much theatrical enjoyment, especially in schools and universities. In light of this, and hopefully for the benefit of future appreciation of this remarkable work, it seems highly desirable to consider as closely as possible how far it can be seen as coherent.

A number of critics have set out unifying features amongst whom Gardner (1974), Helterman (1981), Robinson (1991) and Stevens (1987) have been most stimulating in this study. Gardner, for example, describes the text as being 'one writer's plan', and sees the Wakefield Master as an overall reviser (2–3). The design he perceives reaches a climax in *Harrowing* (25) and *Resurrection* (26), which he characterizes as recognition and reversal on an Aristotelian model (120); he sees *Conspiracy* to *Dicing* as a tragic phase, and the following *Harrowing* to *Judgement* (30) as a triumphant one.[1] Alternatively, the work of A. C. Cawley, whose *The Wakefield Pageants in the Towneley Cycle* (1958) remains one of the most

perceptive and enduring contributions to the study of the plays, has often
led, paradoxically, to the separate consideration of the plays on which he
focused and to leaving the rest of the cycle to be relatively neglected.[2]
One of the objectives of this study is to attend to the qualities of plays
he did not discuss. We should also add that Cawley's book consolidated
the idea that the Towneley plays, named after the Catholic family who
possessed the manuscript from the seventeenth to the nineteenth centuries,
were firmly linked to Wakefield.

Beyond this there has been more recently a significant line of enquiry
which emphasizes disjunction. The perception of the variety within the
corpus goes back as far as the Surtees Society editors of the first printed
edition who commented in 1836 upon the diversity of language and
style. Rosemary Woolf also noticed the diversity commenting that 'even
when allowances are made for the accidents of transmission, it is fair to
judge Towneley an uneven and disjointed work'; she further comments,
'The only cycle in which the different styles and stages of revision have
not grown together into an organic whole is the Towneley Cycle.' This
comment is valuably perceptive, even though we might not be quite so
convinced about the organic wholeness of the other cycles as Woolf was.
David Mills, seeking to find some coherence, called it an 'idiosyncratic
assemblage of material'. However the more recent interest in disintegration
comes in part as a result of the REED project, which has revealed some
material which disturbs previous views of the cycle and also, significantly,
does not corroborate the well-established and persistent belief that Wakefield had and performed a cycle like the one at York. Instead the emphasis,
notably in the work of Barbara Palmer, has shifted towards a diversity
of possible origins and the proposal that Beverley and Doncaster, in Yorkshire, and Whalley Abbey, in Lancashire, were possibly points of origin
for different parts of the cycle. Such a concept has the interesting effect
of widening the possible provenance of the plays and in principle this
seems credible. Perhaps the most valuable outcome of this scepticism
about a unified practice is the view that we need to look at each play on
its own terms.[3] Much of what follows in this study is concerned with
doing just that.

However the critique on the idea of cyclicity embodied in Palmer's
approach, understandable in polemical terms, needs some qualification,
and this too will be a persistent theme here. The fact is that someone, the
compiler we may call him, saw this work as a whole, and in assembling
the parts at his disposal, he was striving to create something coherent. In
the main part of this enquiry I shall explore the idea that the uniformity

in respect of the copying of the manuscript, even if it is as late as the Marian period as has been recently suggested, points at least to a nominal unity.[4] Someone wanted to put together a cycle of plays recognizably like that in the York Register, whose existence dates from 1461–73, and perhaps of the Chester Cycle too. Whether this happened before or after the York Register was compiled is a matter of some speculation. However diverse the provenance of individual episodes, and however varied the conclusions we might reach about the authorship and intentions of individual episodes, there is no doubt in my mind that what we have was intended to be a cycle and to conform with a design from Creation to Judgement even if some or all of the individual plays were initially composed without a conscious purpose of contributing to such a cycle. This, I suggest, holds true even if the accumulated plays were never comprehensively performed in the form in which we now find them in the manuscript. Moreover, the process occurred even though recent comment arising from the revelations of the REED project has made it clear that cycle plays were comparatively rare in England – much less common than in parts of France and Germany in the corresponding period.[5]

Thus in some respects this cycle resembles the N Town Cycle, which, one could say, is held together partly by its ill-fitting banns, in as much as both seem to have been assembled without a direct connection with known arrangements for performance of the whole or of parts. Yet the same characteristic obtains for both. They were in the late medieval period apparently meant to be cycles and their existence is predicated upon contemporary assumptions about what a cycle ought to be like. But it is apparent that this intention to assemble a cycle did not necessarily result in a uniformity of texture. As Stephen Spector has put it, in discussing the rather similar state of the N Town Play, 'The eclecticism of the text does not preclude the possibility of thematic and artistic unity.'[6] A more pragmatic theory for the genesis of the cycle is offered by L. M. Clopper: 'Perhaps the Wakefield Master, or a disciple, prepared a passion sequence and the *Judicium* as Wakefield's Corpus Christi play and his Shepherds and Noah plays for other occasions; or perhaps there was a collection of Old and New Testament plays performed at Wakefield but not the entire sequence in the manuscript.' He adds, 'A substantial number of these texts are somehow associated with one another.'[7]

In the context of modern critical thinking the idea of unity is admittedly unfashionable in that so much critical theory has been directed towards deconstructing literary works even where they are apparently the work of an individual writer whose intentions might be plainly conceived, and

whose work may be measured against them. But the recent preoccupation
that a given work is formed and effective in as much as it is part of its
own time can help us in the consideration of the Towneley Plays, if only
we can identify with sufficient precision the features of the time of its
composition likely to bear upon it. If in the end the study undertaken here
does not confirm unity, it may, nevertheless, help us to describe more
accurately what we are actually experiencing when we encounter the text
and in this way to construct a meaning for it.

We may therefore begin by putting the problem of the unity of the
Towneley Cycle as simply as possible. It has survived in only one manuscript, now in the Huntington Library in California (MS HM1). This is
apparently coherent in that most of it is written in the hand of one scribe
who clearly saw the work through, more or less as one continuous process
from start to finish. Though there is some evidence that the scribe changed
or evolved his procedures somewhat as he went along, there was an unmistakable attempt to make the manuscript look all of a piece, not least
by means of the elaborate illuminated capitals at the start of most of the
individual plays, which were allowed for in the management of space on
the pages, and by other general features of the layout.[8] The work is written
in Yorkshire dialect throughout and it presents the Christian narrative of
salvation from the Creation to Judgement Day, though there are some
queries about the sequencing of certain individual episodes. The linguistic
characteristics in the text allow us to be fairly certain that it originates in
or near Wakefield, and when we come to look at it in some detail later
on we shall find that there are a number of features which distinguish its
linguistic practice with some consistency from that of the York Plays. We
shall also be considering some minor topographical details in the plays
which point to a Wakefield provenance.

Although the date of the extant copy is somewhat controversial, it seems
likely that the text was written out in the mid-sixteenth century, perhaps
in the reign of Queen Mary. But the possible date or dates for the composition of the individual plays within the cycle is a much more thorny
problem to which we shall return. We come to greater uncertainty when
we consider varieties of literary and dramatic style between plays and also
within individual plays themselves. This is in marked contrast to the much
more even style and versification found, for example, throughout the
Chester Cycle. Our study of the Towneley plays will not allow us to pre-
sume unity of dramatic style for them. The exploration of such differences
and discontinuities in this cycle is one of our chief objectives here. In part,

such irregular features of Towneley turn upon the contribution of the so-called Wakefield Master whose individual, not to say idiosyncratic, contribution is palpable in about one-third of the plays, but whose influence may have extended more widely through the cycle, though this is a matter of some debate.[9] In dealing with this writer we need to look at two general aspects which are not too easy to separate. On the one hand there are the verbal characteristics of his work, and on the other there is the dramatic imagination which informs his choices about types of scene and types of theatrical effect. The overall impact of his interventions must depend in some degree upon the interaction of these.

It is also imperative, however, to be aware of the many plays which do not bear evidence of his characteristic work. In fact these make up the majority of the cycle, as reference to Figure 1 makes clear. As we shall see in Chapter 1.2 there are fourteen plays in this category, and taken with the six which are substantially borrowed from York, this gives a total of twenty plays out of thirty-two.[10]

This manuscript may have been conceived as a continuous piece, a written work to be read; since it was put together almost entirely at a specific and relatively short time, it provides an insight into how someone conceived the cycle at that particular moment, whatever the longer history of its parts. But when we come to consider the relationship between this written text and the performance which in all probability was the chief experience of it, a number of fascinatingly complex issues arise. We have to consider how the plays might have been presented, what the characteristics of performance may have been, and whether there is coherence in the theatrical imagination underlying the *mise-en-scène* as distinct from the composing process by which the cycle was put together as a text for reading. We may ask whether the individual plays are conceived for performance on the same type of stage. There is also the possibility that though there may have been a Corpus Christi Cycle performed at Wakefield in the mid-sixteenth century, as the very limited non-dramatic documentation suggests, it is not necessarily the case that this surviving text conforms with what was actually to be seen in performance at that time.

The study of the non-dramatic records at Wakefield has in fact been a rather muddled affair. It now seems that certain items invented by J. W. Walker have misled scholars as to the nature of the local arrangements. His inventions appeared to bring the practices at Wakefield much closer to those at York than can now be justified. The authentic records are these:

1556

Item a payne is sett that everye crafte and occupacion doo bringe furthe /
theire pagyauntes of Corpus Christi daye as hathe bene heretofore used and
to / gyve furthe the speches of the same in Easter holydayes in payne of /
everye one not so doynge to forfett / xl s.

1559

Item a payn ys layd þat gyles dollefe shall brenge In or Causse to be broght
þe regenall of Corpus Christy play befo[re] þis & wytsonday In pane . . .
Item a payn ys layde þat þe mest[er]es of þe Corpus Christi playe shall
Come & mayke thayre a Countes before þe gentyllmen & burgessus of þe
to[wn] / before thys & may day next In payn of evere on not so doynge –
xx s.[11]

These entries confirm that there was a Corpus Christi sequence of plays
at Wakefield in the middle of the sixteenth century. They also link the
plays with the craft guilds, though independent corroboration for this is
somewhat scanty. It does not necessarily follow, however, that the text
we have is that authoritative one which was to be brought forth by Giles
Dolleffe. The 'regenall' of 1559 may be a text of a whole cycle, but it
could also be the text of one play for one guild. Indeed the 1556 phrase
'gyve furthe the speeches' may mean only 'issue the actors' parts to the
actors', as Peter Quince does in *A Midsummer Night's Dream* (1.2.80–1).[12]
There are thus doubts about whether the Towneley manuscript has a similar
status as that compiled at York. Nevertheless, further evidence that a play
sequence associated with Corpus Christi, though not necessarily performed
on that feast day, did exist at Wakefield may be found in the letter from
the Ecclesiastical Commissioners at York of 17 May 1576. For ideological
reasons associated with Protestant orientation, this placed restraint upon
an intended performance in Whitsun week of 'a plaie commonlie called
Corpus Christi plaie, which hath bene hereto fore used':

> . . . that in the said playe no Pageant be used or set further wherein the
> Maiestye of god the father, god the sonne or god the holie ghoste or the
> administration of either the Sacramentes of Baptisme or of the lordes Supper
> be counterfeited or represented / or any thinge plaied which tende to the
> maintenaunce of superstition and idolatrie.[13]

Objections have rightly been raised about whether this fully corroborates
the Burgess records. What is said here constitutes a presumption about
the existence of a cycle, rather than proof that one actually existed. The
reference, unfortunately, does not tell us what the writer actually knew

about what was in fact performed at Wakefield. He may not have known very much, but he does imply a large Corpus Christi play with 'pageants' within it.[14]

In trying to focus these matters we should consider, in a preliminary way and rather briefly, the relationship between the Towneley Cycle and other surviving examples of cycle plays, or their remnants; in an approach to the question of authorship, we should also address some ideas about the function of an author in medieval times. This is not the place to attempt a full account of the development of cyclic form, but we should note that if Towneley were created in the fifteenth century in a form which is similar to that preserved in the manuscript, it must have been a relatively early example, and as we shall see there were very few identifiable precedents other than the York Cycle.[15]

There is indeed little doubt that York is the closest analogue to Towneley. The language of the two has a great deal in common and the distance between York and Wakefield is but little (about twenty-five miles). This means that anyone working on the composition, compilation or presentation of Towneley could hardly have been unaware of the other cycle, which was indeed generally well known by the mid-fifteenth century, if not before. The intimacy is such that in six individual episodes the York version has been taken over in close detail, though we shall consider later that the nature of the incorporation is not uniform. There is also the possibility that several other episodes were influenced by details from York, as we shall see. It seems likely from the York records that by 1415 an extensive cycle was in existence there and it is one which bore a substantial, but not comprehensive, resemblance to the surviving text, which has been dated 1463–77.[16] But the nature of the York manuscript differentiates its function sharply from its Wakefield counterpart. The York codex is an accumulation of texts from about fifty identifiable guilds and its function was to be a register, a standard even, against which subsequent versions for performance could be measured or checked. Its compilation was no doubt a civic act, one by which the city corporation sought to maintain control over what was already happening in the streets. It was not meant to be a book for reading, so much as a work for reference and practical use, and as such there are distinct signs of updating, some of it well into the sixteenth century, a generation and more after the manuscript was first assembled.[17] In all probability the guilds owned the text of their individual plays and the York Register was a means of stabilizing all such texts, especially as there were changes from year to year; we also know from the records that performances were undertaken frequently, though not quite as frequently as every year without fail. The authorship of York is varied, as can be seen by the many different dramatic and literary textures to be found throughout, though Richard Beadle, its most recent editor, has expressed interest in many homogeneous features of its language.[18] There can now be little doubt that the mode of performance at York was processional, each play being performed following a regular route through the city on or from a pageant wagon at each of the twelve or more locations designated by the city ahead of the day of performance. Moreover, there was a close link with the feast of Corpus Christi: it was normally performed on that day throughout its history.

It has long been tempting, then, to see Towneley as parallel to York, but the truth is that its differences are remarkable both in terms of the purpose of the text and in the possibilities of performance, and the evidence for continuous presentation over more than 150 years found at York cannot be equalled at Wakefield. Nevertheless we need to bear in mind that in some respects Towneley follows York, especially in the selection of incidents. Further parallels can be adduced from the two other extant cycles in English, N Town and Chester.[19] But once again though these cycles support Towneley as being similar in some respects, and as evidence that Towneley was part of a recognizable mode, they also show that each cycle has many individual characteristics and that the surviving texts cannot be treated as though they had the same status, or relate to a uniform mode of performance. Moreover, the relationship between the surviving texts and possible performance is a variable and often uncertain one.

The N Town cycle has not been satisfactorily located in a town or city, though its language is demonstrably that of East Anglia, probably not far from Norwich. Its manuscript, dating from late in the fifteenth century, is largely the work of one scribe, most probably an ad hoc compilation of work already in existence. It does follow the pattern of Creation to Judgement Day, and it includes many of the episodes common to the other known cycles, including Towneley and the lost cycle from Beverley (also in Yorkshire). Although there is a rich accumulation of stage directions in some episodes, there are many problems about the nature of performance of this cycle as a whole, and it is tenable that there never was a performance of the kind implied in the banns and the extant text. The existence of the text in this form is an important reminder that we should not take the status of Towneley for granted in terms of the nature of its manuscript and the possibility of performance. The late records pointing to performances at Wakefield in and after 1556 tell us little or nothing about the development of the cycle in the fifteenth century. Moreover the nature of the relationship between the surviving Towneley text and any possible performances is problematic, particularly, as we shall see, over the question of the differences in dramatic texture in the cycle and the question of whether there ever was any one performance of the cycle in its present form. There is also doubt about whether putative performances were processional like those at York and Chester, or whether some or all of the individual plays might have been conceived for a fixed location with a number of centres of interest. Such a contrast in methods of perform-ance does indeed seem to be true for episodes in N Town, especially in the Passion sequence. The reference quoted above for 1556 may suggest that there was a processional performance by the guilds at Wakefield, though it leaves many doubts about what went on.

If it were indeed the case that Towneley was generated in the fifteenth century, alongside and in touch, so to speak, with the development of York, it comes at a very early point in the development of the cycle drama. It is possible that there was also a precedent at Beverley, which is about forty miles from Wakefield, but the evidence is not conclusive. There are early references at Beverley to a pageant of the play of Corpus Christi in 1377 and 1390, with thirty-eight named guilds participating. But there is no list before 1520 to indicate which episodes were included in perform-ance, and no text has survived. Perhaps because there were as many as thirty-eight plays before 1400, and because the Saddlers had a *Creation* in 1441, we may suppose that there was a cycle comparable to York's early enough to provide a model for the Towneley compilers.[20]

The nature of the Chester Cycle cannot be substantiated much before 1422, and scholars have dated all the surviving complete texts as later than 1590 with the strong possibility of a three-day original which may have been created in the period 1521–31.[21] It remains distinctly problematic as to whether Chester was comparable to York in the fifteenth century. Even though this cycle is largely independent of other surviving examples, there must be a possibility that its compilation was dependent upon other models, such as York, and, it must be said, possibly Towneley.

The only other serious contender for chronological precedence in England is the *Ordinalia*, the cycle in Cornish. This may be as early as the last quarter of the fourteenth century.[22] However, it has to been seen as rather separate from the cycles in English in terms of its selection of incidents, which runs from the Creation to the Resurrection, and omits the Nativity and the Last Judgement. It is also very distinctive in its playing arrangements which were apparently intended for performance in the round using a circular arena (the *plen-an-gwary*) with fixed locations, whose designations could be changed for the three days required for performance. We can only speculate whether the remoteness of Cornwall was a barrier to imitation at Wakefield, but it is clear that a number of features of the *Ordinalia* are shared with continental plays, especially in France and the German-speaking states. In these there were some developments in the fifteenth century such as the *Passion d'Arras*, though the most significant in France does not occur until Arnoul Gréban's *Passion* written in about 1450.[23]

These considerations suggest some specific contextual features for Towneley. It is virtually certain that it was dependent upon York in a number of aspects; we shall explore these more fully in Chapter 1.2. Other precedents are more remote and the evidence for there being significant forerunners, other than York, is limited. At most we can say that there was some possibility that if Towneley originated before the middle of the fifteenth century there might have been a staging tradition other than the York processional mode that could have been an influence.

The act of creating the manuscript, even if it is as late as the reign of Queen Mary, may be better understood by considering medieval approaches to authorship. In the pre-printing era making a manuscript was part of a disseminating process and this role very often involved passing on what had been said before. This meant that a book was often an embodiment of the work of others which it was desired to reproduce, but also perhaps to change somewhat. The distinction between *auctores*, authors or authorities, and *compilatores*, those who compiled or arranged books, was an important one and had a significant function. The compiler, who often placed the responsibility for the material in the work on the authorities upon which he relied, was engaged in the arrangement of the work, especially the relationship between parts, making them significant and accessible.[24] In spite of the deference shown to authorities, this often added much to what was being transmitted. As Towneley has substantially only one scribe it is quite possible that he was the compiler following this well-established function. Underlying his work is the creative work of the poet or poets, itself in part a re-handling of other poetical work, and beyond that, the authority of patristic writings and exegetes and finally of the Bible itself, especially the Gospels. In this particular case there are also the substantial transplanted items from York, which were in fact modified in the transcription in various ways. But we are dealing here with a special form of writing, a play text, which by its very nature tends to remove the voice of the compiler and substitute instead the many voices of participants in the performance.[25] There is also the input of actors, who then as now, no doubt, wanted to change whatever the writer offered them.

It is not at all clear whether the principal scribe was in fact the compiler of the Towneley Cycle. He obviously was able to copy his material consecutively from beginning to end, with a few very minor discontinuities. Such a process would be consonant with both copying an existing manuscript and also putting the individual plays in the order he chose once he had assembled them from whatever source, ready for copying. Whichever was the case, the manuscript as it stands follows some of the conventions of its medieval predecessors. As Stevens has pointed out, the scribe begins the manuscript with a prayer: *In dei nomine Amen. Assit principio sancta Maria meo.* [In the name of the Lord, Amen. May Holy Mary be present at my beginning.][26] The stage directions are often in Latin, presumably because the volume was meant to be read. A number of the plays begin with the conventional words 'incipit' and 'explicit'. The illuminated capitals which begin most of the plays are also a significant feature of the visual impact of this manuscript, and they obviously could have had nothing to do with performance and no relevance to it. It is apparent that frequently these capitals, which in some cases almost fill the page, were put in first and the text was then fitted in around them (as the frontispiece shows). Moreover their elaborate decoration does not appear to have any specific relation to the plays themselves. The presence of rubrication within the manuscript is another visual feature with scribal precedents. In short, the preparation of the manuscript seems to have been governed largely by conventions of late medieval book making. We need to weigh this alongside the difficulty of regarding this particular text as the 'regenall' mentioned in the 1559 record noted above. While it may embody some theatrical practice, these features suggest that it was manifestly not made primarily for use in a performance, and it shows very little sign of having been marked or annotated in the light of the exigencies of performance such as we find with John Clerke's additions to the York Register.[27]

We may of course regard this book-making process as unifying at least as far as the text is concerned, but in order to consider the unity of the cycle as a whole we need to examine a number of the features raised here in more detail. In Parts I and II we shall therefore review the nature of the manuscript and the theatrical possibilities of its contents. This will be followed in Part III by an approach to a variety of themes which appear in a number of plays and may help to link episodes together. Part IV brings the earlier discussion into focus by evaluating the relationship between the unifying elements so far considered and some of the disjunctive factors.

# I

## THE TEXT

# 1

# Prologue:
# Place and Date

**B**oth the attribution of the cycle to Wakefield and the date of its composition have proved controversial, and since the arguments are by no means over, it seems best to set out at this point what can be regarded as secure. The references to plays at Wakefield in 1556, 1559 and 1576 quoted in the Introduction attest the acting of a Corpus Christi play, but they are sufficiently imprecise to leave some doubt about whether the plays in the manuscript are the ones concerned. As a term 'Corpus Christi Play' covers a multitude of differences, it is best to interpret it as something that was presented on Corpus Christi day and not necessarily a Creation to Doomsday cycle by any means. The 1576 letter from the Ecclesiastical Commissioners in particular seems rather remote from the plays as we have them and it is composed in such general terms that it may be asked whether the writer of it really did have a grasp of what was actually going on, in spite of the political need to impose restrictions to which he was responding. One can, however, say that these documents support the idea that that there was a play at Wakefield in the mid-century, and they give some indication that guilds were involved in performance, even though the nature of the performance is uncertain.

The manuscript itself has been held to add some corroborating detail. The word 'Wakefeld' [*sic*] appears at the end of the heading of *Creation* (1) and *Noah* (3). This may give some support to the attribution, but there is still the doubt that placing this word at the beginning of *Noah* as well as at the beginning of the first play may imply that the other plays in the manuscript could not be so attributed, and this difficulty has given some support to the idea that the cycle was collected from a number of places around the manor of Wakefield which was its centre.[1] We note elsewhere that since a quire is lost from the beginning of the manuscript *Creation* may not have been the first play.

In other places the text does have some further local allusions which Cawley has linked to Wakefield, though it must be admitted that they are thinly spread and may not apply to the whole. These are 'Gudeboure at the quarell hede' (2/369), a reference to Goodybower Lane near a former quarry; 'ayll of Hely'(12/352), pointing to the place-name of Healy in the West Riding; and 'Horbery shrogys' (13/657) after Horbury, a town three miles south-west of Wakefield.[2] Specific though these may seem, only the first is in Wakefield itself. Two further references offered by Cawley are rather less convincing: the 'crokyd thorne' (13/581), thought to refer to a tree in Mapplewell or Horbury, seems rather too vague to be conclusive. The mention of Watling Street by Second Demon, on his way to Judgement Day, is also somewhat uncertain (30/186). Even though the *Oxford English Dictionary* allows a wider use for Roman roads than exclusively the main route from Dover to Wroxeter as it is commonly referred to nowadays, the dating of the examples given are rather late for these plays, and there is a possibility that in mentioning it the poet had in mind not a Roman road in or near Wakefield, but the Milky Way which was another referent for the name. However, all these possibly local references do come in passages which can be attributed to the Wakefield Master. That in itself may hide another limitation. Even if he wrote extensively in the corpus and he did come from Wakefield, it does not follow that all the plays necessarily did, nor is it certain, from this topological evidence, that the compilation of the whole codex was necessarily made there.

Although the date of the manuscript offers some problems, the dialect in which it is written may point to Wakefield. We shall hope to show that this language, which is interestingly differentiated from exemplars written at York, does seem to indicate that the scribe was using some north Midland forms rather than the northern forms found in the York Cycle. This may not point certainly to Wakefield itself but it does help to indicate the area in which the text was copied, and perhaps reflects the area of composition. It makes it more likely that whatever was the precise nature of the Corpus Christi play the York Commissioners warned about, the extant text is probably related to it in some way.

The *terminus a quo* for the plays would seem to be the first half of the fifteenth century. This was suggested by Frampton on the grounds of some aspects of clothing and fashion in the passage interpolated into the York original by the Wakefield Master. He finds the women's horned headdress (30/391), pleated and stuffed gowns (30/419–20) and the short haircuts, bristled like hogs (30/459), all point to a period around 1420–40, which match quite well the indications about copying from *York*.[3] But the evidence he gives does not necessarily mean that all the plays were written at this time. If we assume that the compilation was much later there is plenty of scope for individual parts to have been written at different times – indeed at very different times – over more than a century. In his edition of the plays written by the Wakefield Master, Cawley has produced some useful evidence regarding the dating of the language of these parts of the cycle.[4] From this it appears that they were composed in the fifteenth century. Once again this opens up a wide gap of time for changes to take place before the copying of the manuscript in its present form.

To sum up these considerations we can say that there are distinct probabilities in both place and date. It seems likely that parts of the text were associated with Wakefield and that the dialect does not make this impossible. Similarly some of the plays were probably written in the fifteenth century. On the other hand the uneven texture of the plays and the limits of the evidence mean that we ought to extend these conclusions to the whole cycle with some caution. This is in line with doubts raised about coherence we have noted in the critical record.

Let us now turn to the provenances of the work and a more detailed consideration of features of authorship.

# 1.1

# The Manuscript

To begin with, we need to review the manuscript to see how far it supports and suggests unity and gives indications of coherence and structure. We can do this by first discussing the layout and conventions so as to observe the objectives of the compiler. Then follows some consideration of the discontinuities in the text: some of these are accidental and need to be seen as such. Finally there are some deliberate alterations which may reflect purposeful changes of intention.

Before embarking on these topics, however, we should deal with a few general aspects. As regards the date of the manuscript itself, recent work has suggested that the traditional date of late fifteenth or early sixteenth century needs to be moved later than had previously been thought: perhaps to the reign of Queen Mary.[1] The implications of this view are considerable because it separates the manuscript by a long period from the presumed date of composition of some parts of the cycle which lies in the mid-fifteenth century.[2] It would mean that there was plenty of time for change and development before the compiler put this text together, albeit that in our present state of knowledge we have very little with which to fill such a gap.

Two features bear upon this. One is that at one point the Towneley *Harrowing* is apparently drawn from an earlier version than the corresponding wording of the York Register. It is all the more impressive because John Clerke, the Common Clerk at York, emended the York text in a way which brings it back to the version in Towneley. The wording of Towneley was probably derived from a guild text at York which was in existence before the York Register was copied in 1463–77.[3] The second aspect is the physical state of parts of the manuscript which show what Wann called 'hard use'. Several pages are very worn and thumbed and this suggests that for some reason or other they were much handled. Since these pages are rather isolated it is quite difficult to explain this, but it does mean that the text was not simply laid aside once it was created. It may well be that this feature points away from this version of the cycle being the one used as 'regenall', as mentioned in the 1559 note.[4]

The other preliminary is to attend briefly to the history of the manuscript after the sixteenth century. This is covered in detail by Wann (150–2) and by Stevens and Cawley (*Plays*, p. xvi), but it is useful here to note that it came into the possession of the Lancashire Towneley family, who were Catholic. The pressmark on the first page indicates that the volume was owned by Christopher Towneley (1604–74).[5] It was no doubt the Towneley family's religious allegiance which led them to preserve the volume after the mystery cycles had gone out of fashion and performance had been discontinued. Without this, and in the light of the very limited amount of non-dramatic documentation, we would have had very little idea of the nature and scope of this cycle. It was only when the family first parted with the text in 1814 that the importance of its survival began to be appreciated more widely in the nineteenth century.

Turning now to the layout and structure of the manuscript, we find that there are a number of features which are consistent throughout and which thus argue for the coherence of the compiler's and the scribe's intentions. It should be said that if the text was indeed written out in the mid-sixteenth century we can show that conventions for play manuscripts had by then become quite well established. For example, the speech headings are uniformly arranged in black to the right of the page, and the speeches are separated by means of red horizontal lines across the page.[6] The use of red for this latter purpose is fairly consistent, but sometimes it occurs in all or part of individual names. Red is also used for the word 'explicit' at the end of twenty-one plays, and the same word appears in black for all the other plays, except that we cannot check the five plays whose ending is lost. The use of 'incipit' is rather less consistent. It is present in sixteen plays, having a decorated initial 'I': plays 8–25 (except 18 and 23). Cawley and Stevens suggest that the scribe's use of rubrication changed after play 7 (*Prophets*), which has lost its proper ending. Besides the first appearance of 'incipit', in play 8 and most of those following, there occurs a miniature 'E' (red capital) inside the 'E' of 'Explicit' at the end of play 8 and all the remaining plays except 31, and from play 8 onwards the formula 'Explicit' plus the name of the preceding play comes at the end of each item.[7] From play 8 onwards the first speaker's name is in red. The effect of these changes in procedure is to make the beginning and end of each play more noticeable.

The metrical structure is indicated by the bracketing of rhymes in black ink, though in a few places this breaks down, and it is likely that the scribe occasionally had some difficulty in managing his copy. This may be a reflection of the very complex versification in some passages.[8] At present there are 132 leaves in the manuscript. Twenty-eight have been lost for various reasons, and the complete text had a total of 160 leaves in twenty quires of eight. There are quire signatures throughout and from these it is clear that the first quire has been lost. This means that there is no main title page and we do not know how the compiler wanted the book to be named. Nevertheless, he has been careful with the individual play titles which are consistently large in size, up to about one and a quarter inches in height. They are all in red, except for the title for *Judas*, play 32, the anomalous and incomplete last play.

The elaborate initial letter of each play, which we have already mentioned, is a significant feature of the manuscript. This forms part of the visual effect which is essential to this text. For *Creation* (1) and *Mactatio Abel* (2) these first letters are in a neatly boxed form, perhaps copied from blocks used in a printed book, but thereafter the initial letters of all the succeeding plays are in complex and varying designs with strapwork. This practice begins with a fairly modest specimen for *Noah* (3), but the artist became more and more adventurous as he went along and his inventiveness led his pen through increasingly fanciful but non-realistic decorations. By the time he reached *Thomas of India* (28) the initial 'H' stretches over about two-thirds of the page. This progression in design suggests that the writer was pursuing a plan of integrating the whole work as he went along. Such was the importance attached to the design of these initials that they were usually written or set out first as he came to the start of each play, and he then fitted in the lines of text around the embellishment of the initials. It is not clear whether these decorated capitals are the work of the scribe himself or a specialist artist working closely with him.[9] Each individual letter seems to have been designed *in situ* following a generic similarity, but where the same letter is required, as for 'P' on fols 17v and 21, the design is different. Cawley and Stevens show that these may have been derived from models in printed books, but although there were examples in French and German before 1500, the comparable English examples are later (*Facsimile*, pp. xv–xvi, n. 12.)

It appears from this practice with the initials, then, that the compiler's sense of the coherence of his work developed as he went along. We can appreciate this further by considering an intricate correction he made. At the top left of fol. 80, before he had written any text on the page, he

made a mistake in creating an illuminated capital 'D'. It appears that
he originally meant to start *Buffeting* (21) with this letter at the beginning
of quire m (now fol. 73), but he discovered that he had not completed
*Conspiracy* (20) which he went back to do, following it with another,
differently designed initial 'D' for *Buffeting* now on fol. 73v. He boxed
the erroneous letter, and, having refolded the sheets, used this page, which
now became fol. 80, for copying part of *Scourging* (22), setting the text
around the now unwanted letter, where it still stands. He subsequently
adopted a new practice to help avoid the mistake of misplacing the start
of the plays. For the next seven plays, *Crucifixion* to *Ascension* (23–9),
the first two lines are in a slightly different hand from the rest of the texts,
and the likelihood is that these were done in advance so as to avoid a
repetition of the error on fol. 80 above. It is not clear from the hand
whether this is the work of a supervisor or whether it is a self-correcting
device by the scribe himself.[10]

We are now looking at features of the manuscript which show changes
of intention. There are some more of these, but they do not necessarily
point to a coherent approach throughout the cycle. One of these is the
ascriptions to guilds which have been added to five plays in four different
hands. These are 'Barker' for *Creation* (1), 'Glover pa . . .' for *Mactatio
Abel* (2), 'Litsters pagonn' and 'lyster play' for *Pharaoh* (8), 'fysher pagent'
for *Pilgrims* (27) and 'Lysters pag' for *Judas* (32). Their appearance makes
for further uncertainty, and on balance they separate this particular
manuscript from performance rather more than establishing a connection.
It was clearly not the compiler's intention to include them in the first
place, and they have been added apparently by others. But we have seen
from the 1556 evidence that there may indeed have been a well-established
association with guilds 'as hathe bene heretofore used'. Moreover the
ascription of two separate plays to the Lysters must raise some doubt as
to whether both are correct. Altogether these added notes seem rather
tentative and they may reflect some uncertainty on the part of those different
people who made them. It does not seem at all likely that the manuscript
was created in order to incorporate information about a production by the
guilds at Wakefield and these additions cannot be regarded as anything
but superficial, and they may not be very reliable.[11]

The order of the plays as they appear in the manuscript needs some
attention. As we have seen, the manuscript runs continuously from *Creation* (1) to *Judgement* (30), a precedent established at York by 1415, but
there are several irregularities. Chief of these are the misordering of some
incidents and the addition of *Lazarus* (31) and *Judas* (32) at the end. Unlike

York, where each play begins on a new sheet, Towneley was written more or less continuously, with one play starting directly below the end of the previous one, no internal space being left in which insertions could be made. The only exception to this is at the end of *Prophets* (7), which is incomplete and stops some distance from the foot of fol. 19v. The recto of the next page (20r) is blank, whilst its verso once had writing on it which has been erased. The erased wording was apparently the first page of *Pharaoh* (8), which now appears on fol. 21r. It looks as though the scribe stopped copying *Pharaoh*, miscalculated the space he needed to complete it, and did not go back to fill up the omission. There is a distinct possibility that the scribe decided to stop copying *Prophets* because he realized that he had made an error in starting it before *Pharaoh*, a play which ought to precede it chronologically.

Different explanations are required for the location of *Lazarus* and *Judas* at the tail end of the manuscript. The latter has been judged an interpolation not properly connected with the rest of the cycle. It is written in a script which has marked differences from that of the main scribe and it is incomplete, even though another person has annotated it with *finis huius* (32/97).[12]

The placing of *Lazarus* is more controversial. On the one hand it is undoubtedly written out by the main scribe and it is presented deliberately with scribal characteristics which fit in with the rest of the manuscript, such as the 'incipit' and 'explicit', the ornamental capital and the general layout of dramatic speech. The scribe's reason for placing it at the end may have been that it was not available for copying when he was ready for it at the point where it might fit in normal order, after *Baptist* and before the Passion begins. But he does not give any indication that he thinks there is anything anomalous in putting this episode after *Judgement*, and it is entirely possible therefore that he really did intend this to end the cycle, however unexpectedly.[13] In support of this we may note that there is no other episode from the Ministry of Christ, and the play might have been isolated if placed there. But it is perhaps more convincing to consider the style of the piece. The first half shows the exchange between Jesus, Mary, Martha, Thomas, John and Peter, culminating in the point where Jesus weeps (31/88sd) and calls Lazarus from the grave. The speech the resurrected Lazarus makes is closely based upon John Bromyard's sermon on the fate of the dead, in places word for word.[14] It is possible that the scribe, having begun his copy with a prayer on fol. 1, wanted to end with a final devotional emphasis. Such a decision might accord with the bookmaking aspects of this document and would further identify its intention as devotional rather than theatrical. In saying this it would be wrong to polarize these two aspects, but it seems that a great deal of the evidence we have reviewed indicates that the greater emphasis may well have been on creating a book.

The inclusion and marking of stage directions is somewhat irregular and may support this intention. All but one are in Latin, the exception being 14/510sd. Twelve plays have none at all. There are fifteen plays having them in black ink, while two have them entirely in red and three have a mixture.[15]

One further group of changes also contributes to our understanding of the unity of the cycle, though here the effect is rather more towards disintegration. There are a number of lacunae in the manuscript and some of these are presumably the result of Protestant attempts to make the manuscript acceptable to the Reformers. These are part of a series of interventions which included tearing out a passage from *Resurrection* (26/345–50), which probably dealt with the subject of transubstantiation, and removing two leaves, perhaps affecting the narrative of the Virgin, at the end of *Purification*, and twelve leaves between *Ascension* and *Judgement*, probably concerned with highly emotional events at the end of Mary's life.[16] There were also some small alterations to the text. Among these are erasing the word 'pope' (16/381) and deleting in red a passage on the seven sacraments, with an accompanying note reading 'corected & not playd' (19/193–200). In the light of the proposed Marian date, the occasion and timing of these becomes rather a puzzle. If the cycle was performed in 1556–9 and the manuscript was written out in association with this but not directly for it, we might ask when it became necessary to make the alterations. The last phrase just quoted suggests that playing was at least in mind when the cut was made. It points to a stage life, real or intended, after the end of Mary's Catholic regime in 1558. The presence of these anti-Catholic measures does rather militate against the possibility that the manuscript was created for the Towneley family. If it were it becomes more difficult to account for Protestant intervention unless in some way the manuscript passed out of their possession and then back into it.

**Figure 1: Towneley Cycle – York elements plays and Wakefield Master stanzas**

| 1 | 2 | 3 | 4 | 5 | 6 | 7 | 8 |
|---|---|---|---|---|---|---|---|
| 1 | *Creation* | | | | | | |
| 2 | *Abel* | | | | | W2? | |
| 3 | *Noah* | | WM | | | | |
| 4 | *Abraham* | | | | | | |
| 5 | *Isaac* | | | | | | |
| 6 | *Jacob* | | | | | | |
| 7 | *Prophets* | | | | | | |
| 8 | *Pharaoh* | **Y11** | | | | | |
| 9 | *Caesar* | | | | | | |
| 10 | *Annunciation* | Y | | | | | |
| 11 | *Salutation* | Y | | | | | |
| 12 | *1 Shepherds* | | WM | | | | |
| 13 | *2 Shepherds* | | WM | | | | |
| 14 | *Magi* | Y | | | | | |
| 15 | *Flight* | Y | | | | | |
| 16 | *Herod* | Y? | WM | | | | Herod, Soldiers |
| 17 | *Purification* | | | | | | |
| 18 | *Doctors* | **Y20** | | | | | |
| 19 | *Baptist* | | | | | | |
| 20 | *Conspiracy* | Y | | | W6+4? | | Pilate, Soldiers |
| 21 | *Buffeting* | | WM | | | | Caia., Ann., Torts. |
| 22 | *Scourging* | **Y34** part | | W27 | | | Pilate, Torturers |
| 23 | *Crucifixion* | | | | | W1? | |
| 24 | *Dicing* | ?(from lost Y) | | | W9 | | Pilate, Torturers |
| 25 | *Harrowing* | **Y37** | | | | | |
| 26 | *Resurrection* | **Y38** | | | | | |
| 27 | *Pilgrims* | Y | | | | W1 | |
| 28 | *Thomas* | Y | | | | | |
| 29 | *Ascension* | Y | | | | W2? | |
| 30 | *Judgement* | **Y47**+ | | W40 | | | Devils, Titivillus |
| 31 | *Lazarus* | | | | W7? | | [Lazarus's solil.] |
| 32 | *Judas* | ?(from lost Y) | | | | | |
| | | 4+2[+2] | 5 | 2  + | 3  + | 4 | |

| Column 3: | Plays **completely** or **largely** borrowed from *York*. |
|---|---|
| | Plays with briefer borrowings are marked *Y*. |
| Column 4: | Plays entirely in the WM stanzas. |
| Columns 5–7: | Count of interpolated WM stanzas. |
| Column 8: | Characters speaking WM stanzas (selected). |

# 1.2

# York and Towneley

The presence in the Towneley manuscript of a large quantity of material which can be demonstrably identified with various passages in the York text (the Register) raises a number of issues regarding the development of the plays at Wakefield and the interaction between the two cycles, and it has a bearing upon our understanding of the coherence of Towneley. Although from one point of view the origin of material hardly matters when it is fully absorbed into a new scheme, if such a process is less than perfect and comprehensive, the details of such an incorporation may be more significant and revealing. The manuscript of the York Register was compiled at some point in the years 1463–77, but it reflects nearly a century of development beforehand. Though the Towneley text is now thought to have been written down in the mid-sixteenth century, its origins, as we have noticed, appear to lie in the fifteenth century, perhaps in the first half. There would thus have been plenty of opportunity for interaction with York, and not necessarily on one single occasion, or indeed in one direction. We may assume that the texts of individual York plays were never in a permanently fixed state, even if religious sentiment acted conservatively: we might regard them rather as bases for change. That being so, we usually cannot tell with any precision what the base text was for any Towneley derivation. However, there is now very little to be offered in support of the main conclusion by M. C. Lyle in her extensive study that the Towneley version was in fact the earlier, York being dependent upon it.[1] In broad terms, and in spite of evidence which may support the possibility of several authors and clear indications that the present text is the product of a number of changes, York is remarkably homogeneous,[2] and it seems far more likely that the similarities between the two cycles were the result of borrowing by those who created or managed the Towneley plays, whose texture is far more uneven. But the situation is admittedly difficult to rationalize because it is hard to arrive at a positive date for the composition of Towneley. Nor are the dates at which individual plays came into the York Cycle easy to ascertain. Furthermore it is not clear how far the document we now have is the result of various stages of composition and how many of these there might have been. Indeed there must be some probability, even a likelihood, that the gathering of material took place over a period of time. Moreover we recall that there are no supporting civic records at Wakefield earlier than the 1550s to cast any light on the generation of the cycle there. The argument against an extensive development of the cycle in the fifteenth century is attractive on the grounds that Wakefield was a small place at that period. The evidence given by M. G. Frampton suggests that there was a rather slow growth in the population, and that the town was not really prosperous in the wool trade until late in the century.[3] This makes a performance of the whole cycle hard to envisage for the fifteenth century.

In reviewing the similarities we shall deal first with the five Towneley plays which show extensive similarities with the York versions: *Pharaoh* (8, with Y11), *Doctors* (18, with Y20), *The Harrowing of Hell* (25, with Y37), *Resurrection* (26, with Y38), and *Judgement* (30, with Y47). We shall then look at the other, lesser links, which, in themselves, may somewhat complicate the position, but also illuminate it. The five chief plays were identified by Lucy Toulmin Smith in her edition of *York Plays* (1885), where both versions are conveniently printed together on the same pages. It is apparent, however, that the process by which one play was imitated by another was by no means uniform. This means that judgement and selection were being exercized by the Towneley authors. We shall also see that there is a strong case for considering the Towneley *Scourging* (22) along with them.

The Towneley *Pharaoh* is the closest to its York counterpart. It follows the York version throughout with only occasional variations amounting to twenty-six additional lines in all. The largest change, in itself still but a minor one, is that the Towneley version gives the last word to Moses, who honours the Trinity (422–9), whereas the York has a boy lead into an anthem. The change might accord with the discussion in Chapter 2.3 below about the relative poverty of music in Towneley. There are differences in spelling to which we shall return later. Since the York *Harrowing* is also closely followed in Towneley, it is interesting that the verbal links between these two plays at York are also found to have survived in the Towneley versions.[4]

With the other four plays we have to leave open the possibilities that the differences might have been the result of incorporating earlier material now lost, or that there are specially created interpolations within them to change the emphasis of the individual York plays. In *Doctors*, for example, there is a difference between the two beginnings. The extant York version starts with a dialogue of seventy-two lines between Mary and Joseph during which they realize that their son is not with them. Once they discover this they decide to return to seek him. The Towneley version, which is incomplete at the beginning and amounts to forty-eight lines in quatrains, shows two 'Magistri' discussing the prophecies of the birth of Christ as Emmanuel. The texts then run parallel until the young Jesus begins his version of the Ten Commandments at T18/145. Here the versification changes from the characteristic York septenars (having twelve lines) to quatrains, and these Towneley quatrains are much more explicit and pointed in their phraseology about sin.[5] Compare, for example: 'The viij$^{te}$ lernes 3ou for to be lele, / Here for to bere no false witnesse' (Y20/185–6) with:

The viii byddys the 'Be true in dede,
And fals wytnes looke thou none bere;
Looke thou not ly for freynd ne fede,
Lest to thi saull that it do dere'.    (T18/169–72)[6]

After the passage containing the Commandments the close parallel is resumed at T18/185 and continues to the end at T18/280.

We may take *Harrowing* (T25) and *Judgement* (T30) together because both Towneley versions place additional emphasis upon devils. *Harrowing* follows the York version very closely for the most part, taking over twenty-three out of thirty-four septenar stanzas, and adding about ninety lines.[7] Apart from some minor additions to the part of Jesus, the chief addition involves the devil Rybald, whose name actually appears in the form 'Rebalde' in the York version, though not as a proper name (Y37/99). In some places, lines attributed to another devil are switched to him (T25/101–5, 107–8, 120), but he is also given additional speeches which are not in the York text (as at 121–4). His main function is to show defiance to Christ and to support Satan's confrontation with him in the longest continuous interpolation (T25/121–52). This latter passage is partly composed in the York septenars, and it is therefore possible that it preserves some lines which have dropped out of the existing York text. But even so, the change towards the enlargement of devils' activity fits in with other changes, such as those we find in *Judgement* where there is a much larger injection of new material. In this play, about one-fifth of the

Towneley version follows York closely, these lines being in substance the part of Jesus and they form a structure which is essentially the same as that of York (Y47).[8] Most of the additions are in the thirteen-line stanzas and characteristic verbal style of the Wakefield Master, and they are the medium for vigorous and elaborate dialogue by three devils, First and Second Demon, and Tutivillus (T30/131–559). Their role is to illustrate some of the many sins which have to be accounted for at the Judgement. Tutivillus claims he has brought ten thousand souls, whom he found in an hour (T30/312–5), and he speaks with great fluency and much telling detail of the corruption and folly of those who are to be condemned. It is questionable, though, whether this passage adds much to the York narrative even though it makes the devils seem much worse and elaborates the extent of human misdeeds.

Apart from the devil sequence, the Towneley *Judgement* also varies at the beginning. Unfortunately, the text is deficient at this point because some pages have been removed; where the speeches do begin, in quatrains, they show that the parts of the damned souls have been elaborated and distributed among four speakers, as distinct from York's two. This suggests that at some point there were more actors available for a performance of Towneley than there had been at York. At T30/27 the York text is resumed verbatim, in the original eight-line stanzas, here in the voice of 3 Malus. After another enlargement for 4 Malus and the descent of the Angel and Jesus, who speak in the York stanzas, there begins the interpolation of the devils already noticed (T30/131–559). In the lost portion at the beginning of the Towneley episode, it is likely that the play was begun by Deus, as in York. If this were so, it would form a parallel with his initiation of *Creation* and *Annunciation* earlier in Towneley.

The relationship between the Towneley (T26) and York (Y38) versions of *Resurrection* points to a heavy revision, even though the basic structure of the two plays, the core so to speak, is the same and contains virtually the same text. This comprises the preparation for the Watch between the Centurion, Pilate, and Caiaphas (T26/41–50, 85–217), followed by the visit of the three Marys (351–446) and then the awakening of the soldiers and their second encounter with Pilate, Annas and Caiaphas (447–579). To this is added in Towneley an opening boastful speech by Pilate (1–36); an introductory speech by the Centurion which recognizes that he who was crucified was 'That Lord veray' (line 66 in the passage 51–75); a long and lyrical speech to the audience by Jesus who draws attention to his wounds and to his love and mercy (230–350); and a scene between him as supposed gardener and Mary Magdalene, which ends the Towneley version and elaborates the presentation of Christ's sanctity and sacrifice (580–659).

It is clear from these details that in these five plays, which are those taking over most material from York, that the process of incorporation was not necessarily coherent, nor did it follow the same rationale. This needs to be considered alongside some of the incorporations which do seem to point in the same direction, such as the tendency to enlarge the part played by devils, and the interest in developing initial boasts, which we discuss in Chapter 3.4. Both these tendencies might have implications in terms of moral/theological objectives, as well as being an increase, or at least a change in theatricality.

When we turn to the many other places where Towneley has material from York, but on a lesser scale, we find a wealth of similarities, but again it is difficult to identify many broad tendencies. The number of minor correspondences is very large but many of them might well be seen as highly subjective. M. C. Lyle's painstaking study is a useful point of departure, but unfortunately many of her examples are open to question and a significant proportion rely upon only one or two common words in a chosen passage, which can hardly be conclusive.[9] In some cases one might well suspect that similarities result from a common linguistic inheritance, with scribes using formulaic expressions. But perhaps we should make something out of the uncertainty some of her examples generate. The inexact matches show that to be precise about imitation of derivation is difficult. It should be noted here that Stevens and Cawley proposed that there was a coherent re-editing of the whole cycle by a redactor and that their summative view of the process was as follows: 'The likelihood is that the Towneley redactor had access to the guild copies of many of the York pageants and that he revised and rewrote them to fit into their new context in the Towneley cycle.'[10] I shall return to this possibility of one coherent reviser later. In the following review, which works progressively through the cycle, I propose to illustrate the kinds of similarity by means of a limited selection and to try to give a broad indication of how many plays reveal some signs of direct verbal parallels, and to show how extensive these are. It is striking that apart from *Pharaoh* the interaction is largely concentrated upon the plays dealing with the scriptural narrative from *Annunciation* onwards, with little occurring in the Old Testament plays.

In the following discussion of plays I shall consider some of the lesser parallels. The distribution of the elements from York is shown in Figure 1

together with the extent of the interventions by the Wakefield Master, as
discussed in Chapters 1.3 and 1.4 below.

## Annunciation (10)

The following examples are perhaps close enough to suggest copying or
recollection, but they are very short, and the two versions of *Annunciation*
are structured very differently.

þase games fra me are gane.   (Y13/196)
The gams fro me ar gane.   (T10/169)

Sir, Goddis and youres.   (Y13/103)
Syr, Godys and yowrs.   (T10/195)

was I neuer filid.   (Y13/215)
was I neuer fylyd.   (T10/206)

## Salutation (11)

This contains a possible parallel in wording and the use of rhyme.[11]

My saule sall louying ma
Vnto þat lorde so lele,
And my gast make ioye alswa
In God þat es my hele.   (Y12/237–40)
My saull lufys my Lord abuf,
And my gost gladys with luf,
In God, that is my hele
. . . And kept me madyn lele.   (T11/49–51, 54)

## Magi (14)

One twelve-line stanza (T14/595–606), spoken by the Angel, is a close
parallel with one in York (Y16/369–80). The last three lines are differently
arranged in Towneley (Stevens and Cawley revert to York's order):

And yf 3e aske hym bone,
Youre beelde ay will he be
For þis þat 3e haue done.   (Y16/378–80)

And if ye ask hym boyn,
For this dede that ye haue done,
Youre beyld ay wyll he be.   (T14/604–6)

Besides this one stanza, it has been pointed out that the rest of the play
is written in the six-line stanza (aaabab) which is one of the staple forms
used in the York cycle.[12]

## Flight into Egypt (15)

There are a number of parallel passages which suggest that the compiler
of this Towneley play was aware of the York text even though his version
differs in some ways, including the versification and the character of
Joseph.

A, myghtfull lorde, whateuere þat mente?
So swete a voyce herde I neuere ayre.   (Y18/41–2)
A, myghtfull God,
Whateuer this ment,
So swete of toyn?   (T15/11–13)

For Herowde þe kyng gars doo to dede
All knave-childer in ilke a stede,
þat he may ta
With 3eris twa
þat are of olde.   (Y18/55–9)
For Herode dos do dy
All knaue-chyldren, securly,
Within two yere that be
Of eld.   (T15/21–4)

His harte aught to be ful sare,
On slike a foode hym to forfare,
þat nevir did ill
Hym for to spill,
And he ne wate why.   (Y18/139–43)
His hart shuld be full sare
Sich-on for to fare,
That neuer yit dyd yll
Ne thoght.   (T15/86–9: Stevens and Cawley emend the manuscript
                         from 'fare' to 'forfare' (87).)

## Herod (16)

One passage suggests that the Wakefield Master, who wrote most of this play afresh, might have been aware of the York version, but this example also illustrates that it is difficult to be categorical about whether the Towneley version is really a copy:

> I saie for they are past.
> What, forthe away fro me?
> 3a, lord, in faitht ful faste.   (Y19/100–2)
> Lord, thynk not ill if I
> Tell you how thay ar past;
> I kepe not layn, truly
> Syn thay cam by you last,
> Anothere way in hy
> Thay soght, and that full fast.   (T16/209–14)

## Conspiracy and Capture (20)

Lyle adduces a number of minor similarities of phrase with the York counterparts, but there are many dissimilarities, including a different characterization of Pilate. Of these possible parallels the most convincing is:

> His maistreys schulde moue 3ou youre mode for to amende.   (Y26/63)
> Sir Pylate, mefe you now no more,
> Bot mese youre hart and mend youre mode.   (T20/174–5)

The remainder, however, are less close. Nevertheless the origins of this long play may well be diverse. Because in the manuscript it is called 'Conspiracio' at the beginning and 'Capcio' at the conclusion, it is likely that it originally consisted of two plays. It may indeed have been even more at some stage, since the unusually large accumulation of incidents approximates to three plays at York (26, 27, 28): they are the Conspiracy, the Betrayal, the Last Supper, the Agony in the Garden and the Arrest. There is also a large range of verse forms, including twenty-two septenar stanzas (78–337) like those found in the York plays but here without verbal parallel.

## Scourging (22)

This play contains a substantial passage in the stanzas of the Wakefield Master (twenty-seven stanzas in 1–351) as well as extensive but selective borrowings from York (nine ten-line stanzas from Y34: T22/106–35, 190–9, 230–49, 260–99). The former passage comprises, in a complete sequence, another boast by Pilate together with the accusation, scourging, crowning and condemnation, and ending as the Torturers lead Christ away with the cross. The York borrowings appear as three sequences in Towneley: the first is part of a speech by John to the Marys (T22/352–71); the second shows the Torturers threatening the Marys (486–95); the third shows the Torturers pressurizing Simon of Cyrene (504–63).[13] There are other elements in this later sequence, and it is quite possible that some of the present Towneley text comes from lost York passages. One of the intriguing aspects of the revision of York in this play is that if it was revised by the Wakefield Master, as the first 351 lines suggest, he did not re-write the cruel sequences from York at 486–95 and 504–63 in his usual verse and style; they remained in the York form and paralleled the language directly. In passages not apparently by him, the Towneley version shows Pilate more crafty and malicious.

## Pilgrims (27)

There are a few verbal similarities between the York and Towneley versions of this play, but they do not suggest extensive borrowing. The following may be evidence for a common source or perhaps some interconnection before the current state of the two texts:

All nyght we thynke for to bide here;
Bide with vs, sir pilgrime, we praye 3ou.   (Y40/143–4)
Now, sir, we pray you, as oure freynde,
All nyght to abyde for charité.   (T27/246–7)

Saie! Wher is þis man?
                    Away is he went –
Right now satte he beside vs!   (Y40/161–2)
... Where is this man becom,
Right here that sat betwix vs two?   (T27/297–8)

## Thomas of India (28)

This is a complex and effective play, coherent and organized, without signs of the Wakefield Master. The action of the Towneley play is more elaborate than that of the York version, suggesting that the latter is perhaps

the older version. There are a few verbal similarities which may be evidence
for some common original.

> And se þat I haue flessh and bone.
> Gropes me nowe,
> For so ne has sperite none . . .   (Y41/57–9)
> Grope and fele flesh and bone
> And fourme of man well-wroght;
> Sich thyng has goost none.   (T28/133–5)

> To grope hym grathely, bloode and bone
> And flesh to feele.
> Such thyngis, Thomas, hase sperite none,
> þat wote thou wele.   (Y41/153–6)
> Man has both fleshe and bone,
> Hu, hyde, and hore thertill;
> Sich thyng has goost none.
> Thomas, lo, here thi skyll.   (T28/379–82)

> Are schalle I trowe no tales betwene.
> Thomas, þat wounde haue we seene.
> 3a, 3e wotte neuere what 3e mene,
> Youre witte it wantis.   (Y41/163–6)
> For we say that we haue sene,
> Thou holdys vs wars then woode;
> Iesu lyfyng stod vs betwene,
> Oure Lord that with vs yode.
> I say ye wote neuer what ye mene.   (T28/489–93)

## Ascension (29)

The two versions differ markedly in size and scope, but there is one
sequence where similarities may be noted.

> 3e men of þe lande of Galilé,
> What wondir 3e to heuene lokand?
> þis Jesus whome 3e fro youe see
> Vppe-tane, 3e schall wele vndirstande,
> Right so agayne come doune schall he,
> When he so comes with woundes bledand.   (Y42/217–21)
> Ye men of Galylee,
> Wherfor meruell ye?

Hevyn behold, and se
How Iesus vp can weynde . . .
Right so shall he securly
Com downe agane truly,
With his woundys blody.    (T29/290–3, 302–4)

Besides these plays which show various but minor similarities with York, we should also take note of *Dicing* (24) and *Hanging of Judas* (32). There has been some argument over whether the former is a survival from York. Though there is no such play in the York Register, the records indicate that one existed in 1422–3, and the description of it is much like the incidents in the Towneley play.[14] Separate plays about the incident of gambling over Christ's seamless garment are rare. The incident is also present elsewhere in Towneley, rather briefly, as part of *Crucifixion* (T23/560–71). There the Torturers draw lots. In *Dicing*, a second and longer version, they play at dice and draw lots, and in this the play apparently follows the York episode, where Pilate was also one of the gamblers.[15] The *Hanging of Judas* may also be a survival from York. Though it is not present in the Register, a play of that name did exist in 1422–3, and the Towneley version is written in the six-line stanza used for some York plays (as noted in *Magi* above).

This review shows that there was a positive process whereby some York elements were incorporated and that in a few places the Towneley episodes are intimately dependent upon York. But the presence of the minor examples we have noted means that influences came about in a very unsystematic manner. Some of the similarities are so small and so isolated that it is difficult to be sure whether they really do imply the York version or rather something in the source material or the scriptural narrative. These differences may mean that the composers or compiler of Towneley did not actually have an organized approach to incorporating York elements. One possibility is that some of them may have occurred through odd flashes of memory, entirely a matter of chance, even though in the event they are theatrically potent. The phrase above from *Annunciation* (T10/195) seems especially so. As it can be shown that the York Cycle was frequently performed in the fifteenth and early sixteenth centuries, there would have been plenty of opportunity for such details of phraseology to have become familiar.

But for the larger adaptations we may also be in doubt as to reasons. It should also be borne in mind that other plays might have been used at Wakefield if there were a long and changing performance history, but in effect this is hard to be sure about. Meanwhile the adaptation of the four chief imitations (excluding *Pharaoh*, which we have seen is almost word for word) show active selective procedures whereby verse forms are changed, incidents enlarged or contracted, characters re-drawn and sometimes different episodes added or substituted. We also have to leave open the problem of why particular choices were made as to whether a York episode or sequence should be incorporated. It might have been that certain texts were conveniently to hand when a gap had to be filled. But here we might ask whether it was a gap in performance or a gap in the process of compiling the manuscript. Such a distinction depends upon the reason for compiling the manuscript in the first place. It does seem likely that access to written York material would have been physically and chronologically feasible, but since the York Register was not put together until 1463 at the earliest, it is perfectly possible that the Wakefield writers were allowed access to the texts held by individual guilds and that these could easily have been earlier than the Register.[16] If the generation of the Towneley cycle antedates the York Register this must necessarily be the case.

The real uncertainty, which it is admittedly difficult to surmount, is whether the York copies used by the Towneley dramatist(s) had already been altered, so making them closer to the existing York text than they originally were. Moreover, it is almost impossible to decide whether the Towneley adaptations were made at the same time as one another. The argument presented by Meredith makes it very likely that the Towneley versions were not made from versions later than the York Register, since there is no annotation of changes in the individual York plays concerned. This means that common clerks checking the texts in the York Register saw substantially the same plays year by year well into the sixteenth century.[17]

I should now like to consider another factor relevant to comparing the York items with the Towneley text. It will be evident from the extracts given above that though the words may be the same, they were changed in the process of transcription because the Towneley scribe was working in a somewhat different dialect and also, in all probability, at a different time. His dialect has been characterized as being a combination of northern and Midland elements, and some of the changes from the York material are in line with this.[18] Indeed some characteristics of the language of Towneley increase the likelihood that, whenever the cycle was originally conceived and written down, what is actually left to us is a sixteenth-century document closely associated with the area in which Wakefield is located.

The changes in word formation are generally consistent from York to Towneley, though there are some places where this is not sustained. This is especially interesting in respect of the study of variation in regional forms by M. L. Holford. He shows that the principal York scribe (designated 'B' by Richard Beadle in his edition) was inconsistent in his use of northern forms.[19] The chief implication of the regular changes by the principal Towneley scribe is that they enhance the unity of the Towneley manuscript, and in doing so they underline the idea that the scribe, even where he took over material which was manifestly extraneous or diverse, sought to bring it to conformity with the linguistic forms that he found in the rest of his exemplars or that he imposed on them. Trusler holds that the scribe was methodical in his approach, and she gives as examples, among many others, the Midland forms 'before', 'more', 'bore', whereas the northern forms would have been 'befare', 'mare', 'bare'.[20] But it is also true that specific York forms were carried over for rhyme, for example 'than' (T8/93) to rhyme with 'began', 'man', 'wan', following the York original, whereas the more usual form in Towneley is the Midland 'then' (as at T12/26, T13/96, 563). Another example occurs in *Pharaoh* with 'wrang'/'wrong': the York version uses 'wrang(e)' which it rhymes with 'lang'/'gang' (Y11/284, 351); Towneley follows at T8/296, 360, but it substitutes 'wrong' at T8/149 for 'wrang' in Y11/137 in a location within the line where there is no need for rhyme. Where consistency occurs it may suggest that the scribe was copying from exempla which had already been standardized. However, we might note that the Wakefield Master does have a substantial vocabulary of northern words.[21] Moreover, where changes from York to Wakefield forms are not consistent because linguistic stock is not always different, scribes may have been sharing an inheritance which they followed unconsciously as a result of memory rather than systematic and deliberate choice.

The following list is based upon a sample of about one hundred lines from each of the six plays with large York elements: *Pharaoh* (8), *Doctors* (18), *Scourging* (22), *Harrowing* (25), *Resurrection* (26) and *Judgement* (30). The York forms are given first in the first column followed by the Towneley form, and the references in the second column are to the plays and lines in the Towneley text. Where the form is repeated in the sample from each play the second and further instances have been disregarded unless there is no example in the other plays. The third column gives references of the location attributed to each word as given by A. McIntosh et al., *The Linguistic Atlas of Late Medieval English* (A + volume and page), or to J. Wright, *The English Dialect Dictionary* (EDD).

**Figure 2:  Some linguistic changes from York to Towneley**

| | | |
|---|---|---|
| als > as | 8/12 25/65 26/170 | |
| brennand > burnand | 8/105 | |
| busk > bush | 8/105 | |
| er > are | 8/36 8/48 | A2.83[22] |
| ey > ee (eye) | 30/46 | A4.622 |
| fadir > fader | 8/5 | |
| gud > good | 8/90 | A2.281 |
| haly > holy | 8/4 18/175 | A4.200–1 |
| herdes > hyrdys | 8/62 | |
| knawen > knowne | 8/11 | |
| maistir > master | 8/27 18/95 22/251 | EDD |
| mone > moyn (moon) | 26/119 | A4.316 |
| noght, no3t > not | 8/72 22/552 25/101 | A2.197 |
| pepill > people | 8/18 | |
| sall > shall | 8/65 8/66 | A2.95, 101[23] |
| schall > shall | 25/32 26/90 30/44 | A2.101, A2.153 |
| schulde > shuld | 22/549 26/96 | A2.107 |
| snow > snawe | 25/81 | EDD |
| sone > soyn (soon) | 8/28 18/71 22/504 | |
| such > sich | 22/537 25/98 26/107 | A2.41 |
| suld > shuld | 8/28 | |
| suthly > sothly | 8/38 | |
| swilke > sych | 8/72 18/110 26/140 | A2.41 |
| þame > theyme, thayme | 8/28 22/366 | A2.29 |
| þan > then | 8/137 18/56 | A2.137 |
| þes > thyse | 25/102 | A2.5 |
| ther > thare | 8/82 22/488 26/114 | A2.35 |
| thurgh > thrugh | 8/29 25/14 26/131 | A2.227 |
| walde > wold | 8/30 | |
| whan(ne) > when | 8/56 22/559 26/101 | A2.223 |
| whilke > which | 18/146 | A2.45 |
| woll > will | 30/124 30/127 | |
| worldly > warldly | 8/107 | |

Though this is only a sample, the cumulative effect of the changes and their consistency both suggest that on linguistic grounds the attribution of the manuscript to the Wakefield area cannot be doubted.

As a tailpiece to this account of the links between York and Towneley we may add that there are several reasons for thinking that the Wakefield Master, whose work we shall consider in Chapter 1.4, was familiar with much of the York Cycle. This is apparent in the plays where his work is interrelated with existing York material, as in the *Last Judgement* (30). But as J. W. Robinson has pointed out, even where he has written a completely new play, the structure or outline may still preserve the York version, as in *First Shepherds* (12). He also points out that the Towneley *Herod* (16) follows York (19) in isolating the 'Slaughter of the Innocents', and that the Towneley *Buffeting* (21) has a similar outline to the York *Christ before Annas and Caiaphas* (29), where the dramatic silence of Christ may well have been developed by the Wakefield Master from the York precedent.[24]

# 1.3

# Provenances and Authorship

As with all the English extant mystery cycles, Towneley presents difficulties when we come to identify authors. To some extent this is
endemic in the genre, assuming that we accept the model of its being
an urban drama developed and used over a long period by a variety of
entrepreneurs and performers, to the extent that the texts have to be seen
as fluid entities. Our attempts at understanding them are circumscribed
by the necessity of looking through such particular and constricted
windows as the surviving manuscripts allow, and this attempt is rather
like taking a photograph of the water passing in a river. Such a photograph gives us some certainty about how the water appears at one moment
but the rest of its existence can only be grasped with the help of a heavy
measure of speculation and deduction. We should add here, however,
that there are some particular difficulties, discussed elsewhere, in accepting this model for Towneley, especially in view of the presumed late
date of the manuscript.

Since Gayley named a particular contributing poet as the Wakefield
Master in 1903,[1] it has become almost impossible to think of this cycle
without bearing in mind what this dramatist might have contributed. The
present investigation into the coherence of the cycle requires that we re-
assess the nature and importance of this writer's work; it cannot be ignored.
Even though Gayley's designation has been challenged by some because
it perhaps exaggerates his skill towards the level of genius, it seems only
practical to persist with it on the ground of familiarity, though it remains
preferable to try to describe his work this side idolatry. To do this enables
us to avoid the uncertainty engendered by Stevens and Cawley who refer
variously in their edition to the Wakefield Master, the Wakefield Author
and the Wakefield Redactor. This confusion is partly a reflection of their
proposition that this particular individual, however named, was in fact a
reviser who oversaw as a compiler the whole manuscript as we now have

it.[2] The discussion which follows does not finally support their point of view: indeed it will become apparent that if this author did set out to do this, he has left an extraordinarily large number of untidy ends.

We shall approach the authorship and provenance in a sequence of three phases by discussing first the episodes which do not contain any direct evidence of his composition; by doing this we should establish that there are a number features implying that a large part of the cycle is independent of him. To some extent dealing with these first is a polemical decision aimed at emphasizing that there were other writers exercising distinctive literary and dramatic skills. It is important to underline these. This goes along with the implication already established, that the borrowings from York discussed in the previous section help in the perception of the limits of his contribution. Secondly, we shall look at the plays which may be regarded as, to all intents and purposes, entirely his work (Chapter 1.4.I). The third part then turns to the plays which show rather more limited indications of his work as well as much that is not characteristic of him (Chapter 1.4.II). In this group his interaction with the work of other writers presents us with some particularly useful information regarding the unity of the cycle.

The evidence of his participation depends firstly upon the use of the thirteen-line stanza, as identified by Cawley and others. We shall return to its characteristics in the next section since the stanzas do vary somewhat, but its significance as evidence is supported by a number of broader criteria, including some features of language and aspects of dramatic style as manifested in character, plot and concept. It follows, however, that where an intervention is minimal, such features may not always be unmistakably identifiable. In practice, it is the presence of the stanza form that provides the best clue to his participation. This has to be seen against two other matters: one is that there is a very large number of other stanzaic forms in Towneley, and the other is the fact that prosodic versatility showing itself in the use of complex stanzaic forms was a feature of several large-scale medieval plays, especially in the York and Towneley Cycles and *Castle of Perseverance* in *The Macro Plays*, pp. 1–111. This practice suggests that there was an abiding interest in the opportunities offered by such structures and the possible variations. Though these have been frequently and routinely documented by editors, there have not been many attempts to relate their use to dramatic effects. It is also worth noting that a surviving interest in the alliterative prosody of Anglo-Saxon poetry played a significant, though intermittent, part in the success of these complex verse forms.

The accompanying table (Figure 1, p. 24) shows that the plays without signs of the Wakefield Master are largely those dealing with Old Testament subjects together with the life of Christ up to *John the Baptist* (19). There are fourteen of these: *Creation, Abraham, Isaac, Jacob, Prophets, Pharaoh, Caesar, Annunciation, Salutation, Magi, Flight into Egypt, Purification, Doctors* and *John the Baptist*. Five plays have to be excepted, *Mactatio Abel* (2), *Noah* (3), *First* and *Second Shepherds* (12 and 13) and *Herod* (16), and for these he appears to have written complete individual plays. Nevertheless, it looks as though much of this poet's interest was concentrated more persistently in the Passion sequence and rather more intermittently thereafter. As we shall see, there are varying amounts of his influence in nine of the remaining thirteen plays. Only *Harrowing, Resurrection, Thomas* and *Judas* from the last part of the cycle will appear in the first part of the discussion of plays not showing it. Altogether his work is found in fourteen plays and there are eighteen to be considered first where his influence is not apparent.

The plays in the Old Testament sequence show a considerable variety of poetic method and dramatic style and it seems unlikely that, as they stand, they are the work of the same author. Nor is there consistency in the prosody, though we must beware of the assumption that any individual poet would necessarily confine himself to one metrical form, a point which needs to be borne in mind in relation to the work of the Wakefield Master as well. In the first part of this study it will be apparent that there is no overriding principle for the selection of verse forms, but there is some deliberate and skilful manipulation of them in places.

As we turn first to the dramatic characteristics of these plays, which are manifestly varied, we need to recollect that the evidence for performance of the cycle as a whole is practically non-existent until the mid-sixteenth century, and if individual plays were initiated at some point in the fifteenth century, as can be assumed on linguistic grounds, there is really no basis for assuming that they were necessarily conceived for cyclic performance. Their appearance together in the conventional English sequence from *Creation* to *Judgement* in the manuscript may well be a matter of subsequent convenience or rearrangement rather than of initial conception. This does not necessarily mean, however, that a high degree of coherence could not be achieved. We can best consider the dramatic approaches of the writers by looking at the Old Testament episodes in sequence, and at the same time noting the relationship of verse forms to the action.

*Creation* (1), which has only 265 lines, there being four leaves lost at the end, comprises the work of Deus creating the world, the boast and fall of Lucifer, the creation of Adam and Eve, the warning by the Cherub and Lucifer's preparation for the temptation. Deus and Lucifer both speak eloquently, and the shifts in the action are marked with four Latin stage directions. It looks as though the decisions about verse forms were intended to relate closely to the speakers and their functions. The two passages for Deus, creating first the world and then Adam and Eve, are in the same rhyme scheme, which is used for these alone (aabccb, with a concluding close variant aabaab). Lucifer has a different stanza for his boast (aabab) and all the rest of the fragment, which is largely dialogue as distinct from monologue, is in couplets. Though we shall find other plays in the cycle where the varieties of metre may suggest cutting and pasting passages from different provenances, it seems very likely that in this play such changes are closely related to the writer's theatrical intent. They may be difficult to detect in a performance but they are an unmistakable part of the play's rhetoric. It seems that this feature may have been underestimated in the quest for fault lines in the composition of the plays in general.

*Abraham* (4) offers hints of a similar approach to verse forms in that they are related directly to the speakers and that it seems that this is the underlying principle rather than any question of revision. Though the ending of the play is missing, it is composed entirely in the same eight-line stanzas (abababab) except for one speech in couplets by Deus (also of eight lines) in which he resolves to test Abraham. But in his uses of the main stanza the dramatist shows great versatility, frequently breaking up individual stanzas with striking effect. The drama involves much more interactive dialogue than *Creation* and the two main characters are given very human characteristics. The following stanza comes at the crisis, when Abraham tells Isaac of his fate:

| | |
|---|---|
| *Abraham* | Isaac! |
| *Isaac* | Sir? |
| *Abraham* | Come heder, bid I; |
| | Thou shal be dede, whatsoeuer betide. |
| *Isaac* | A, fader, mercy! mercy! |
| *Abraham* | That I say may not be denyde; |
| | Take thi dede therfor meekly. |
| *Isaac* | A, good syr, abide! |
| | Fader! |
| *Abraham* | What, son? |
| *Isaac* | To do youre will I am redy, |
| | Wheresoeuer ye go or ride.    (4/177–84) |

The pressure continues in the next three stanzas but in each case the interweaving of the two voices is differently arranged to reflect the increasing emotional tension.

Though the play is primarily concerned with God's relationship with man, the detail of the dramatization concentrates upon the depth of feeling in the two characters and the intricate interrelationship between them. The dramatic tension is heightened because Abraham is reluctant to tell his son what God has required, and he conducts the preliminaries with an outward harshness even though he is clearly suffering within. On the other hand Isaac, though he may prefigure Christ as victim, is actually terrified of what is going on, and he is much less a figure of obedience than in dramatizations of this episode in other cycles.[3] *Abraham* reveals much subtlety in its characterization but it is notably free from any satirical intent, a feature which distinguishes this treatment of Abraham from that of the Wakefield Master in the presentation of a fallible Noah. Structurally, however, its collocation of God and Abraham followed by Abraham and Isaac provides a strict examination of the test of obedience. The absence of an ending impedes our evaluation but after he is released by the Angel, Abraham's contorted sentence structures articulate his primary anguish about his son; 'To speke with the haue I no space, / With my dere son till I haue spoken. / My good son, thou shal haue grace, / On the now will I not be wrokyn' (4/273–6).

It is appropriate to consider the next two plays, *Isaac* and *Jacob* (5 and 6) together because they are similar in language and dramatic style. Though the beginning of *Isaac* is lost, they form a continuous narrative closely related to their biblical source (*Genesis* 27–8: 13) and are written entirely in couplets. The dialogue is tightly written and the dramatic intention is largely directed towards portraying the close interaction between the characters. The beginning in *Jacob* is rather more elevated in style. Like *Noah* and *Abraham*, this play begins with a prayer. Deus responds to Jacob's plea for help, by undertaking the traditional scriptural role of unrelenting support: 'All that I say, I shall forth, / And all the folkys of thyne ofspryng / Shal be blyssyd of thy blyssyng. / Iacob, haue thou no kyns drede; / I shall the clethe, I shall the fede' (6/24–8). The two plays seem to fit together in another way, in that they both deal with the feud between Jacob and Esau, as Stevens and Cawley point out (*Plays*, 2.457), and they are both concerned with reconciliation: Isaac kisses Jacob, and Jacob kisses Esau. These parallel climactic moments are marked by stage directions near the end of each play (5/65sd and 6/122sd). Such integration is remarkable and it may suggest that the plays had a previous independent and interrelated existence as a single play but, as the texts now stand, they have been neatly incorporated into the manuscript and there is little in the dialect to suggest a different provenance, even though the dramatic style is distinctive. Moreover, the dramatic style, which is carefully provided with Latin stage directions about places and movement, does not suggest that of the Wakefield Master. Unfortunately, these stage directions tell us little about the configuration required for the staging of the play. These will be considered below, together with the staging requirements implicit in the text.

The next three plays in the manuscript, *Prophets*, *Pharaoh* and *Caesar Augustus* (7, 8 and 9), bear no sign of the Wakefield Master and they bring very different information about provenance and the possible unity of the cycle. The dramatic texture of *Prophets* is unique within Towneley, though it bears some resemblance to corresponding elements in other cycles, as for example, *Jesse Root* (7) in N Town. Unfortunately it is incomplete, though in this instance it looks as though the scribe discontinued copying for some reason, as there is some space below the last line in the text on fol. 19v, and there is no 'explicit'. There is a distinct possibility that he became aware of an obvious irregularity in that this play appears in the wrong place. It would follow more naturally after *Pharaoh*, the next play in the manuscript, itself the last of the episodes historically located in the Old Testament.

The action of *Prophets* comprises a procession of prophets, each of whom makes a statement about the messianic hope. There does not appear to be any further action which might be described as dramatic, and the text breaks off during, or possibly at the end of, the speech of Daniel, who follows Moses, David and the Sibyl. As each of these passages is prefaced by a brief Latin prologue, Stevens and Cawley were able to relate the play to a *lectio* used for the Matins of Christmas or elsewhere in Advent, ultimately deriving from the fifth- or sixth-century pseudo-Augustinian *Sermo contra Judaeos*. In accordance with this, it is suggested that the original may have contained another nine speakers.[4] The verse forms in the episode show a measure of uniformity. The whole fragment is in six-line stanzas, and once again there seems to be an intention to use variations for specific speakers. Thus Moses is linked to David by the same rhyme scheme (aabaab); the Sibyl and Daniel are given the same variation (aabccb). In addition, the part of Moses' speech expounding the Ten Commandments is also put into the latter variation.

The content of the individual prophecies most probably seemed attractive since eschatologically it suggests unifying thematic material. The four speakers each bring specific concepts which refer to other items or episodes in the cycle. Thus Moses tells of the coming of the prophet Christ, who will be supreme over all other prophets and who will redeem Adam 'and all his blode' (7/6) from hell. David confirms that this will be the Son of God, and he concentrates particularly on his status as 'kyng of all' (7/127). The Sibyl foretells the Last Judgement and shows how it reflects upon the present. Daniel anticipates the Incarnation through the virgin birth. The general impression given by this episode is that, although it may be differently conceived in its dramatic method, it fulfils an important teleological role in the cycle's structure and it is one fulfilled by corresponding episodes in other cycles, typically *Jesse Root* (7) in N Town.

*Pharaoh* (8) is one of the plays incorporated into Towneley directly from the York Cycle and as such it has been discussed above in the section dealing with these adaptations. Its presence here, presumably out of sequence in relation to *Prophets*, may suggest some dislocation at this point in the manuscript.

With *Caesar Augustus*, the next play (9), we come to a different set of problems relating to the unity of the cycle. The subject is rare in the English cycle plays and it offers some important links with other elements in Towneley. It shows how the Emperor was shaken by the news that there was a prophecy: 'That in this land shuld dwell a may, / The which sall bere a chylde, thay say, / That shall youre force downe fell' (9/70–2). Caesar's response is to decree that all his subjects shall praise him as their 'lord alone' (9/214) and to demand a penny as homage from every man. There may not be any evidence within the play of work by the Wakefield Master, yet in two respects it does link with his interests. The first is that it is a tyrant's boast, and we shall refer later to his use of similar passages in several plays. Secondly, Caesar repeatedly refers to 'Mahowne' as his particular deity, and this is a convention for tyrants and evil men. For example, it is used for the Towneley Pharaoh in a section in common with York (T8/410–13 and Y12/401–4). It was a convenient device for underlining the wickedness of Christ's enemies. The Wakefield Master frequently followed it, as for Herod (16/1) and Pilate (20/19).[5]

After the initial boast by Caesar, the play concentrates on a tense dialogue between him and his advisers. This shows the unease felt by Caesar and at the same time touches upon some details of the scriptural narrative. The process has the effect of constantly recalling the underlying narrative in a manner characteristic of cyclic form. The play does not show the metrical discrimination we have noted in some other Old

Testament plays. It is written throughout in the same six-line stanza as the major part of *Prophets* (aabaab), and it does not break up the stanzas between speakers in the manner of *Abraham*. Nevertheless, it is clear that the plays in the Old Testament we have considered show a range of dramatic and poetic versatility and their methods can be held to be independent of the plays characteristic of the Wakefield Master. When we turn to the early part of the New Testament, from *Annunciation* to *Baptist*, we find a comparable independence and variety.

*Annunciation* is a play of some weight in Towneley because it seems designed to initiate a new start in the narrative. It is a play of substantial length (374 lines), and it is prosodically similar to the following play, *Salutation* (11), which is rather shorter (ninety lines). The action begins in cyclic fashion with an extended monologue by Deus, seventy-six lines in couplets. He first recalls the creation of Adam, 'Lyke to myn ymage', the Fall and the expulsion, and then the promise of mercy: 'Bot yit, I myn, I hight hym grace. / Oyll of mercy I can hym heyt' (10/8–9).[6] He now intends the Incarnation and the writer constructs an image which seems to encompass the whole narrative of the cycle in a figurative mode:

> For reson wyll that ther be thre –
> A man, a madyn, and a tre.
> Man for man, tre for tre,
> Madyn for madyn; thus shal it be.   (10/32–4)

There are several cross-currents in this speech which further underline the importance of this initiative at this point in the cycle. Deus refers to his conflict with the 'feynd of hell', and he places repeated emphasis upon Mary as 'Madyn'. As he instructs Gabriel he draws another contrast with the 'feynd': 'He was foule and layth to syght, / And thou art angel fayr and bright' (10/63–4).

Once this long and comprehensive speech is complete there is a change in the verse form, the rest of the play being in six-line stanzas of the type found in *Prophets* and *Caesar*. These are sustained in the form aabccb through the encounter between Gabriel and Mary and also for the episode of Joseph's doubts about Mary. The only exception is the single stanza where Gabriel takes leave of Mary: for this the rhyme aabaab reappears, and the lines are shortened to trimeters for Gabriel and dimeters for Mary:

> *Gabriel*   Mary, madyn heynd,
> Me behovys to weynd;
> My leyf at the I take.

> *Mary*    Far to my freynd,
> Who the can send
> For mankynde sake.   (10/149–54)

Once again it appears that the manipulation of the versification is dramatically significant, and there is very little reason to suppose that the changes are merely the result of cutting and pasting older fragments.

The third section of the play, the episode of Joseph's doubts, is treated rather more severely than in some other cycles, and there seems to be less recourse to the comic possibilities of Joseph's incredulity and the comedy of the old husband and the young wife. However, Joseph does regret the untrustworthiness of young women and his own difficulties because of his age. The main part of his long speech is mostly narrative, as he recounts the story of the purity of Mary's upbringing in the temple and how there was heavenly intervention obliging him to become her husband by means of the miraculous flowering of his wand (10/255). He also tells of his discovery of Mary's pregnancy. By this method of presenting the details the dramatist avoids direct confrontation, and the narrative presentation of this part of the play matches that implied in the initial speech by Deus. Together they give the impression that this poet was interested in making this episode carry great momentum in the cycle as a whole. However, there is also a significant active element in the dramatic method, for Joseph is about to slip away in despair at the end of his long narrative monologue and he is prevented only by the appearance of the Angel who tells him the truth about God's Son. This leads to a further twist in the play as Mary receives his apology with tenderness. Hence it does seem that in this play the dramatist was prepared to work towards linking with other episodes in the cycle, or filling in complementary narrative details.

This emotional tone in *Annunciation* is sustained in *Salutation* (11), which is next in sequence. A short play, it has much more limited dramatic objectives, and tradition suggests that the episode was often closely linked to Joseph's reaction as seen in play 10. Here there are only two speakers and the tone is an intimate one related to family life, though the actual familial relationship between Mary and Elizabeth is not made clear. Elizabeth has also heard an angel (11/37–40), a detail not found in other versions, and this, together with the movement of the child in her womb, who 'makys joy as any byrd', does have the important effect of affirming the angel's message (11/46–8). Once this point is reached Mary gives her version of the Magnificat, looking forward to her special role in spite of her sense of her own unworthiness. The play ends with a kiss between the two women, its sole participants.

We now come to *Offering of the Magi* (14), a play not apparently the work of the Wakefield Master, but one bearing some resemblance in places to its counterpart at York (16). The play contains little variety of stanza, most of it in a form which rhymes aaabab, and one which Stevens and Cawley note is common in plays 7 to 10. However, there is a special device in the first six stanzas bearing much of Herod's boast. Each is linked or concatenated to the next by means of verbal echoes, as in 'The lord am I, / Lord am I of euery land' (14/6–7). His boast is also heavily alliterated. This is a feature common in the York Cycle, as for example by Pilate in *Death of Christ* (Y36/1–39). Once again there is reference to Mahowne, and here the sense of his allegiance is strengthened because he sends out his followers to apprehend those not serving this 'deity'.[7] The boast is thus somewhat reminiscent of the Wakefield Master's practice, but it may well have originated from a common antecedent such as those boasts in *York*.

Although much of the play is centred on Herod, the kings are vividly portrayed. The initial prophecy of the first king is followed by his meeting with the others. They follow the star, continue to prophesy and are met by Herod's Nuncius.[8] For most of their dialogue the kings speak in strictly numerical order. After leaving Herod they approach the infant Christ in the stable and make the scriptural offerings. They are warned to depart by the Angel whose speech comprises a single stanza copied closely from its York counterpart (T/595–606 and Y16/369–380, rhyming abababcdcd, a common York form). The play ends with the separation of the kings, the last with a pious wish, 'Saue vs from fowndyng of the feynd / For his pausté' (T14/641–2). Thus this play does not reflect the demotic inventiveness of the Wakefield Master, but it has its own rhetorical characteristics.

*Flight into Egypt* (15) is a coherent and tightly knit play. It begins with the Angel's warning to Joseph against Herod (1–52), and the main action shows how Joseph tells Mary that they must leave and comforts her when she is distressed by the news. Joseph himself is much concerned to begin with and shows weakness and uncertainty, but he does speak bravely to Mary in spite of his age and anxiety. Mary's part is emotional, and it was perhaps inspired by the Sorrows of Mary, one of which traditionally was indeed the Flight into Egypt. Metrically the play is interesting in that it is written in a thirteen-line stanza, but one which is not the same as that by which the Wakefield Master is known. All but two of the thirteen stanzas follow the pattern ababaabaabcbc, with the eleventh line as a 'bob' of only two syllables. The variations occurring in the first and the penultimate stanzas are so small as to appear insignificant or accidental.

There are some features which relate this play to the corresponding York version (Y18). These are at the level of similarities in idiomatic phrases of which the following are examples:

> Awake, Ioseph, and take intent   (T15/1)
> Wake, Joseph! and take entente!   (Y18/37)
>
> A, leyf Ioseph, what chere?   (T15/57)
> A, leue Joseph, what chere?   (Y18/85)

It is tempting to suppose that these similarities in demotic speech are the result of memory by participants or audience. They argue interaction between Towneley and York at some point, but it is not clear whether this implies that Towneley reflects an earlier version than that in the York manuscript, or a common antecedent. However, there are significant differences, as the York play is in twelve-line stanzas and there is a marked difference in the characterization of Joseph, the York version being less emotional. Any similarities were thus subject to radical revision.

As we now approach the transition from plays about the Infancy of Christ to the group centred upon the Passion, a number of important issues arise regarding the unity of the cycle and the possibility of an overall design. We need to consider these here, independently of the work of the Wakefield Master, to see how far there is coherence. The next three plays, *Purification* (17), *Doctors* (18) and *John the Baptist* (19), contribute differing evidence about the design. *Purification* is out of chronological sequence, as its events must have preceded *Flight into Egypt*, but, as Stevens and Cawley point out (*Plays*, vol. 2, p. 530), its placing fits the liturgical order and its present position makes it the first of the three plays dealing with Christ's early life before the Passion. The actual Purification was no doubt to be found in the two leaves missing from the manuscript and one may attribute their absence to Protestant iconoclasm directed against Marian sentiment. The surviving part prepares the action by means of Simeon's monologue (1–72). This speech contains an elaborate description by Simeon of his decrepitude, a conventional theme for his character in the mystery cycles and in the non-dramatic sources. This is apparently treated seriously and not as an object of mockery, its purpose perhaps a conventional one underlining human frailty.[9] There is also a teleological view of the coming of Christ which is linked to the words of the prophets (Simeon was traditionally included among them) and to the redemption: 'And becom man for oure sake, / Oure redempcyon for to make, / That slayn were thrugh syn' (17/62–4). The speech is written in eight-line tail-rhyme stanzas (aaabaaab), but when the two Angels appear to announce the arrival of God's Son the metre changes to aabaab for the rest of the fragment. This is the form used for the part of Deus in *Creation*, the whole of *Prophets* and Gabriel in *Annunciation*, and its occurrence here seems motivated by dramatic or rhetorical considerations rather than conflation. There is also a liturgical aspect in this play, as a stage direction (l. 132) instructs the Angels to sing *Simeon iustus et timoratus*, an antiphon for the Feast of the Purification.[10] The next play, *Doctors*, is largely borrowed from York and has been discussed in the appropriate section above, but we should note here that its inclusion at this point in the cycle makes a significant impact upon the development of the overall narrative. Because it has the young Christ recite the Ten Commandments, it also contributes to the continuing theme of the law.[11] *John the Baptist* is consistent throughout in its metre. It is written in eight-line stanzas (abababab), the same as *Abraham* (4). One notable variation is that for the critical stanza during which the baptism takes place, John speaks in trimeters instead of tetrameters (19/185–92). The content of the play reflects its importance for the cycle as a whole in a number of ways. John at first speaks retrospectively, going back to the Creation and the Incarnation, but his elegant and dignified speech also looks ahead to the Crucifixion and the Resurrection:

> Thise Iues shall hyng hym on a roode –
> Mans saull to hym it is so leyfe –
> And therapon shall shede his bloode
> As he were tratoure or a thefe,
> Not for his gylt bot for oure goode,
> Because that we ar in myschefe;
> Thus shall he dy, that freely foode,
> And ryse agane tyll oure relefe.   (19/33–40)

These momentous events he links with the folly of Adam and Eve (19/61). He twice indicates in this speech that his mission as a 'forgangere' is to teach Christ's laws (19/10 and 29). The story of the baptism is a natural place for emphasizing the notion of the sacraments and this dramatist certainly makes much of this. Christ, mentioning the oil and cream, and John himself both refer to the idea of the sacrament (19/116, 130).

The action of the play culminates in the moment of baptism, distinguished by the rhythmic change noted above. The sacramental element in the play was apparently noticed by Reformers, who deleted the next stanza (19/193–200) with red lines and annotated in the margin 'corected and not playd'. It contains another reference to oil and cream and one to the six other sacraments. However, the significance is underlined shortly afterwards when Christ presents John with the lamb, which signifies Christ himself ('the lamb of me'), and anticipates Christ's sacrifice to come.

After this sacramental element is firmly established Christ tells John towards the end of the play that he must go forth and preach. It is here that the human aspects of John's characterization are emphasized. Unlike the York version, the dramatist offers a character who must take up a role independent of divine power, yet still be supported by it.[12] Christ associates this role with the sinfulness of man and his own death, 'For it I mon dy on a tre' (19/242), and he presents an image of Mary's grief: 'My moder certys that sight mon se; / That sorowfull sight shall make her maytt, / For I was born of hir body' (19/244–6). These lines recall the human dimension of the Incarnation, but they also suggest its transcendental importance. Stylistically they may recall the poetic directness of *Annunciation* (10), as in the quotations above.

The elements of retrospect and anticipation draw attention to the pivotal nature of this episode and this is enhanced when we consider the choices made by the person who arranged the manuscript, and perhaps of those who managed the performances. The Towneley text is unique in its genre in the absence of plays dealing with Christ's Ministry. After *John the Baptist* the next episode is *Conspiracy and Capture* (20), a highly complex play which begins the Passion itself. It must remain a possibility that this omission is purely a matter of chance but as it stands the effect may be considered significant. Towards the end of *John the Baptist*, as we have seen, Christ sends John to preach, and this may well epitomize his own contact with the people. The content of the episode also points very notably to grim aspects of the coming Passion and the evil it was meant to overcome. Thus there is directness in moving from this episode with its stress upon a series of dominating themes to the cruelty and violence in the catastrophic events which were to follow. The sacramental preparation here against such a future is valid and persuasive: it provides a sort of spiritual antidote and perhaps encourages us to look for its reiteration during the many stresses of the Passion.

As I have noted, most of the plays in the Passion sequence and after it (20–4, 27, 29–31) bear some evidence of work by the Wakefield Master and will be considered separately. In addition, *Harrowing* (25) and *Resurrection* (26) are substantially York plays, which leaves only *Thomas* (28) and *Judas* (32) for consideration here.

The first of these, whose full title is *Thomas of India*, is a complex one. Altogether its various episodes form part of the sequence of appearances of Christ after the Resurrection, and in this play he is by no means as silent as he appears in the Passion, indeed he speaks in a rich and poetic language. The incredulity shown by Thomas is only a part of the whole, and the play is substantially concerned with the manifestation of Christ himself in new circumstances. However there is some indication that this play as it stands is the result of compressing two or more separate elements. Unlike some of the changes in metre we have already noticed, the switch at line sixty-five from a six-line stanza (aabccb) to an eight-line form (abababab) occurs when Mary Magdalene has withstood mocking anti-feminist disbelief by Peter and Paul about her report of her meeting with the risen Christ. At this point Peter suddenly changes his mind and the mocking tone disappears. Perhaps the transition has not been carefully worked out. One reason for using this short episode as a prelude to the play, however, was perhaps that it registered Mary's belief in contrast to the subsequent incredulity of Thomas, and there is also the possible advantage of resuming the narrative suspended at the end of *Resurrection* (26), where she had indeed met the risen Christ.

Once Peter changes his mind, the play settles down into a more serious and formal mode, with three distinct phases. After Peter and Paul have lamented Christ's death, he appears, sings a liturgical song and leaves (28/104sd).[13] This portentous event helps to set the mysterious, not to say miraculous, tone of the rest of the play, and it also suggests a distinctly formal and ritualistic aspect, as manifested in the red clothing he wears (28/109). Following an appeal he reappears, singing the same song and makes two long speeches. He establishes that this really is a bodily resurrection and displays his five wounds. He makes a series of references to past events but his main purpose is to hold out the promise of mercy for sinners, a point subsequently emphasized by two Apostles who confirm that he has banished sinful despair (i.e. 'wanhope', 28/248, 250). He gives to the Apostles the scriptural power to bind and loose sinners, and he leaves them having breathed his power over them (28/234sd, 240sd). The Apostles thereupon confirm the truth of his bodily resurrection.

The second section switches to a different place, where Thomas laments Christ's death. Again there is a ritualistic tone to the references to his sufferings. When he returns to his brethren a long dispute begins as he elaborates his incredulity. Each of the ten Apostles tries in turn to persuade him, in the course of which they recall details of the life and Passion. Even though this routine is performed twice, Thomas refuses to believe and claims more than once that they have seen a ghost, the point being that this would not have been a resurrection: 'That he rose bodely, / For nothyng trow I may' (28/543–4). The amplitude of this repetitive structure gives scope for a great deal of retrospective detail, including references to the vinegar and gall, the wound by Longeus, the empty sudary and the meal at Emmaus, all potent and arresting images of suffering.

The third section starts with the return of Christ, who immediately allows Thomas to put his hand into the wound made by Longeus, and he himself condemns 'wanhope' (28/565–8). But the pace of the speeches continues to be expository. The main speech by Thomas is an elaborate plea for mercy, which Stevens and Cawley have compared to the genre of penitential lyrics. Fifteen of the forty-eight lines begin with the word 'Mercy', and the passage is rich in emotional imagery. As he casts aside his own rich clothing, Thomas says:

> Iesu, that soke the madyns mylk,
> Ware noght bot clothes of pall,
> Thi close so can thai fro the pyke,
> On roode thay left the small.   (28/605–8)

Christ's final speech is equally compelling:

> Mi saull and my cors haue knytt
> A knott that last shall ay;
> Thus shall I rase, well thou wytt,
> Ilk man on Domesday.   (28/621–4)

Thomas's incredulity is made part of the promise of salvation as in Scripture. In this play the author has found a distinctive voice.

The last play in Towneley is the fragment of *The Hanging of Judas* (32). It is not in the hand of the main scribe and is thought to be late in relation to the rest of the manuscript. Its dramatic mode is also in question since there are no speech headings and the fragment consists of a retrospective monologue by Judas, spoken after his death. The subject matter concerns his early life and the text breaks off before any contact is made with Christ. Judas does however refer to himself as 'Camys kyn' (32/17). Though this text is thus developing as a portrait of perhaps the most evil of men, and the story of Judas was well known from the *Legenda Aurea*, there is no distinctive evidence of the work of the Wakefield Master in it.[14] However, links with the other plays are few, and its function in the cycle as a whole remains obscure. Were it inserted into the historical narrative it might find a place in the Passion sequence on the analogy of the *Remorse of Judas* (Y32) in the York Cycle. There it is placed between the *Trial before Herod* and *Christ before Pilate 2*. Possibly the rather unsatisfactory attempt to include it in Towneley may have been prompted by this precedent.[15]

In spite of the inadequacy of *Judas*, it is apparent that the cumulative effect of the plays not marked by the work of the Wakefield Master is considerable and varied. It bears some distinct signs of organizing intent as between plays, and in places gives a sense of continuity. Individual plays are often distinguished by a distinctive dramatic style. Though this is rather variable in complexity and impact, there can be no doubt that many of the individual plays are clearly conceived and effectively constructed. We can also note a broad variety of emotional, linguistic and dramatic effects which argue competent theatrical imagination. This extends to characterization and also in a number of places to rich linguistic skills. Our study has also been concerned with the effective use of versification which we have frequently noted is closely linked with dramatic structure, and it has been a practical way of distinguishing individual voices.

In addition to such positive qualities in these episodes we find that in most of them there is an absence of certain elements entirely characteristic of the Wakefield Master. Besides his stanzaic preference, these include linguistic aspects as well as some ideological elements, particularly in relation to the oppression of the poor. Let us now look at these in more detail, starting with the plays which are entirely his.

# 1.4

# The Wakefield Master

*I*

In considering the six plays attributed to the Wakefield Master, *Abel* (2), *Noah* (3), *First Shepherds* (12), *Second Shepherds* (13), *Herod* (16) and *Buffeting* (21), we shall look at three aspects: some diagnostic characteristics, which help to establish the reality of his contribution to the cycle; the dramatic texture of these plays; and, in the conclusion of this chapter, his awareness of the rest of the cycle, the compatibility, so to speak, of his work. In due course this leads in the next section to the extent and nature of his participation in a considerable number of other plays in the cycle. But first we need to dwell upon the specific importance of these six plays for the cycle as a whole. They represent six coherent pieces of dramatic composition with all that implies, including inner resonances, which are sustained by the design and structure of each. Although the construction of these plays is not exactly the same, and there are significant variations of tone between them, it is apparent that these plays are each complete in themselves and they show a similar dramatic creativeness which runs through all of them, though with different results. This is supported by the unity of style within each. There is also the question of where they are placed in the cycle.

## Diagnostic Features

These establish the extent of the Wakefield Master's contribution to the Towneley Cycle. The readiest of them is the stanza form: stanzas of thirteen lines usually rhyming abababababcdddc. In the study of this stanza it is important to recall that Stevens and Cawley in their recent edition have decided to print the stanza as thirteen-liners, rather than the nine-liners common in previous editions. Such a form is not greatly dissimilar to many other generally distributed forms in the early drama, as for example the elaborate stanzas in the York plays and *Castle of Perseverance*. This suggests that the skill in manipulating such verse forms was considered appropriate and desirable. The dramatist here sticks very closely to his chosen pattern in all the six plays, except for *Abel*. But it is not only the frequency of use which distinguishes the versification: throughout its occurrence there is a marked versatility in the ways in which it is exploited. Sometimes the stanza is used without a break and this allows a great deal of variety in the way sentences can be sustained throughout a stanza. This is especially found in places where there is only one speaker and the rhetorical force can run uninterrupted, as in Herod's boast and the intro- ductory bravura by his Nuncius which precedes it (16/118–208, 1–91). Similarly it can be used lyrically as in the sequence where the Shepherds hail the infant Christ in a form which recalls established poetic convention (12/660–98, 13/1024–62).[1]

It is when we come to consider interactive dialogue that we see the complexity of use which is most characteristic and reflects extraordinary technical boldness. To some extent this goes with an interest in group dynamics since, as we shall see later, there is much gained by differentiating within the groups of Shepherds and Torturers. In his analysis of the form Stevens has shown that the speakers may change at almost any point in the stanza and this adds great flexibility to the ways in which they interact. In supporting this, the statistics in his table also refine the point by showing that about a quarter of the changes comes before the first line of the stanza and significant totals come before lines three, five, and seven: altogether he shows that 59.4 per cent of changes come at these four points. The other frequent places are before lines ten, eleven and twelve, which account for 23.94 per cent.[2] But the outstanding feature of the data he has compiled is that the poet was interested in spreading the change of speakers through the stanza and the effect of this is undoubtedly to create many differing opportunities for varied effects in the interactive dialogue. In *Second Shepherds* the stanza which embodies the recognition of the stolen sheep in the cradle allows for rapid interaction of the three speakers as well as giving sharp attention to some words like 'snowte' and to key moments in the action like 'Ay, so!':

> *3 Pastor*  Gyf me lefe hym to kys
> And lyft vp the clowtt.
> What the dewill is this?
> He has a long snowte!

| *1 Pastor* | He is markyd amys. |
| | We wate ill abowte. |
| *2 Pastor* | Ill-spon weft, iwys, |
| | Ay commys foull owte. |
| | Ay, so! |
| | He is lyke to oure shepe! |
| *3 Pastor* | How, Gyb, may I pepe? |
| *1 Pastor* | I trow kynde will crepe |
| | Where it may not go.   (13/842–54) |

Stevens also points out that in many instances speeches do not end with the stanza but there is frequently a continuity from one to another, the change of speaker occurring within the next stanza. The following exchange illustrates the continuity, enabling the fierce intention of Caiaphas to use violence against Christ to be pinpointed in two words:

| *Annas* | Youre wordys ar bustus; |
| | *Et hoc nos volumus,* |
| | *Quod de iure possumus.* |
| | Ye wote what I meyn – |
| | |
| | It is best that we trete hym |
| | With farenes. |
| *Caiaphas* | We, nay! |
| *Annas* | And so myght we gett hym |
| | Som word for to say.   (21/309–16) |

Another significant feature, which is brought out by the decision to show the stanzas as thirteen-liners, is that, in contrast to the stanza forms of the York plays and *Castle of Perseverance*, the lines are mostly quite short. This has the effect of making the rhyme a more prominent feature, and in this it is apparent that words are made to echo and repeat upon one another. Such verbal cross-reference is one of the fundamental characteristics of rhyming as a device and it is potent here. It may well be that such complexity introduces a certain artificiality into the sound of the words, a sense of contrivance. It required great ingenuity to sustain the requirements of the rhyme structure. The challenge of the complexity was no doubt an opportunity rather than a burden. When we consider this along with the often restricted and harsh vocabulary the effect is very striking. We may observe this in the following stanza spoken by Herod. At the same time, in this example we notice how the ninth, usually the shortest line and often a dimeter, is emphatically arranged, bringing some kind of poise, dwelling momentarily upon the sense.

*Herod*     For if I here it spokyn
           When I com agayn,
           Youre branys bese brokyn;
           Therfor be ye bayn.
           Nothyng bese vnlokyn;
           It shal be so playn.
           Begyn I to rokyn,
           I thynk all dysdayn
           For-daunche.
           Syrs, this is my counsell:
           Bese not to cruell.
           Bot adew! – to the deuyll!
           I can no more Franch.  (16/729–41)

Whilst the verse is not entirely dependent upon alliteration, it is apparent that some of its effect is achieved by the presence of alliterated groups of words, another device which tends to bring out remarkable sound effects. This can be seen in lines 731–2 and 740 in the stanza just quoted. In considering these aspects of the verse we should not forget that these are play texts, meant for performance. Much of the theatrical effect would no doubt be related to the sense of highly organized language which this form of versification facilitated, and its sheer virtuosity. This structured sound would also be integrated with the semiotics of action, movement and gesture.

Of the six plays attributed to the Wakefield Master in their entirety, *Abel* does not conform in terms of its versification. About half of the play is in couplets and the rest is in irregular stanza forms of nine, ten, eleven and twelve lines, some of them quite similar to the usual form. Only one stanza has thirteen lines and matches it exactly (2/452–64). However, the other diagnostic aspects we shall discuss here are strongly persuasive for its inclusion in the group. The most significant of these is the language. On the one hand there is no doubt that that the Wakefield Master was writing in Yorkshire dialect, but this is shared with the other plays in the cycle. Indeed it is a remarkable feature of the York, Chester, N Town and Coventry Cycles that they all depend upon the dialect of the locality in which they originated. It is a measure in each case of the way in which the cycles formed a part of the culture of their times, and it is hard to imagine them operating in circumstances separate from their roots in their respective communities. The dramatic effects, which can still be appreciated, are intimately associated with the sense of place engendered by such local language. But with the group of plays we are concerned with

here, there are features of language which distinguish them from the rest
of the Towneley Cycle.

The choice of language must be intimately related to the kinds of
dramatic situations and the course of events which the dramatist chooses
to portray. We have already suggested that in some places the plays are
concerned with lyrical expression, especially in relation to the Nativity.
It also occurs, with clear simplicity, in the rejoicing at the end of *Noah*.
Here the alliteration is not harsh, but delicate:

> As he in bayll is blis,
> I pray hym in this space,
> In heven hye with his
> To purvaye vs a place    (3/798–801).

But much of the business of the plays, the dialogue and the events portrayed
are tinged with the suffering, tribulation and human folly of the temporal
world, and these aspects determine a good deal of the expression. Even in
the two Shepherds plays, where the final mood is a joyful celebration of
the Nativity, the process by which this is reached is fraught with discomfort, folly and evil. The dramatist's taste for words is characterized by an
interest in harsh sounding and ugly names or attributions. These are found
in the six plays: 'all-wyghtys' (13/202), 'bewshere' (16/395), 'byll-hagers'*
(12/83), 'brodels' (16/118), 'dottypols'* (16/335), 'gedlyngys'* (2/14),
'holard'* (16/518), 'land-lepars'* (16/241), 'losell' (16/193), 'lurdan'
(16/710), 'scapethryft'* (2/386), 'wryers'* (12/85), and 'wragers'* (12/85).[3]
The abusive interchanges between Noah and his wife contain insults: 'ram-
skyt' (3/313), 'Nicholl Nedy' (3/585). In their strife the colloquial language
is laced with vigorous action and menace:

| *Vxor* | Spare me not, I pray the, |
| | Bot euen as thou thynk; |
| | Thise grete wordys shall not flay me. |
| *Noe* | Abide, dame, and drynk, |
| | For betyn shall thou be |
| | With this staf to thou stynk.[4] |
| | Ar strokys good? say me. |
| *Vxor* | What say ye, Wat Wynk? |
| *Noe* | Speke! |
| | Cry me mercy, I say! |
| *Vxor* | Therto I say nay. |
| *Noe* | Bot thou do, bi this day, |
| | Thi hede shall I breke!   (3/547–59) |

Even as she is beaten the Wife's defiance shows in her responses, and the short lines are managed in close coordination with the changes of feeling. Notice here how line nine is reduced to one word. In this sequence there is also an interplay between the comic and the menacing. The comic language is partly a matter of witty inventiveness, a feature of the long list of food consumed by the Shepherds:

> Here is to recorde
> The leg of a goys,
> With chekyns endorde,
> Pork, partryk to roys,
> A tart for a lorde –
> How thynk ye this doys? –
> A calf-lyuer skorde
> With the veryose.   (12/335–42)

This witty texture of the language also shows itself in the use of the proverbs distributed through the plays. B. J. Whiting pointed out long ago that this cycle is rich in proverbs, though these are distributed somewhat unevenly. He found that some eleven plays had very little proverbial material of any kind, and for our purposes his indication that there is a concentration of them in the plays by the Wakefield Master is significant as a diagnostic feature.[5] Many of them are used by the people of lower rank such as Pikeharness (Garcio), the Shepherds and the Torturers, and this fits in with the preoccupation with showing the biblical events in terms of the contexts of everyday life. The particular advantage of the pithy concentration of proverbial language is appropriate to both the comic and the serious in what these characters have to say.

The bitterness of Cain finds expression in the sharpness of a proverb: 'How! let furth youre geyse; the fox will preche' (2/86). And: 'Yey, ill-spon weft ay comes foule out' (2/438). This last example reappears in *Second Shepherds* just as the Second Shepherd spots the stolen sheep in the cradle (13/848–9, quoted above, p. 58). It is also the case that some other expressions used by Cain, which cannot be designated proverbs, still have the appearance of being such, as in 'Ther is a podyng in the pot' (2/388). Such colloquial language is a recurrent feature. Herod's threats are accompanied by a proverbial threat: 'Styr not bot ye haue lefe, / For if ye do, I clefe / You small as flesh to pott' (16/141–3).

The dramatic texture of the two Shepherds plays is remarkably similar, and this is sustained by the frequency and efficacy of proverbs within them. In *First Shepherds* the initial speech by the First Shepherd is built around the contrast of fair and foul – 'Now is fayre, now is rayne' (12/106) – in a notable example of the construction of a thirteen-liner. The theme it announces can hardly be a matter of chance because the action of the play turns upon the misfortunes of the Shepherds, earthly men, transformed by the Incarnation – 'We mon all be restorde' (12/716). The wisdom embodied in proverbs is consonant with the Shepherds: 'Nothyng is inpossybyll / Sothly that God wyll' (12/541–2). Yet this occurs in a play where the polarization of folly and wisdom is integral to the action.

In the *Second Shepherds* play the incidence of proverbs is even higher, a point made by Whiting (p. 18). Like *Abel*, this play contains a forthright presentation of an evil character in Mak, who is in many ways similar to Cain, and who resolutely pursues his evil intentions: 'We must drynk as we brew, / And that is bot reson' (13/722–3). J. W. Robinson has pointed out an ingenious play on a proverb when Mak invites the Shepherds to check his sleeve for theft (13/571–2): 'to stuff one's sleeve with a fleece' meant to deceive.[6] But it is the Shepherds themselves who are given most of the proverbs. The same contrast of good times and bad reappears – 'Now in weyll, now in wo, / And all thyng wrythys' (13/181–2). The consequences of uncomfortable marriage are a theme: 'For thou may cach in an owre / That shall sow the full sowre / As long as thou lyffys' (13/141–3). The perception of Mak by the Third Shepherd carries special weight: 'Fare wordys may ther be, / Bot luf is ther none / þis yere' (13/823–4). He says this as they leave Mak's cottage before they return to discover the sheep. This sententiousness is no doubt part of the traditional characterization of the Shepherds, notable in other cycles. It may be part of the wisdom they show and it supports their customary function as prophets before the Nativity.

But in spite of this, the incidence of proverbial expressions among the evil characters remains a remarkable feature of these plays, and this is sustained in *Buffeting*. One of the most dominating dramatic effects of this particular play is the silence of Christ. Indeed his silence is at the heart of the dramatic action. Theologically it is important here because in other parts of the cycle everything depends upon what Christ, the Word, says. But here his silence is eloquent and the wicked characters around him, Annas, Caiaphas, the two Torturers and the boy Froward, all try to break it. The assault is anticipated by the Second Torturer in the third stanza: 'Many wordys has thou saide / Of which we ar not well payde; / As good that thou had / Halden still thi clatter' (21/36–9). As they all press upon Christ their language is rich in proverbs, which are shared among them as follows:

| *First Torturer* | It is better syt styll |
|---|---|
| | Then rise vp and fall.  (21/40–1) |
| | He lyes for the quetstone.  (21/116) |
| | As cokys in a croft.  (21/514) |
| *Second Torturer* | He settys not a fle-wyng |
| | Bi Syr Cesar full euen.  (21/137–8) |
| *Annas* | All soft may men go far.  (21/306) |
| | *Et hoc nos volumus,* |
| | *Quod de iure possumus.*  (21/310–11) |
| | When it com to the pryk.  (21/380) |
| *Caiaphas* | Of care may thou syng!  (21/188) |
| | He gettys more by purches |
| | Then bi his fre rent.  (21/233–4) |
| | Kyng Copyn in oure game.  (21/241) |
| | Yei, bot all is out of har.  (21/304) |
| | Bot gyftys marres many man.  (21/635) |
| *Froward* | I may syng 'ylla hayll!'  (21/543) |

These expressions articulate the brutality of this episode, yet they are commonplace phrases, in themselves without threat. The cruel effect of these words may actually be a function of the brevity of what they say: the bite is in the neat accuracy of expression. Their presence and effectiveness in this context reflects the writer's interest in showing these cruel events by contemporary means. This is characteristic of his work in the six plays and in many of the other contributions he made to the cycle. Proverbs, it should be said, are distributed widely in the early English drama and the critical question is to account for their attraction to dramatists. For the Wakefield Master, we may suggest, this lay in the closeness to demotic speech, which was essential to his emphatically contemporary setting. But beyond this there is a poetic force in such expressions: their brevity, their pertinence and also their ambivalence, which made for poetic strength and the richness of linguistic experience.

Our analysis so far has drawn attention to the presence of demotic speech in many places in these six plays. It is found in the words of the Shepherds, the Torturers and Garcio. There is some contrast with the more educated speech by Annas and Caiaphas in *Buffeting*. These two are clerics and they are given some status by their language, as in the use of Latin. They are also differentiated in that Annas is subtler in his approach, seeking to calm down the violence threatened by Caiaphas. This configuration is

reversed from the York version where it is Annas who is the more severe.[7]
Here he stands by the law as recorded in Scripture (John 18:31):

> Annas    *Sed nobis non licet*
>          *Interficere quemquam.*
>
>          Sir, ye wote better then I
>          We shuld slo no man.    (21/389–92)

Caiaphas also stands upon his status:

> Caiaphas   Lad, I am a prelate,
>            A lord in degré:
>            Syttys in myn astate,
>            As thou may se.    (21/222–5)

But his hypocritical speeches are littered with crude threats and just as
his pretensions are undermined by them, so it is Annas who finally gives
way and orders the Torturers to carry out the beating: 'And that kyng to
you take, / And with knokys make hym wake' (21/465–6). Such manipulation enriches the poet's vision of these events and we also note how he
slips in the word 'kyng' at this critical moment. It may be sarcastic in the
part of Annas, but it reminds us who this victim is.

The six plays show a preoccupation with evil and folly, on some
occasions combining the two. This is not to say that evil appears in all of
them in exactly the same mode. Nevertheless, if the dramatist sees salvation
ultimately, he spends a great deal of dramatic time and emphasis upon
a detailed representation of much that is wrong in the human condition.
This is a continuum from the sufferings of the Shepherds as poor men
with little to enjoy in their lives, through their troubles in marriage, which
they share in some ways with Mak and with Noah, to the active cruelty
of the high priests and to the ultimate evil in Cain who does not seek
forgiveness and who cannot be forgiven. Even with the Shepherds, much
of the outlook is bleak. In the *First Shepherds* play the first two Shepherds
lament their poverty, the illness of their animals and the oppression they
have to endure from landlords and those who exploit them. Here there is
even a threat of consequences if they refuse to comply with requests
(12/105–17). In the *Second Shepherds* play the dramatist finds the opportunity to explore some of these themes before he becomes involved with
the intrigue surrounding Mak, the sheep stealer. The anticipation of this
in itself is another of their tribulations, and it is made apparent that they

are wary of it even before Mak begins his attempt. Eventually in both plays the mood changes, but before this the *First Shepherds* play is conspicuous for its exploration of folly, first by the unnecessary quarrel over where some entirely imaginary sheep should be pastured, and secondly by the device used by the Third Shepherd to reveal the follies of the other two, during which demonstration he wastes all his meal. This in turn is exposed by Jak Garcio: 'Of all the foles I can tell, / From heuen vnto hell, / Ye thre bere the bell' (12/266–8).

The sense of the oppressiveness of labour is shared by Cain and his boy. Their troubles with the plough team are enacted. Their relationship is bitter and destructive. Cain does not hesitate to strike Pikeharness and to make light of it when he complains:

> *Garcio*  All the day to ryn and trott,
>          And euer amang thou strykeand;
>          Thus am I comen bofettys to fott.
> *Cayn*   Peas, man! I did bot to vse my hand.   (2/392–5)

Perhaps the most perverse episode between them is when Cain forces Pikeharness to accompany his proclamation of the king's peace for himself, but in a passage of alternating speeches Pikeharness turns the proclamation into ridicule (2/421–39). Cain threatens to hang him if he is disobedient.

In *Herod* the concentration upon evil is unrelieved up to the very last moment. Herod's reputation is heralded by the lengthy introduction by Nuncius, a bravura passage in itself. He introduces the idea of Mahowne in the first line and this link with Herod runs through the play as though Mahowne was the deity he worshipped (as it appears in the moment of triumph at 16/665 and 685–6). The poet probably picked this motif up from the York plays, but he has made much of it here and elsewhere.[8] Notably the speech by Nuncius is thick with alliteration: twelve of the lines in the first stanza (as printed by Stevens and Cawley) contain an example. The substance of what Herod has to say is concentrated upon his menacing kingship, with the same underlying hint as in the speech by Caiaphas noted above: 'Carpys of no kyng / Bot Herode, that lordyng' (16/48–9). He repeats the phrase later more specifically referring to Christ (16/114). He also uses the phrase 'kyng of kyngys' (16/52) in a kind of inverted parody. It undermines Herod for the audience while glorifying him in the world of the play and this exposure is the basic dramatic impulse of the play.

When Herod appears he follows the preparation, but adds the rage which is traditional in his character: 'Me thynk I brast / For anger and for teyn' (16/169–70).[9] Sustaining his harsh language he hears news of the rival. The dramatic technique here is to give details of the prophecy of Christ's coming in the scornful words of his advisers. The proposal to kill the 'knaue-chyldren' comes from them and Herod is eager to follow it. The evil he embodies is backed up by the acts of the soldiers who carry out the slaughter of the innocents. There is no doubt that the enactment of this was shockingly visible: 'Alas, my hart is all on flood, / To se my chyld thus blede' (16/545–6). But the underlying purpose is no doubt to anticipate the Crucifixion and the lamentations of Mary after it. However, Herod's final speech (16/729–41, quoted above) makes him look ridiculous, especially when he tells his listeners not to be too cruel (16/739). In this speech his instability makes him look pointless and barren and the portrait suggests a pathological instability.

In *Noah* the evil element is handled more flexibly. Noah is initially apprehensive about the evil which has arisen among people, and he summarizes the Creation and Fall and God's promise of the oil of mercy. He points to the prevalence of the seven deadly sins (3/75–8). God follows this and, calling down destruction on the world, he repents full sorely that he ever made man. But the characterization of Noah in relation to his wife is managed in such a way as to show his own shortcomings. He anticipates that she will be quick to anger, and he is ready to respond to her challenge. In fact it is he who strikes the first blow and the quarrel between them has a series of violent episodes. It is their three sons who finally intervene to criticize both their parents and so bring the strife to an end. When they complain (3/599–604) Noah accepts the rebuke and the hostility ceases: once they are aboard the Ark he trusts his wife with the steering and consults her opinions. This association of Noah with the corruption of the world may indeed underline the necessity of grace at the end of the play. Along with this, his wife's refusal to come into the Ark may suggest the sinner who refuses salvation, an idea which turns upon the identification of the Ark with the Church.[10] Ultimately she does enter the Ark willingly, and this is another means of allowing for grace.

One significant pointer in these plays to the poet's deep concern with the presentation of evil is the persistent references made to the devil by the characters associated with sin. Cain refers to him frequently, associating it with obscenity: 'And kys the dwillis toute!' (2/65); 'Yei, kys the dwills ars behynde; / The dwill hang the bi the nek!' (2/268–9, and again at

2/89). There is a sort of mindless banality in most of his allusions which fits with the overriding barrenness of his actions and character. Similarly Herod refers to the devil seven times as his frustrated rage develops (16/170, 192, 207 (Lucifer), 218, 252, 326, 740). These are interwoven with the references to Mahowne already noticed. There is undoubtedly a symbolic resonance to this characterization: perhaps because of his misuse of royal power and his identity as a false king and an association with Antichrist, a close ally or manifestation of the devil. In *Buffeting* there is a series of references to the devil, but they are confined to Caiaphas. It may well be that as he was the manifestly more evil of the two high priests in this presentation this was a valuable distinction. He refers to the devil seven times (21/192, 210, 216, 235, 246, 446 and 637). None of the other characters in this play makes a reference.

With Mak, the devil references are more ambiguous, and it is apparent that the critical evaluation of this character has been uncertain, even though he attracts a great deal of attention. Instead of actually calling upon the devil, most of his asseverations are to do with God. Indeed he is quick to call blasphemously upon the Divine in a number of circumstances. In his first speech he calls upon God twice (13/274, 280). He says ironically to the Shepherds: 'God looke you all thre!' (13/317). When he awakes from his pretended sleep he says; 'Now Crystys holy name / Be vs emang!' (13/545–6). These phrases are indeed blasphemous, but their very use does bring God into the consciousness of the audience, albeit obliquely. Noticeably when the Shepherds reach Mak's cottage and the deception is highest Mak again calls upon God and in this he is joined by his wife. This domestic scene, in itself a parallel, even a parody, of the Nativity, is enriched by these verbal devices and there is a sacramental suggestion also at work, even though, chronologically speaking the Eucharist was not yet in being.

| Mak | As I am true and lele, |
|---|---|
| | To God here I pray |
| | That this be the fyrst mele |
| | That I shall ete this day.   (13/751–4) |

A few moment later his wife asserts in similar sacramental parody:

| Vxor | I pray to God so mylde, |
|---|---|
| | If euer I you begyld, |
| | That I ete this chylde |
| | That lygys in this credyll.   (13/773–6) |

But Mak's practice of magic in casting a spell upon the Shepherds while he steals the sheep, using false Latin in calling upon Pontius Pilate as a conjuration, sets a quite different tone. His ultimate fate, being tossed in the blanket, is a kind of reconciliation – both he and his wife know the penalty for sheep stealing was hanging – and it is recognition of humanity in Mak rather than a condemnation of a figure manifesting the devil, such as we have found in Cain and Herod. His treatment also brings a revelation about the Shepherds. Their kindness and mercy, in spite of all the difficulties they face and the folly they exhibit, become an act of charity and it is a holy response to the wickedness introduced by Mak. There is no way back for Cain and Herod, but there is for him. We should also question whether his offence is a crime or a sin. To steal a sheep, in the circumstances in which Mak is placed, is a deed of a different order from the sins of Cain and Herod. Thus the treatment of evil is a potent element in the Wakefield Master's work, but in spite of some very unremitting villains to whom he pays extensive attention and to whom he gives individualized language, he is also interested in fallible human beings who are not monsters.

## Dramatic Techniques

Our appreciation of the six plays wholly attributed to him will be strengthened further by looking at their dramatic texture. To this end we shall consider the nature of the dramatic dialogue in the plays, some action sequences, the use of groups, music, boys and servants.

The verse structure allows close interaction in the dialogue and we have also seen some very short speeches in the exchanges. These are often closely related to the action on the stage which at times is intricate and specific. The Shepherds talk about their actions as they approach the sheep in the cradle and Mak and his wife have urgent consultations about what to do next. In *Buffeting* after Froward, the boy, has brought a stool for Christ to sit upon so that they can reach him more easily with their blows, the Torturers give instructions to Froward about the veil to blindfold Christ. The dialogue suggests that they are watching his every move, and his tentativeness is apparent:

| | |
|---|---|
| *Froward* | Here a vayll haue I fon; |
| | I trow it will last. |
| *1 Tortor.* | Bryng it hyder, good son. |
| | That is it that I ast. |

| | |
|---|---|
| *Froward* | How shuld it be bon? |
| *2 Tortor.* | Abowte his heade cast. |
| *1 Tortor.* | Yei, and when it is well won, |
| | Knyt a knot fast, |
| | I red. |
| *Froward* | Is it weyll? |
| *2 Tortor.* | Yei, knaue.   (21/560–9) |

Interplay such as this, where each speaker picks up quickly on the previous speech is characteristic of the close interaction within the groups
of Shepherds and Torturers. Whatever the circumstances and tone of
performance, it looks as though the poet felt that he could rely upon the
players for whom he was writing to accomplish such effects, and he wrote
dialogue accordingly.

In the longer speeches there is a clear interest in the rhetoric which
sustains them. This is achieved by repetition of phrases and by the accumulation of items in lists, as in the Second Shepherd's description of his
various enemies (12/79–91). Long speeches could also contain critical
items of direct speech which no doubt provided opportunity for mimicry,
as in 2/419, 3/93–4, 12/227, 13/134, 16/330–1, 21/248. Throughout such
speeches there seems to be an interest in the potential for performance by
the actor. One special example of this is the device of direct address to
the audience, when the actor crosses from impersonation to sharing
thoughts with the onlookers. This is an integral part of the speeches. For
Pikeharness, at the beginning of *Abel*, there is the need to suppress the
audience, a variant of the 'make room' convention of medieval drama in
general (2/1–13). Similarly, Nuncius forces his warning upon the audience.
The threat embodied by Herod is presented as a threat to the audience as
though they were his subjects, but this is part of the theatrical game here:

Take tenderly intent
What sondys ar sent,
Els harmes shall ye hent,
And lothes you to lap.   (16/10–13)

The *First Shepherds* play begins with two addresses to the audience.
The First Shepherd speaks alone on the stage. The direction of his words
is not to the audience as such: rather the audience overhear what he says
about his distress as a victim of poverty. He is interrupted by the Second
Shepherd, who does not see him. This approach to the audience is quite
different:

Bensté, bensté
Be vs emang,
And saue all that I se
Here in this thrang!
He saue you and me,
Overtwhart and endlang,
That hang on a tre,
I say you no wrang.   (12/66–73)

The Second Shepherd then goes on to elaborate a picture of oppressors, but in doing so he associates the audience as though they too were at risk. The *Second Shepherds* play also begins with two soliloquies. The First Shepherd begins with a lament about the oppressors, 'thyse gentlery-men', and he confides in the audience about his sufferings and the difficulties he has encountered. Again there is some business whereby the Second Shepherd speaks separately to the audience. Cawley notes that he is deaf, which accounts for his ignoring the First Shepherd until the latter interjects, having blessed the audience: 'God looke ouer the raw' (13/157). The Second Shepherd addresses the audience, this time on the troubles of marriage.[11] The introduction of this theme echoes the relationship between Mak and his wife, and it anticipates the farcical element in what is to come. He specifically addresses young men, bidding them to be aware of wedding, and ends with the proverb quoted above ('For thou may cach in an owre', 13/141–3).

In *Noah* the attitude implied towards the audience is more complex. Both Noah and his wife address them and each makes them a part of their anxiety, of husband against wife, and vice versa. The speeches occur as they come to fighting and once again one feels that a farcical element is present as they take up conventional positions in the war of the sexes. Noah's wife speaks to the audience after Noah's threat. She first responds to him defiantly and then turns to the audience: 'We women may wary / All ill husbandys' (3/299–300). Noah is equally specific in his address to husbands:

Yee men that has wifys,
Whyls thay ar yong,
If ye luf youre lifys,
Chastice thare tong.   (3/573–6)

Action sequences in these plays are inventive and distinctive. They suggest that the dramatist could visualize what might happen on the stage and that he created sequences which would work. There is a strong possibility that he had an interest in mime. Thus the many items which the Shepherds produce for their feast may well have been non-existent and actions would be used to suggest them. If this was not the case and the items were real then there would have to have been a sort of conjuring performance whereby the items appeared from packets and packs. Later in the same play there is the bag of meal which the Third Shepherd empties to illustrate the folly of his companions (12/244–5). It is possible that this was a real property, but once again mime might have been the best solution. Similarly there is an interesting problem about the plough team of eight horses and oxen in *Abel*.[12] A good deal of the dialogue is about them, and at one point Cain asks whether he has got to hold as well as drive, implying that one man's place was to hold and direct the plough from the back while the other concentrated upon urging on the animals. But it does seem unlikely that eight beasts were used. As with the Chester *Noah*, the Ark has to be built on the stage here. To begin Noah takes off his gown, and the construction appears to take only two stanzas if we note the verb tenses. He begins by saying he *will* make the top and the sail; then he says driving the nails through the boards *is* a good device ('nobull gyn'); and finally he says that window, door and three chambers *are well made*, adding that 'It is better wroght / Then I coude *haif thoght*' (3/377–416, original emphasis).

The theatrical inventiveness appears also in a number of sequences. These include the sequence at the cradle of Mak's 'baby' and especially the turning point when an act of charity makes the Shepherds return to discover the theft. In this sequence and the extended buffeting of Christ it is notable that the actors have to work in a closely coordinated manner. The dialogue they are given creates an extraordinarily tense atmosphere. A third episode comparable for its close working between characters and active dialogue is the murder of the innocents in *Herod* (16/458–573). The stanzas here are often divided between many speakers, up to six at one point (16/482–94). From a performance point of view the timing must be of primary importance. In this episode the emotional content is high as the lamentations of the mothers are met by the insults of the soldiers. It is worth noting at this point that passages of such close interaction are not unique to the work of the Wakefield Master. It may well be that he was influenced by similar passages in the York plays dealing with the Shepherds and the Soldiers at the Crucifixion. In the latter there is a great deal of writing for a group working closely together, in terms of actions as well as words. But we can say that in some of these six plays there is a deliberate attempt to exploit this kind of theatrical invention.

Music is apparently confined to the two shepherds plays among the six. There was undoubtedly a tradition that the Shepherds should sing in the cycle plays, and the York manuscript shows that this was established by the fifteenth century.[13] Such a tradition may have arisen because of liturgical precedents and also by association with the scriptural account suggesting that the Shepherds heard the song of the angels.[14] The occurrences of songs are quite similar in the two Wakefield plays: the first occurs at a secular moment, one after the Angels appear, and another as an exit at the end of the play. However, the *Second Shepherds* play adds an apparently unpalatable lullaby by Mak for his 'child'; one which enhances the farce, perhaps as a parody of the Angel (13/643, 688–90). Unfortunately there are no musical texts in the manuscript, nor are there any words, except for the Angel's. But the dialogue is informative about what is to happen and it reveals that the poet was interested in elaborate musical effects based apparently upon considerable knowledge, and also upon an appreciation of what constituted good or bad music.

In the *First Shepherds* play the secular moment is associated with drinking, perhaps in line with the gluttony manifested in the preceding feast. After the Shepherds fail to drink equally and fairly from one bottle, the Second Shepherd produces another from which 'Whoso can best syng / Shall haue the begynnyng' (12/383–4). The First Shepherd, however, hijacks the competition: when they have all sung – perhaps a drinking song – he drinks first without waiting for adjudication and in spite of complaints from the other two (12/385–94). Shortly after this they fall asleep and are awakened by the Angel. In the text there is only a speech from the latter but a subsequent comment makes it clear that there was also a song, presumably a 'Gloria' (12/426–38, 589–90). The Shepherds discuss the musicality of what they have heard – and this goes with the idea that the actors might also have been trained singers – and apparently they now repeat the Angel's song, completing it at line 621.[15] After they have visited the Child, the Shepherds end with a cheerful song 'With myrth and gam' though it is not clear whether this is sacred or secular.

Some of these plays show an interest in exploiting relationships between masters and servants. Perhaps this should be linked with the complaints about oppression that we have noticed, but it is also possible that there was a precedent at York for including the relationship with a rather subversive boy as with Brewbarret, Cain's servant in York (Y/73–9).[16] In the *First Shepherds* play Jak Garcio has been looking after the flock but he arrives in time to mock the others as the fools of Gotham. There is some doubt about the consistency of his presence because he fades out unnoticed, but here at least he is separate from the others and he says 'Ye thre bere the bell' (12/268).[17] But also the Third Shepherd (Slawpase) has a subordinate status and complains of ill-treatment (12/290–1). There remains a possibility that there is a textual flaw here. In the *Second Shepherds* play the Third Shepherd (Daw) is clearly established as a boy of subordinate status (13/212–5, 252) and he refers to himself as a servant (13/222). He has an extensive complaint against his masters, particularly about the poor and belated payment for his labour (13/222–47). It is noticeable that he does the hard work.

There are two other examples in the six plays. Pikeharness introduces Cain in *Abel* with some obscenity and sustains his quarrels with his master throughout the play. Like Froward in *Buffeting* he complains of his harsh treatment (2/430–2 and 21/549–55). Froward is described as 'euer curst' (21/548) and his part in the cruelty shown to Christ is sustained at a critical time in the play, and he derives satisfaction from it: 'In fayth, syr, we had almost / Knokyd hym on slepe' (21/610–2).

## II

We now turn to the other plays where there is evidence of intervention by the Wakefield Master. As reference to Figure 1 shows, this is apparently intermittent in so far as the occurrence of the thirteen-line stanza is a criterion and the extent varies from play to play. But this raises another difficult issue in as much as a short palpable intervention – writing a few lines in his trademark stanza – may also imply his approval of what he does not interfere with or change. It seems that it is upon this that the claim advanced by Stevens for the Wakefield Master's overall and final redactorship is based. But it is evidence by default rather than by being irrefutably positive. Moreover, the date of the Wakefield Master's work is usually thought of as being mid-fifteenth century and such a redactorship would not fit well with the comparatively late date now advocated for the manuscript as a whole. Apart from the special case of *Abel* already discussed, the plays in which the thirteen-line stanza occurs intermittently are *Conspiracy, Scourging, Crucifixion, Dicing, Pilgrims, Ascension* and *Judgement,* such interventions being focused within the Passion sequence. An approximation to the stanza also occurs in *Lazarus,* a play whose position in the manuscript is anomalous. Our concern here is to establish what the Wakefield Master does to the plays in which he does intervene.

The high incidence of thirteen-line stanzas in *Scourging* and *Judgement*, twenty-seven and forty stanzas respectively, points to a virtual re-writing of these two plays and results in a significant shift of emphasis. Both, however, have retained a substantial amount from the corresponding episodes at York. *Scourging* begins with a complete episode by the Wakefield Master enacting a boast by Pilate followed by the scourging and mocking of Christ and the departure for Calvary (22/1–351). The boast is not unlike that for Herod in play 16 (i.e. before the slaughter of the Innocents. The later Herod, who participates in the Passion, is absent in Towneley). Pilate also shows allegiance to Mahowne as the earlier Herod had done. It should be noted, however, that the first eight lines of each stanza in his fifty-two lines are much longer than is usually the case with thirteen-liners. Once the dialogue with the Torturers begins, this part of each stanza returns to the more usual shorter lines. One feature here is that in these speeches there is a deliberate attempt to recreate some of the earlier events lying outside this play, a cyclic function of some importance. What is said by such evil characters is meant to blacken Christ's name, but in fact the miracles and the healing are actively recalled in a positive manner despite this ostensible objective. Pilate does not attach much importance to such accusations until there is a threat to report the outrages to Caesar, whereupon he capitulates and orders the Crucifixion. For the scourging there may be some reliance upon the York Crucifixion where the close interaction between the Soldiers is notable. The following stanza shows the Towneley Torturers at work and it also recalls the Torturers in *Buffeting:*

| | |
|---|---|
| *2 Tortor.* | Now fall I the fyrst |
| | To flap on his hyde. |
| *3 Tortor.* | My hartt wold all to-bryst |
| | Bot I myght tyll hym glyde. |
| *1 Tortor.* | A swap, fayn if I durst, |
| | Wold I lene the this tyde. |
| *2 Tortor.* | War! lett me rub on the rust, |
| | That the bloode downe glyde |
| | As swythe. |
| *3 Tortor.* | Haue att! |
| *1 Tortor.* | Take þou that! |
| *2 Tortor.* | I shall lene the a flap, |
| | My strengthe for to kythe.   (22/170–82) |

The point should be made that this interaction between Torturers is a widespread convention: it is found for example in Gréban's *Passion* which originates in northern France *c*.1450.[18] In the next section of the play the text shows extensive direct borrowing from York play 34, a passage reproduced in the York ten-line stanza. The sequence also adds some stanzas which are presumably derived from York but which do not appear in the York manuscript as we now have it. This might suggest that this play or this sequence within it originated before the York Register was written. The subject matter here is John's report to the Virgin and the Marys, together with their lamentation as they see Christ be led away. Near the end of the play the Torturers re-appear, now in direct imitation of York. However, the last stanza shows the three Torturers again working closely to drag Christ off, and they speak a nine-line stanza reminiscent of their earlier speeches composed by the Wakefield Master:

| | |
|---|---|
| *3 Tortor.* | Now, by Mahowne, oure heuen kyng, |
| | I wold that we were in that stede |
| | Where we myght hym on cros bryng. |
| | Step on before, and furth hym lede |
| | A trace. |
| *1 Tortor.* | Com on, thou! |
| *2 Tortor.* | Put on, thou! |
| *3 Tortor.* | I com fast after you |
| | And folowse in the chace.   (22/564–72) |

If he did write this passage, as seems likely, it looks as though one of his concerns was structural and in doing this he may have been working towards reconciling different and distinctive parts.

The revision of *Judgement* is so large that the whole tone and balance of the York play from which it derives are changed. The latter was intensely devotional in intent and concentrated upon visual effects associated with the iconographical effects. The participation of the devils is minimal in the York text, though we cannot be quite sure how large was the visual impact: potentially dragging Bad Souls off to hell might have been a major spectacle, perhaps by tradition. Though some of the iconographical intent survives, especially when Jesus spreads his hands and shows his wounds (the Towneley text adds a stage direction to this effect, 30/575sd), the additional material in thirteen-line stanzas is entirely concerned with the devils and in particular their response to the summons to the Judgement. The expression in these passages shows the familiar characteristics, with its deliberately ugly phraseology and harsh sounds and rhythms, often alliterative. The new devils do three things: the First and Second Demons describe the records of sins in the form of rentals or catalogues, which will be used at the Judgement, and the failure of sinners to see the effect of their deeds (30/131–299); Tutivillus details the wicked ways of many individual sinners (30/300–559); and after the condemnation by Jesus, the devils take the damned off to hell, tormenting them verbally with their misdeeds and with the threat of pains to come (30/706–821). There are a number of touches here which recall the details we have noticed in the work of the Wakefield Master. The two demons operate a master–servant contrast interestingly noted by Stevens and Cawley in the uses of 'thou' by the First Demon, who is superior, and 'you' by the Second Demon (174, 179 notes). Tutivillus is apparently small in stature, probably a boy, and although he has an extensive catalogue of sins he is apparently subservient to the others. There is a distinctly anti-feminine trait in his list. In terms of the plot of this play these hardly make any difference, but the Judgement is an inherently difficult subject in terms of its actual events since the outcome is rather expected. But the emotional effect of these additions is undoubtedly cruel and grim, one which might be associated with the threats and deeds of tyrants in other passages by the Wakefield Master. The two demons sing a song as they begin to drive away the Bad Souls: the Second Demon (the servant) has the tenor part, and the other the mean (30/715–16). Unfortunately the song is lost, but Tutivillus's next speech sets the mood: 'Youre lyfes ar lorne / And commen is youre care!' (30/719–20). The outcome of *Judgement* as a whole is that the final effect is more threatening than the triumph of divinity at York.

The inclusion of Tutivillus intensifies the cruelty, but the poet was drawing upon a well-established tradition in Christian literature.[19] The fact that Tutivillus identifies himself as a 'master Lollar' (30/311) also points to the orthodoxy of the poet. We shall return later, however, to the subversive aspects of his work.

In *Conspiracy*, *Dicing* and *Lazarus* we find distinctive evidence of the work of the Wakefield Master, but if we confine ourselves to the incidence of thirteen-liners it is limited and specific. However, this broad judgement needs qualification. *Conspiracy* is one of the most challenging texts in the corpus: it clearly contains a mixture of effects and there is the strong possibility that it was assembled from a number of different sequences. It is one of the longest plays in the cycle, with 779 lines in the Stevens and Cawley edition, and it stands at the beginning of the Passion sequence, initiated by Pilate's boast in thirteen-line stanzas typical of the Wakefield

Master. From there it works through a number of episodes including the conspiracy between Pilate, Annas and Caiaphas, with the proposed betrayal by Judas; the Last Supper, though Towneley is unique in not including the instituting of the Eucharist; the move to Olivet; Pilate's despatch of the soldiers, there being four thirteen-line stanzas as part of this sequence; the arrest, including the incidents of the kiss by Judas and Peter's cutting off the ear of Malchus, and the decision by Pilate to send Christ to Caiaphas. As the play is headed 'Conspiracio' but the explicit refers to 'Capcio' there is some grounds for suggesting the compiler was to some extent in two minds faced with this large variety of material. There is also a duplication of references to Peter's denial (20/402–5 and 448–51). Internal changes in verse form also suggest some discontinuity. Most of the play is written in a language which is not suggestive of the Wakefield Master, but there is one passage where Pilate is preparing to give instructions for the arrest written in quatrains like much of the rest of the play. Here the expression takes on the minatory tone of the Wakefield Master's Herod and Pilate found elsewhere, but it must be said also that there are tyrants in York and elsewhere whose language is not dissimilar. The following extract is characteristic of the passage:

> Peas! I commaunde you, carles vnkynde,
> To stand as styll as any stone!
> In donyon depe he shal be pynde
> That will not sesse his tong anone.

> For I am gouernowre of the law:
> My name it is Pilate.
> I may lightly gar hang you or draw;
> I stand in sich astate
> To do whatso I will.   (20/584–92)

Although there is some reliance here upon alliteration, this speech does not have the resonance and the intensity of the Wakefield Master's work elsewhere, especially if we compare it with the opening boast in this play (20/1–77).

*Dicing* presents us with a number of issues relating to the intervention by the Wakefield Master into plays not entirely written by him. It has been convincingly suggested by some scholars that the original was the lost play belonging to the millers at York, which they discontinued after 1423.[20] As it does not appear in the York manuscript, comparison is difficult but it is likely that the central section (24/180–371) is derived from the

millers' pageant chiefly because the description of the events in the lost
pageant corresponds closely to what actually happens in the Towneley
version: Pilate and the Soldiers play at dice for the garments, draw lots
for them and then divide them amongst themselves.[21] On either side of
this passage the work of the Wakefield Master is apparent and a comparison
with some of his other interventions is valuable. The play begins with
another boast by Pilate in five thirteen-line stanzas: this time one of them
is entirely in Latin and the other four are macaronic, but the familiar
threats are apparent:

> Bot ye youre hedys
> Bare in thies stedys,
> Redy my swerde is
> Of thaym to shere now.   (24/49–52)

In the later passage of four thirteen-line stanzas the Wakefield Master
springs a surprise, yet it is in line with some of his interventions elsewhere.
The Torturers, having given the garment to Pilate, suddenly express a
moral rejection of dicing and its evil effects. In vigorous language, with
alliteration and the familiar crabbed vocabulary, they give a warning
against it:

> Thise dysars and thise hullars
> Thuse cokkers and this bollars,
> And all purs-cuttars –
> Bese well war of thise men!   (24/387–90)

Swearing by the devil and by Mahowne, they blame Fortune, in a passage
reminiscent of the anxieties of the Shepherds:

> She can downe and vptake;
> And rych
> She turnes vp-so-downe,
> And vnder abone.   (24/398–401)

There are, however, some signs that the interventions extended beyond
these passages. Stevens and Cawley note that the scribe's normal practice
of connecting rhyme words by means of brackets breaks down here,
and there is evidently some uncertainty about the prosody. The editors
have had to reconstruct the seven-line stanzas used in lines 287–314. This
irregularity occurs in a passage where seven-line stanzas take over from

a variety of other forms. In some of them the language and the sentiments are similar to those we find for the Wakefield Master, and some of the shorter stanzas also are rhythmically similar to his work. At the end of Pilate's boast we find: 'Loke that no boy be to bustus, blast here for to blaw, / Bot truly to my talkyng loke that ye be intendyng' (24/66–7). There is a proverb: 'He has myster of nyghtys rest that nappys not in noynyng' (24/84). And another expression which is bawdy and also probably a proverb: 'I haue brysten both my balok-stones, / So fast hyed I hedyr' (24/166–7). The Torturers give a triumphant account of the sufferings of Christ at Calvary. One of them admits to the name 'Spyll-payn' (24/143; one who wastes bread, perhaps the bread of the Eucharist). We also note that in places the stanzas are distributed between different speakers, sometimes breaking up lines and sometimes using the short line to some effect. The central part of the play may thus have been worked by the Wakefield Master and if it is, its importance lies in the fact that he did not always write in thirteen-liners, however attractive and challenging these might have been to him. With perhaps less certainty than for *Abel* we may assume a considerable contribution here. But then, it is also interesting that he chose not to use the thirteen-liners in these cases even though other aspects of his poetic method are apparent.

The play of *Lazarus* presents us with problems at several different levels and the participation of the Wakefield Master is by no means as certain as it is even in the plays we have just been considering. The play follows *Judgement* in the manuscript, standing remote from its expected place in the narrative, which would normally have been at the end of the Ministry so as to present a prelude to the Passion and the Resurrection. It has been argued by J. W. Earl that a significant part of the content, a warning about hell, may have determined this placing in order to drive home the message of Judgement, and the monologue of Lazarus approximating to a sermon may have been perceived as an appropriate vehicle for this.[22] However, the play begins with a simple dramatization written in couplets, with a distinct narrative structure, as Jesus and his disciples determine to visit Lazarus; this may seem out of place following the *Te Deum* which comes at the last moments of *Judgement*. The possible intervention by the Wakefield Master occurs after the narrative of the play is complete, when the revived Lazarus speaks a monologue. This includes six fourteen-line stanzas which bear prosodic similarity to his usual form, though the characteristic manipulation of the short line (line nine) is not apparent. The rhyme scheme for these stanzas is ababababcccdcd. One thirteen-line stanza follows the usual pattern but it may well be a defective

fourteen-liner (31/181–93). The monologue is unrelievedly mournful and
although the tone might seem to suggest the grimmer aspects of the Wakefield Master's usual view of human ills, the rather conventional presentation
of horrors argues against this. On the other hand there is some irregular
concatenation between stanzas, as in 'vnder' (138–9) and 'goode/goodys'
(166–7), which may suggest his verbal dexterity, even though this device
is not usual for him. The following lines, though they do depend in part
upon alliteration, seem most concerned with invoking conventional disgust
and follow conventional literature about the horror of decay:

> Youre rud that was so red,
> Youre lyre the lylly lyke,
> Then shall be wan as led
> And stynke as dog in dyke.
> Wormes shall in you brede
> As bees dos in the byke,
> And ees outt of youre hede
> Thusgate shall paddokys pyke.   (31/153–60)

If this play does indeed contain an intervention by the Wakefield Master
it may seem uncharacteristically inept. There are further underlying difficulties, the chief of which is the absence of any other plays dealing with
Christ's Ministry, and the suspicion remains that the compiler, or perhaps
the scribe, did not quite know how to deal with the episode, which in
itself lacks continuity.

   Though the indications of interventions in *Crucifixion*, *Pilgrims* and
*Ascension* are rather limited we may regard them as part of a persistent
interest in the Passion sequence on the part of the Wakefield Master.
Starting with *Conspiracy* (20), he apparently intervened in every play until
*Judgement* (30) except for three, *Harrowing*, *Resurrection* (both taken
from York) and *Thomas*. Nevertheless, the possible intervention in *Crucifixion* is somewhat problematic and overall evidence for participation is
somewhat spasmodic. There is one thirteen-line stanza (23/383–95) with
a short ninth line but there are four rhymes in the first eight lines, instead
of the usual two. This occurs in a substantial episode following the raising
of the cross in which John seeks to comfort the Virgin. The passage has
a lyrical strategy with a variety of verse forms and some pattering
depending upon the word 'Alas' spoken by Mary (23/367, 410, 435, 461).
The suggestion by Stevens and Cawley that this is a sustained poetic effect
is certainly credible but whether the Wakefield Master was responsible
for this poetic structure, with its prosodic variation, is open to question.

It does not really recall any of his other lyrical passages, except possibly the 'Hail' lyrics by the Shepherds (12/673–711, 13/1024–62), but even there the resemblance is limited. The passage involving the Torturers is not written in thirteen-liners, but it does contain some closely integrated dialect as they go about their cruel work. Such writing has some similarities with the corresponding passage in the York version, and may indeed have been suggested by it. The following stanza illustrates the mode but it is difficult to attribute it to the Wakefield Master on any positive grounds.

| | |
|---|---|
| *4 Tortor.* | Pull, pull! |
| *1 Tortor.* |     Haue now! |
| *2 Tortor.* |         Let se! |
| *3 Tortor.* |            Aha! |
| *4 Tortor.* | Yit a draght! |
| *1 Tortor.* | Therto with all my maght! |
| *2 Tortor.* | Aha! hold still thore! |
| *3 Tortor.* | So, felowse, looke now belyfe |
| | Which of you can best dryfe, |
| | And I shall take the bore.  (23/191–6) |

*Pilgrims* is a simply constructed play which probably inherits something from the liturgical drama.[23] The plot is very direct and simple, telling the story of how Christ accompanied Cleophas and Lucas, and his sudden disappearance after he blesses the bread at the meal: *Tunc benedicet Iesus panem et franget in tribus partibus, et postea euanebit ab oculis eorum* (27/296sd). At the beginning of the play there is a retrospective passage which functions in a cyclic manner, bringing back the horror of past events. In spite of differences from York there is very little in the way this story is unfolded to suggest the overall intervention of the Wakefield Master. Stevens and Cawley point out that the didactic role of Christ here is more pronounced than in the York version. His speeches are often metrically different from the rest of the play but it is not clear that these are interpolations, as Stevens and Cawley suggest, so much as a means of differentiating his part in a manner similar to other episodes we have noticed elsewhere in the cycle. The only thirteen-line stanza occurs near the beginning of the play, an elegiac retrospect by Lucas about Christ's preaching and the cruelty shown him.

That lord, alas, that leche,
That was so meke and mylde,
So well that couth vs preche,
With syn was neuer fylde,

He was full bayn to preche
Vs all from warkes wylde.
His ded it will me drech,
For thay hym so begylde
This day;
Alas, why dyd they so,
To tug hym to and fro?
From hym wold thay not go
To his lyfe was away.   (27/19–31)

There is some alliteration in this stanza but this is not materially different from the rest of the play, and especially the preceding speech. The first eight lines have three stresses rather than two but the short ninth line, 'This day', works in the normal way and the last quatrain has some of the tense pressure we may expect.

*Ascension* is a well-developed play with strong parts for Jesus and Mary. It contains a spectacular climax, the Ascension being accompanied by singing angels and the speeches suggest that some sort of scenic device was used at this point (29/282–9 and stage directions at 281 and 289). Again there is a strong retrospective element, this time by Jesus himself. After the climax there are two thirteen-line stanzas which are spoken by Bartholomeus and Matheus (29/362–87). Their purpose is to underline the spectacle and meaning of the Ascension. As in the *Pilgrims* stanza there are three stresses in each of the first eight lines. Earlier, during the long speech by Jesus setting up the mission for the disciples, there is one nine-line stanza which, though shorter, is structured similarly. The ingenious, almost strained rhymes in lines 155–6 might just suggest the characteristic skill of the Wakefield Master:

And trowe truly
Mi dethe and rysyng,
And also myn *vpstevynyng*,
And also myn *agane-commyng*,
Thay shal be saue suerly.   (29/153–7: original emphasis)

Apart from these elements, there is very little to suggest that there was a sustained intervention.

Assessing the overall impact of the Wakefield Master on the Towneley plays, we must note that even if the criteria for his intervention can be agreed unmistakably it is apparent that there is much that he did not touch. Other parts of the cycle have their own distinctive characteristics and we have noticed earlier their poetic and theatrical qualities, which differ markedly from his work. Some plays show him to be able to sustain his interest and demonstrate his skills throughout. Others show that he could intervene effectively, and in doing so bring about a considerable shift in emphasis. Beyond this there are plays where his intervention is virtually certain but it is so limited that doubts remain about exactly why he did intervene at all. Lastly, there are places where his intervention remains only a possibility, and the play concerned remains largely outside his range and interests. It is also true that since in several plays his intervention is apparently very small, it must still be conceded that for these he was at least a reviser, adding something to the work of others. However, we cannot be sure that the completely new plays he composed were intended to replace others or that he was initiating entirely new elements.

Within the broad characteristics of cyclic form the Wakefield Master shows in his complete plays an awareness of how it works. He follows the techniques of anticipation and retrospect which are characteristic of it and he reflects its overall preoccupation with grace and salvation. Even though the social aspects of his work seem sometimes subversive, his orthodoxy is not in question and his contributions support the emphasis upon Catholic doctrine spread through the cycle.[24] The episodes which he chose to develop in detail may have his own idiosyncratic marks upon them but his Cain, Noah and Herod, together with the groups of devils, torturers and shepherds, fit in with the York model, which we can assume was available to him. The compiler of the cycle, assuming that he was not the Wakefield Master, must have realized the suitability of the latter's work for his overall intention. The decision to include both the Shepherds plays, however, adds something remarkable in as much as it suggests that his objective was not simply to prepare a text for performance, however pressing that might have been, but to present a text which was cyclic and devotional, and one which recorded what he had to hand and was relevant to his religious purposes.

# II

# Performing the Cycle

# 2

# Prologue:
# Some Questions of Performance

Our study of the Towneley manuscript has made it plain that it has many features which point unmistakably to the possibility of performance. Many of the individual episodes contain stage directions, though these cannot be regarded as systematic, and some plays have none. Where they do occur, they often give specific instructions about gesture and movements on stage, particularly those which involve a change of location or the movement of characters into different situations. The layout of the manuscript itself exhibits some of the characteristics of a play manuscript, and it has many similarities in a number of ways with other dramatic manuscripts of the period. It is apparent that by the time it was written out conventions for writing down plays had been evolved and the scribe was familiar with them and sought to follow them, even if the spectacular decoration of the many initial capitals throughout the manuscript was irrelevant to performance. Beyond this, two references in the Wakefield court rolls make it quite clear that a performance of a Corpus Christi play was intended in the town in 1559, and these are supported to some extent by the 1556 record quoted on p. 6 above which specifies 'that euerye crafte and occupacion doo bringe furthe theire pagyauntes of Corpus Christi daye as hathe bene heretofore used'. These words make it likely that a performance of some sort goes back some way into the now untraceable past and that it was regarded as well established; in addition that the craft guilds were involved in the presentation on Corpus Christi. There may be some residual uncertainty about what exactly was meant by 'pagyauntes' in this record, but the other two surviving references, dated 1559, both use the word 'play', which puts the matter beyond doubt. If the conjecture we noted that the manuscript itself was written out as late as the mid-sixteenth century, such an act would have been very close in time to these records even though we cannot be certain that the text we have was the one which was actually played. Indeed it seems wiser to remain sceptical about what exactly was performed on these occasions and to bear in mind that we have no conclusive evidence that the text as we have it was ever performed as a whole, whatever evidence we are now about to discuss for the inherent dramatic or theatrical qualities it exhibits. Nevertheless, since our primary concern is to focus upon those elements which may shed light upon whether the Towneley Cycle is a consistent whole or an accumulation of parts tenuously related to one another, we shall investigate in this section of our study the ways in which the performance characteristics of the plays are consistent and how far they argue for an overall coherence. In the references noted it is striking that the text involved is called 'the Corpus Christi play' suggesting that it was perceived as a whole and coherent entity, and it is also implied that there were constituent parts.

It will be a major preoccupation in this section as to whether the plays were written for performance on wagons used processionally or for a static playing place. The fact that some of the individual plays are very similar to their counterparts in York must mean that those particular texts were conceived for a processional performance on pageant wagons irrespective of the use that was made of them when they were moved to Wakefield. In the light of this we need to consider how far the plays of Towneley are compatible with such a mode of performance. This would include both physical characteristics of playing as well as the ways in which dramatic language is used in the individual episodes. We shall also be concerned with the ways in which the characters in the plays are managed, and a variety of playing devices involving groups of characters and the ways in which they are engaged with the audience. In addition we need to take account of what stage practitioners and their critics have brought to light in recent years. It seems likely that the extensive essentially practical investigation into the playing of the medieval cycles in the modern period may shed some light on their dramatic and theatrical features.

# 2.1

# Dramaturgy

In this section we shall look at the staging characteristics which can be derived from the text. This will include chiefly a consideration of the stage directions which are found in the Towneley manuscript as well as the ways in which the actual dialogue of the plays indicates aspects of how the plays were to be put on stage in matters like movement, costume and properties. One important matter for discussion will be the ways in which the plays written entirely or substantially by the Wakefield Master differ from the rest of the plays in the collection.

## *Stage Directions*

There are some sixty-eight stage directions in the manuscript, a total which, in view of the length of the whole text, cannot be regarded as plentiful even though they do tell us quite a bit about stage activities in certain circumstances. In the following account the 'incipits' and 'explicits' which are usually present for each play are not included. Of the thirty-two plays, twelve have no specific directions: 2, 7, 9, 10, 11, 12 (one direction was added by another hand), 15, 16, 21, 23, 24, 32. Most of the directions are in black but, perhaps in an attempt to make them stand out, some rubrication is used either by underlining black directions in red or by writing the whole direction in red. However, the practice is not consistent, some directions having no rubrication at all, and there is no rubrication of directions before *Pharaoh* (8).[1] Such rubrication, inconsistent as it is, brings into question the purpose of the manuscript, for it cannot clearly be intended as some kind of acting copy as it is too cumbersome; it may well be that the rubrication is simply a matter of decoration like the elaboration of the initial capitals discussed in Chapter 1.1.

All the stage directions are in Latin except for three in *Magi* (14) and the late one in *First Shepherds* (12).[2] The placing of some of the directions indicates that they were in the copy text as the scribe was able to include them between speeches and without compression, starting from the left margin in line and proceeding across the page, with the dialogue fitted in beneath. Of the sixty-eight some twenty-two are integrated in this way in ten plays: 1, 8, 13, 14, 18, 20, 26, 27, 28, 30. It cannot be ascertained whether the rubrication took place *currente calamo* or whether the scribe went back afterwards to put in the directions, but leaving a space in the latter event means that the scribe knew from his copy that he had to add directions and thus it is likely that they were present in the copy. The remaining directions are placed to the right of the speeches, the majority (thirty-seven) being integrated in some way with the lines of dialogue but distinguished by rubrication as described above and sometimes by being boxed. A small number (seven) show signs of compression in the right margin and these may have been additions by the scribe. Such compressed additions are difficult to evaluate: they may just be simple errors of omission during the initial copying, or they may have become available or relevant after the first transcription work had been completed. It is perhaps significant that this group is so small, indicating, for example, that there was not a large amount to be added after a performance. But we should bear in mind that the method or protocol of the manuscript as a whole was not entirely fixed from the start but developed by the scribe as he progressed with the work.

Two matters regarding the distribution of the stage directions are of special interest: the management of the York elements, and the ways in which the plays showing strong influence of the Wakefield Master incorporate directions. As we have seen in Chapter 1.2 there are six plays showing substantial borrowings from York (T8, 18, 22, 25, 26 and 30) and in these there are no cases where any stage directions can be definitely attributed to York, for there are none in the corresponding York originals. In other words, with three minor exceptions, the changes are all in the same direction: stage directions have been added to the York text in so far as we can regard the extant York manuscript as a source for Towneley.[3] This is not to say that there are no stage directions in York in general, but only that in the passages transferred all the directions now in the Towneley manuscript are not in the York Register. In the light of the suggestion above that many of the directions were clear to the scribe from his copy and could easily be integrated, we may further suppose that this is another piece of evidence that the episodes in Towneley were not copied directly from the York Register. The implication of the apparent insertion of stage directions is that there was a concern with production in the making of the Towneley versions, but that does not clarify whether the latter were created before or after actual performances. Moreover, the fact that we are dealing in total with a relatively small number of additions suggests that the surviving Towneley versions were not much influenced by details derived from performances. We thus need to look for other reasons for the inclusion of the Towneley stage directions besides the relationship with a possible performance.

Stage directions in the plays attributable to the Wakefield Master are rather inconsistent in practice. They occur in only two plays: *Noah* (3) and *Second Shepherds* (13). In the former there is but one: *Tunc perget ad uxorem* (3/273). This appears to ask for a movement across the acting area and it suggests that the play was performed with at least two separate locations, rather than on a wagon. Two of the four directions in *Second Shepherds* mark significant changing points in the action. The first requires Mak's entry wearing a cloak over the rest of his clothes, perhaps a sign of the deception to come (13/273). Since the audience presumably would not be aware of this when they first see him, the stage direction must be there as a warning to the actor about the preparation of his costume, or a deliberate hint to a reader that this character is devious. The second of these indicates Mak's leaving the Shepherds, who are now asleep on the ground as a result of the spell he has cast, so that he can go and steal the sheep ('While the Shepherds sleep he gets up and says' 13/386, translated), again suggesting that there was more than one stage location and Mak was about to move to another. The other two directions are about the Third Shepherd taking Mak's cloak, presumably with some suspicion (13/290), and perhaps picking up on the previous direction at his entry; and a prompt for the Angel to sing the 'Gloria' (13/919). Apart from these two plays there are four others attributed to the Wakefield Master entirely (2, 12, 16 and 21), and they have no stage directions. Similarly, when we examine the passages from plays which bear the marks of his having made a substantial contribution (22 and 30), we again find no stage directions, and the same is true in the much shorter passages he contributed to other plays (20, 27, 29 and 31). It would seem from this that as an author he was not much interested in directing the attention of actors and readers to the details of stage movement in the text itself. This may seem rather surprising in view of the extraordinary theatrical versatility his plays show, as we shall see shortly, but we shall find that his theatrical imagination manifested itself palpably in the dialogue itself.

When we turn to those plays which do have directions we can detect a range of purposes accounting for their inclusion. A considerable number mark changes in the story: stage events like the arrival of a new character or the beginning of a new phase in the action marked by a significant movement. This is especially the case in *Conspiracy* (20), a play we have noted as being composite. In fact, having thirteen, this play has noticeably more stage directions than any other, and they are all completely in red. Several of them mark quite significant detail in the action of the play, such as the moment when they start to eat (375), and the point when Jesus approaches Peter to wash his feet (409). Both these are thoroughly integrated into the copying process, starting at the left margin. In the later part of the play the stage directions are inserted in a compact group to make clear the movements by Jesus as he prays on Mount Olivet, and returns twice to the sleeping disciples (at 523, 527, 535, 539, 543). These individual directions are placed to the right of the relevant speeches, without any sign of compression. It may well be that we need to consider this play as a special case because of the state of the copying. As we noted earlier it appears to be put together rather clumsily, even though it may play well on stage as the narrative unfolds compellingly.

Among the other plays having some stage directions we may identify two groups. In the first, the plays about *Isaac* (5) and *Jacob* (6) are distinctive in a number ways, not least because they are relatively short. Their stage directions are, nevertheless, informative and particular. Incomplete at the beginning, *Isaac*'s remaining seventy lines contain two directions, one for Jacob's exit (18) and the other for the kisses given by Isaac and Rebecca to Jacob (67). *Jacob* is complete, even if it has only 142 lines; yet it contains six directions marking stages in the action and making specific demands upon actors about movement and gesture. The longest is translated thus by Stevens and Cawley: 'And Jacob goes to kiss Esau; Jacob comes, bends his knees praying to God, and rising, Esau rushes into his embrace' (122). The important thing here is that the dramatist, or just possibly someone trying to keep a record of performance, has wanted to fit in this series of actions which the dialogue itself hardly makes clear. In other words, the direction has a narrative function and if the performance is to be complete these actions, with their implied religious and psychological significance, must be carried out.

The second group of plays with directions is rather larger. It comprises the cluster of three plays which occur after the two consecutive borrowings from York, *Harrowing* and *Resurrection*, and consists of *Pilgrims*, *Thomas* and *Ascension* (27, 28, 29). These have three, six and four stage directions respectively. Here there are again some narrative directions rather like those in *Isaac* and *Jacob*. For example the key moment in *Pilgrims* has one: 'Then they shall recline [at table], and Jesus will sit between them. Then Jesus shall bless the bread and break it into three pieces, and afterwards he shall vanish from their sight, and Luke shall say' (27/296, translated). The dialogue does make it clear that Jesus breaks the bread but as it does not mention the three parts, traditionally a reference to the Trinity, the stage direction is intended to carry this expository detail. Similarly in *Thomas* the Sixth Apostle offers food to Christ in a significant detail interpreted as evidence that Christ really is in the form of a human resurrected: 'Let the table be prepared, and the Sixth Apostle offer honey-comb and fish' (176, translated). However, in this case the action is clearly contained in the dialogue which specifically mentions the honey and fish. The remaining stage directions in this group are less concerned with this kind of interpretive narrative detail and focus instead upon significant arrivals and departures, or upon music cues. Thus in *Thomas* the two appearances of Jesus to the majority of the Apostles are noted, together with the anthem he sings twice (104 and 120). These are followed by notice of his breathing of the spirit upon them and his departure (234 and 240). His final appearance to dispel Thomas's doubts is also marked (296). In *Ascension* there is a similar attention to the movements of Jesus, with two entries and an exit, together with a song cue (52, 189 and 281; and 289 at which point the Angels sing *Ascendo ad Patrem meum*). However, we should notice that in these plays the stage directions are not used to mark the movements of characters other than Jesus. The return of Thomas to his brethren is not noted, for example, nor is the movement mentioned by Simon as the apostles leave the hill in *Ascension* (29/420).

It may therefore be that in these three plays a similar protocol bringing out narrative detail and also concentrating upon the actions of Jesus is being sustained for the stage directions. To this we can add some detail from *Judgement* (30) which follows. As we have observed, this is largely a borrowing from York 47 and a considerable number of directions have been added to the borrowed section. This comprises the judgement carried out by Christ during which there are five. These all mark the actions of Christ himself: extending his arms and showing wounds (575); turning towards the Good Souls (607); towards the Bad (648); towards the Good again (697); and finally to the Bad (701). There are no other directions here and the action, taken over and elaborated by the Wakefield Master, does indeed include the removal of the Bad Souls to hell by the taunting devils, as the speeches make clear: 'Do now go furth, [go]' (726). There are no directions for the movements for the devils, even at the point where they cruelly drive the damned to hell. We may therefore conclude that in this part of the manuscript the stage directions are indeed related to some significant actions and are to an extent a guide to or record of performance, but underlying this there is a concern in them with interpretation and also a focus on the actions of Christ himself as distinct from the other characters. In other words, the decisions to put in the directions are not determined solely by staging needs and priorities. They may tell us something about performance, but what they tell us is by no means comprehensive. In that respect, nor are they confined to performance requirements.

## Implicit Stage Directions

Apart from these considerations arising from stage directions there are many places in the texts where details of the staging requirements are to be found. These may be somewhat conflicting, but in many cases we can deduce a great deal about the staging practices.[4] Some of these aspects can be seen to run through several plays, suggesting that in some places the dramatists did have a common view of how the plays were to be performed. In some ways the details revealed by these embedded indications are more reliable than the stage directions which, as we have seen, may have been put in the texts for reasons not solely concerned with the *mise-en-scène*. By contrast the implied stage directions may be informative because they are directly related to unspecified assumptions made by the dramatists as to how they envisage the enactment should take place. Let us begin by looking at a selection of the information which suggests the nature of the playing areas.

In the first place it is striking that many of the individual plays in Towneley require that the characters make a journey or movement from one place to another during the action. In the Old Testament episodes this is very common. In *Creation* Adam and Eve are led into paradise by the Angel (1/195–7). Once there Adam decides he must leave Eve to go and look at another part (1/234). In *Abel* there is very considerable pressure on Cain from Abel to leave his starting place and go to the place of sacrifice. The difference of will about this goes on for so long in the action that for a while it becomes a centre of attention.[5] Eventually Cain agrees to go, with great reluctance. Noah has to make several changes of place and he works on the Ark somewhere separate from where his wife is spinning.

In both these plays a hill is involved: Abel lays down his bundle on one (2/172–3), and Noah's wife sits on one to spin (3/488). The action of *Noah* takes place partly outside the Ark on these two sites and once the flood has arrived events are enacted within it, as when Noah gives the tiller to his wife and himself uses the plumb line. Changes of place are also found in *Abraham*: Isaac is sent home to his mother while Abraham prepares for the journey required by God. Eventually they set off on an ass, accompanied by two boys. When they reach the place of sacrifice, yet another hill, the boys are left behind while Abraham takes Isaac up to the fateful altar (4/148).[6] Meanwhile Deus is in a separate place and as the crisis approaches he sends the Angel to stop Abraham. In the first four plays of the cycle, then, it is apparent from the performance requirements embedded in the text that more than one location was actively required in each case. For our purposes it is significant that two of these plays are attributed to the Wakefield Master, and two are not.

In the New Testament section two plays are especially notable for requiring the characters to undertake movements from place to place. In *Second Shepherds* Mak has to arrive among the Shepherds, and after the spell has been cast he has to collect the sheep and take it home. Then he must go back to the sleepers before they awake and return home again before the Shepherds get there. Finally the Shepherds themselves must first go to Mak's house and then on to Bethlehem. In *Conspiracy*, in itself likely to be an exciting play because of the rich narrative details, there is an accumulation of events which demands a variety of sites as the action shifts between them. At first the arrest is set up at Pilate's house, where Judas arrives for the bargain. The action is taken up by Christ outside the city, from where he sends Peter and John to make arrangements for the supper.[7] When Jesus arrives at this place, he eats a meal and washes the feet of the Apostles before setting out for Olivet. Once there he prays, presumably on a hill, moving back twice to the sleeping Apostles. Judas then starts from the house of Pilate and leads the soldiers to take Christ prisoner.

To these plays with more than one location we should add *Pilgrims* whose structure is essentially a journey. The opening sequence, an elaborate retrospective lament on the sorrows of the Crucifixion, takes place while they are walking along the road to Emmaus. When Jesus appears he speaks of their walking ruefully by the way (27/105). Further individual words and phrases give the sense of continuing journeying as Christ goes along with them: 'gang' (109), 'as ye go' (113), 'walkand' (125), 'farthere fare' (135), 'my iornay' (245), 'no farthere walk' (255). This insistence upon movement may recall that noted above in *Abel*. The structure of this play is very simple up to the moment when they sit down for the meal. During this first part the dramatist is clearly keen to give a sense of the movement of the characters while the serious matter relating to the Crucifixion is explored and explicated. Taking these three plays together, it is notable that *Conspiracy* requires a large cast of speaking characters as well as mutes whereas the others work by means of a much more limited number.

Such journeys may imply that there was more than one location on the stage. As this is a feature of some wagon plays performed at York it does not necessarily follow that multi-centred staging determines that the individual Towneley plays were meant to be staged without wagons, but it does make it more likely. The presence of several locations can be used in a very simple manner by allowing the action to be restarted in another place. The introduction of a new voice is a perfectly effective means of refocusing the attention of the audience. This happens when Moses begins to speak after Pharaoh's opening speech (8/88) and also with Lucifer's first speech (1/69). On many occasions there is careful attention to the naming of places to which characters set out, as in going to Aran (6/58), the Red Sea (8/384), Bethlehem (13/929, 15/443) and Jerusalem (27/370). This may also apply in going to meet other people as when God goes to Noah (3/159) and the Knights go back to Herod after the massacre (16/581). It is a feature of many of these examples that the going is a part of the action. Arrivals, on the other hand, can be very simple and functional, and in many cases they are unheralded. This reliance upon the audience's ability to adapt to such changes is a marked feature of the dramatic code of the plays, and it is something to be exploited.

In considering the frequency of the indirect information about staging it is striking that there are two contrasting practices. In the first of these there are many episodes where we can hardly find any such details. These examples are likely to occur when the action is largely expository or reflective. Such passages are essential to cyclic form and are widely distributed in Towneley even though we have suspected that the whole text may not have been performed. Sometimes the dramatic priority in such dialogue is to establish character and situation. Both the Shepherds plays begin with extensive monologues in which the speakers express their sufferings and discomfort. There is very little action in the first part of these plays, even though the words spoken are compelling. The boast of Herod's Messenger includes the pretensions of his master's power with a list of his dominions, his praise of Mahowne and a fulsome welcome. Before he finishes he also introduces some news of the birth of a king

(16/111–15). There is a more elaborate retrospect at the beginning of *Doctors* as the three Magisters dwell upon the prophecies about the Messiah (18/1–48). The first sequence of *Flight* comes into this category: after the appearance of the Angel the action comprises a highly emotional conversation between Mary and Joseph, but there is very little indication in the text about how this sequence is to be realized. *Baptist* begins with a blessing for the audience and proceeds to John's prophetic role, including a reference to the Crucifixion (19/1–64). In all these cases there is very little activity and the presentation of the characters and their situation or some exegeses are the main concerns.

On the other hand there are some passages where the action is highly complex and the dramatists have imagined its unfolding in some detail even though it is not marked in the text by explicit stage directions. Many of these, as we shall see, come in the work attributed to the Wakefield Master but there are two which stand separate from his work in which there is a sophisticated exploitation of actions embedded in the texts. In *Abraham* there is detail of movement as Isaac is sent home to his mother before the journey to the sacrifice is begun.[8] Father and son then leave the town (4/131) and travel over hills and dales (135). When they reach the mountain they leave their companions with the ass and ascend (145–6). They then go further (161) before reaching the place of sacrifice. When Isaac lies down, his father repeatedly tells him to be still. The shining blade is noticed and this leads to the promise that Isaac shall lie 'groflyngys' (204, face down) so that he shall not see the impending blow, perhaps a more striking invention than the blindfold which appears in other versions. Abraham weeps as he looks at his son who lies still: 'He lyys full still ther as he lay, / For to I com, dar he not styr' (4/231–2). There is no doubt that the emotional content of this passage is very high, but at the same time the dramatist has meticulously embedded the details of the action in the text.

A similar attention to detail is found in *Crucifixion*. Quite possibly the York account was a model for this Towneley dramatist, but the composition is clearly independent. Another possible influence would be the Gospel accounts or metrical adaptations since so much of the detail is dramatized in accordance with them. In phrase after phrase the dramatist keeps attention on the detailed actions and movements. The following phrases from the dialogue may give some impression of its richness and complexity, as the effects achieved are visual as well as conceptual, and they also remind us that the movement of the actors, including that of the silent Christ, are compelling: 'I have a bande' (65) 'drawen fast' (70) 'hamere and nales' (71) 'Knyt thou a knott with all thi strength' (119) 'draw this arme' (120) 'Do dryfe a nayll' (131) 'Hald downe his knees' (140) 'Draw out hys lymmes' (143) 'pull well' (160) 'How draw I' (181) 'Well drawen' (186) 'Pull, pull' (191) 'To lyft' (205) 'fest on all youre hende' (209) 'Up with the tymbre' (215, 224) 'War thi crowne' (227). These references cover only the sequence when Christ is brought to Calvary and fixed to the cross, but the pressure of intense dramatization continues beyond as the narrative of his death is enacted further with the familiar details of the drink, the inscription, the spear of Longinus and on to the removal of the nails during the deposition. We should bear in mind too that although much of the effect here depends on realistic detail painfully enacted, the iconic figure of Christ on the cross is also being brought about. This mixture of practical stagecraft and the evolution of iconic material is particularly effective as theatre.

From what we noticed earlier it is apparent that the Wakefield Master does have some episodes in which there is very little action as such, as in the speech by the messenger in *Herod*. But he also has some sequences which are quite as rich in staging detail as the examples from *Abraham* and *Crucifixion* just discussed. Amongst these we might cite the passages where Cain counts out the sheaves (2/194–225), and Noah's proceedings as he measures the tree, takes off his coat, prepares the sail and drives in the nails (3/365–96). In the last, however, the staging details may not be quite as specific as elsewhere as the actions do not follow one another in a credible order. In this instance it may well be that they are representational rather than mimetic. But even if this is so, it also argues for close attention to how the passage is to be presented on the stage.

When we come to *Second Shepherds* the staging detail after the opening monologues is noticeably specific at times. The interior of Mak's cottage and the door which leads to it are treated carefully, as the dramatist envisages the action. In staging the play, these details could be clearly visible to the audience. Within the cottage we have to be able to see Gyll spinning, her lying down near the cradle, the cradle itself and the movements around it, including the return of the Third Shepherd who examines the 'baby' so closely: 'Gyf me lefe hym to kys / And lyft up the clowtt' (13/842–3). The point here is that, whether or not they were realized in actual production, these details are imagined by the dramatist and embedded in the text. There is further complex detail in the management of the door to the cottage which may illustrate how carefully the details of staging were invented. When Mak first brings the stolen sheep home he cannot get in because the lower half of the door, the 'hek', is

closed and presumably the cumbersome burden of the sheep prevents him
opening it. At his urgent command, as he complains of being left waiting,
Gyll draws the catch, lets him in and sees what he carries:

| | |
|---|---|
| *Mak* | Good wyff, open the hek! |
| | Seys thou not what I bryng? |
| *Uxor* | I may thole the dray the snek. |
| | A, com in, my swetyng! |
| *Mak* | Yee, thou thar not rek |
| | Of my long standyng. |
| *Uxor* | By the nakyd nek |
| | Art thou lyke for to hyng!   (13/439–46) |

A few moments later he tells her to close the door (473–4) and he returns
to his sleeping place with the Shepherds. Once they all wake up, the
Shepherds go to search for the sheep they have now missed, while Mak
returns to the cottage and again he has to ask Gyll to open the door. This
time it is the whole door that has been closed – no doubt for increased
security to hide what is within – and he again complains about being kept
waiting (582–5). Once he is inside, the door is shut once more. When the
Shepherds arrive in pursuit they hear Mak singing from outside and they
too have to ask for the door to be opened (691–2).[9]

The interplay between iconic and functional staging details can be traced
further in the references to properties, though it does not appear that these
are always clearly separable. The lamb which Christ gives to the Baptist
is no doubt the result of an extensive iconographic tradition, and it continues
to be part of the figure of the Baptist today. It derives ultimately from the
Baptist's initial recognition of Christ as the Lamb of God.[10] Christ's speech
directs us towards its power and its iconographical role and once again
we may feel that an icon is being evolved:

It may were the from adversyté,
And so looke that thou tryst;
By this beest knowen shall thou be,
That thou art John Baptyst'.   (19/213–16)

The wounds of Christ, which also have a rich emphasis outside the purely
dramatic context, play an iconic role in some of the plays. Again the
dialogue draws attention to them and to their significance. The wounds
themselves are made during the Crucifixion and we have noted a reference
to them in removing the nails at the deposition. Beyond this they play an

important role in *Thomas* and in *Judgement*. In the former, Christ draws attention to them at his first appearance to the Apostles (28/139). He describes himself as 'Strenkyllid with blood so red' (28/154). Later in the same play the wounds become directly part of the action. In accordance with the Gospels, Christ tells Thomas to put his hand within his side where the spear of Longinus had penetrated, and when Thomas removes it he exclaims 'My hande is blody of thi blode!' (28/565–70). In *Judgement*, following the York version, Christ again exhibits his wounds as the dialogue makes clear, and Towneley has added a stage direction to underline it (30/575–81). The passage continues with a description of his suffering and at the end of it the visual effect is again specified in speech: 'This dredfull day this sight to se' (30/605). In this play the wounds are being used as part of the process of persuading sinners to repentance. The dramatic effect of the wounds is enhanced in a different way by Christ's wearing red clothing. In *Thomas* the Third Apostle refers to it between Christ's first two appearances (109).

The more realistic kind of stage properties are abundant in the dialogue as in the 'chek-bon' used by Cain and the cradle used by Mak's wife. We also find a wand for Pharaoh (8/246), a vestment for Simeon (17/91), lanterns for the Soldiers in *Conspiracy* (20/622, 635) and three dice (24/319). But often even these objects are more than simply mimetic in the way they work. The cradle, for example, is a visual parallel for that in which Mary lays Christ, and the star may reflect the light of heaven (14/83). The gifts of the Shepherds and the Magi, and the oil and cream used in *Baptist* (19/194), though they meet the simple requirements of the narrative, are actually resonant with symbolic meaning regarding Christ's destiny. We should also note that in some plays the actuality of properties is in some doubt. This may well be the case with the plough team in *Abel* and the sack used in *First Shepherds* (12/238). In the latter play there also occurs the feast which may have been presented with the huge accumulation of food as mime. On the other hand, the horses used by the Magi are specific.[11]

There is one other aspect of the implied stage directions which reveals the dramatists' sense of how their plays were to be presented. This comprises costume and other aspects of the physical appearance of characters. Once again we cannot omit to notice that there is sometimes an iconic effect here. Costume is referred to in a number of places. Sometimes the mention is often functional, as when Noah takes off his gown to work on the Ark (3/378), or Simeon puts on his vestment 'in worship' of the infant Christ as king (17/5–6). Herod's knights, when summoned by the

Messenger in preparation for the massacre, are enjoined to put on their 'best aray' (16/506). Similarly, Pilate tells the Soldiers setting out to arrest Christ to dress themselves 'wightly' (20/617). Most of these items imply some sort of change in appearance and there are places where such changes acquire a greater dramatic significance. Lucifer's alteration from being 'bright' (1/78, and repeated at 81) to ugly is made clear by the First Demon: 'Now ar we waxen blak as any coyll / And vgly, tatyrd as a foyll' (1/136–7). This might suggest that the change itself was visibly enacted. Two other striking changes are made which takes the audience beyond the simple demands of narrative. Thomas, having at last recognized the truth of the Resurrection, begs for mercy and in doing so he divests himself of his rich clothing because it makes it more difficult to receive forgiveness. In turn he rejects his staff, his hat, his gay girdle and silk purse as well as his coat. He tellingly contrasts this extravagant clothing with Christ's at the Crucifixion:

> Jesu, that soke the madyns mylk,
> Ware noght bot clothes of pall,
> Thi close so can thai fro the pyke,
> On roode thay left the small. (28/605–8)[12]

The second remarkable change occurs when Lazarus emerges from the tomb. Christ, having wept, orders that the grave clothes be removed:

> Take and lawse hym foote and hande,
> And from his throte take the bande,
> And the sudary take hym fro
> And all that gere, and let hym go. (31/99–102)

In both these examples the dialogue details the stage processes envisaged by the dramatists.

This review of the ways in which the texts of the plays embody approaches to performance leaves us with a series of somewhat conflicting indications. Cyclic form has much strength in its ability to comprehend variety: indeed this is one of its chief characteristics. The Towneley plays as a whole are no exception to this. In the data we have assembled there are certain things which occur again and again. Among these is the interest in complex staging situations and intricately constructed scenes, as well as the exploitation of direct address to the audience in a number of different modes. There is also a tendency to develop iconic aspects in many scenes. This last point is not unique to Towneley; indeed it would be surprising if this cycle did not follow the practices widespread elsewhere. The medieval drama persistently reflects the sense that religion was experienced with the eyes and this awareness was not confined to the stage but ran through many other media. It seems much more likely that dramatists drew upon the non-dramatic cultic practices for their iconography. However, the dramatic idioms can vary greatly between intimate scenes and plays written for a large cast. Some scenes are static with very little action required since the words are dominant, while some range over a series of locations and embody movement as a dramatic feature and not just a convenient way of moving characters from one place to another. Some individual scenes are conceived for finely detailed staging. In several plays there is reference to a hill, and if this was an actual stage feature it suggests that the dramatists had a sense that height, and difference in the playing levels, were useful.

The contribution of the Wakefield Master to the staging is intriguing. In some respects he follows modes clearly established by the other dramatists. This is especially true in his skilful exploitation of multiple locations and the movement between them and in his development of the addresses to the audience in the form of monologues or preparatory speeches. Both of these are manifest in parts of the cycle where his participation is not evident, and they are features of other cycles, notably N Town for the multiple locations, and York and Chester for the direct address. Beyond the mystery cycles these features are present in other genres of drama which may be represented to us in the examples of *Castle of Perseverance* and the Digby *Mary Magdalene*.

Two further conclusions arise. One is that the relationship between the text itself and performance is not entirely discernible: the indications which suggest that the codex was a book for reading are strong and the fact is that some of the stage directions point purposefully towards this. These can indeed give us some ideas about what was envisaged in performance, but they are present in the text for reasons which are not entirely determined by this function. Besides this, which may seem rather an unreliable guide, the plays themselves contain many clues about the performance assumptions of the dramatists and these are rather more revealing of the modes of presentation the writers felt they could rely upon, not least because they are a kind of indirect specification: they are not there to tell the performers explicitly what they are to do, so much being embedded by the dramatic imagination visualizing the text, which the performers would normally follow.

The other conclusion is really an open one. There is some attractive evidence that some of the plays were conceived for multiple staging, but the matter is not easy to resolve. There is no doubt that wagons were used at York and there we find a number of plays where there are more than one location, for example *Dream of Pilate's Wife* (Y30) and *Resurrection* (Y38). It is quite possible that this practice was followed at Wakefield at some point in the cycle's history, perhaps indeed near the end of the life of the plays in the performance referred to in the reign of Queen Mary. We should not forget that processional performance on wagons has distinct dramatic qualities. The fact that the text we have makes us suspect that multiple staging was used in some sequences does not necessarily mean that it was always so. The discussion of modern revivals which follows in the next section may shed some light on the advantages of both methods. But the evidence adduced here points to multiple centred staging for most of the plays rather than not.

# 2.2

# Modern Revivals

The appreciation of the performance characteristics and qualities of the Towneley Cycle in modern times may usefully be seen against the broader interest which has brought about the presentation and exploration of many medieval texts, whether of cycle plays or not, since William Poel staged *Everyman* in the courtyard of the Charterhouse in 1901. To construct a comprehensive history of this remarkable phenomenon is not our purpose here: there is plenty of other material where this may be traced.[1] The two most prominent early practitioners, E. Martin Browne and Nugent Monck, were both interested in the cycle plays. The former produced episodes from N Town at Chichester in 1931 and initiated the regular festival presentation of the versions of the York Cycle in the ruins of St Mary's Abbey in York from 1951. Monck, setting up the Norwich Players in 1910 and creating the Maddermarket Theatre in Norwich opened by W. B. Yeats in 1921, was particularly interested in presenting versions of parts of N Town, especially in 1938 and 1952. Such productions, though they did not always stage complete cycles, usually offered a group of plays allowing the question of interrelationships between individual episodes to be explored for the first time. Monck presented the Towneley *Annunciation* (10) and *Flight* (15) in Norwich in 1910 and *Nativity* at the Abbey Theatre in Dublin in 1912, and he returned to the Towneley Nativity sequence at Norwich in 1919 and 1921.[2] These productions, as we shall see, were partly informed by identified religious considerations and partly by an interest in medieval life and culture, albeit a somewhat idealized one. But there were also many other presentations of individual episodes by professionals and amateurs between the wars. The Towneley *Second Shepherds* attracted a good deal of attention, and it soon became established as the most widely known of all the episodes from the cycle plays. This was somewhat unfortunate from the point of view of the coherence of the cycle because its extraordinary plot, with its dependence upon farce, makes it rather untypical of other plays. The frequency of productions of the Nativity episodes at this time can be partly explained by the restrictions exercised by the Lord Chamberlain over the representation of God or Christ on the stage, which made for severe difficulties in staging the Ministry and the Passion.

The following discussion is aimed at bringing out performance characteristics in Towneley. However, its extensive closeness to York means that in places evidence from the latter's mode of performance is pertinent. Moreover, we should be aware that there was a performance culture surrounding cycle plays at York and this would probably have been available to those concerned with the generation and performance of Towneley. We shall see that the increasing understanding of the cycle in modern times is not only a matter of what was found out by directors, actors and audiences; it was also illuminated by the published evaluations of critics and reviewers.

The 1951 Festival presentation of the York Cycle was paralleled by one comprising episodes from the Chester Cycle at Chester. From this time onwards there have been a very large number of cycle productions of varying completeness: my own count, derived largely from sources mentioned in note 1 of this chapter, gives more than forty up to 2003, but there may have been many more whose details are now difficult to recover. Naturally, each individual cycle presents its own peculiarities but this general interest in producing the cycles has been of importance in bringing out many common characteristics and also allowing us to distinguish more carefully between them. For Towneley itself the most important productions have been those at Bretton Hall, near Wakefield, in 1954; in 1958 and 1967 by Martial Rose, together with those at the Mermaid Theatre in London in 1961 and 1965 (Colin Ellis and Sally Miles); in the streets of Wakefield in 1980 (Jane Oakshott); and at Toronto in 1985 (A. F. Johnston and Garrett P. J. Epp). But there have also been composite productions in which elements of the Wakefield plays were incorporated with material from other cycles, or indeed with modern material. The most significant of these were the extensive performances fitted around the two surviving Coventry episodes in the ruins of Coventry Cathedral from 1978 and the complex National Theatre version of the Passion by Tony Harrison which has had a number of revivals and revisions, particularly in 1985 and 1999.

Running through this large accumulation of theatrical enterprise and experiment are a number of preoccupations. We have already noted the question of whether to base productions upon pageant wagons. This was partly a matter of deciding whether the whole York Cycle of forty-seven plays could really be done in one day in a procession through the streets of York. The urgency of such a problem may have been largely responsible for the staging of the cycle or parts of it on wagons, in deliberate contrast to the Festival productions at the fixed location at St Mary's. The most documented wagon performances have been those in the streets of York in 1988 and 1992 (Meg Twycross), and 1994 and 1998 (Jane Oakshott). So far it has not been possible to perform the whole cycle using the exact route of the fifteenth-century productions but a remarkable amount of experience has nevertheless been gained by directors, actors and their audiences. There have also been two significant wagon productions of the York plays at Toronto in 1977 and 1998.[3] In addition to the question of feasibility there were other practical questions about audibility in the open air, the way in which individual episodes could be made to reflect upon one another, the nature of characterization and how characters should present themselves. There were problems for audiences too, not least the effect upon them of the very large amount of material each cycle contained and the strain watching it might generate.[4] It is also true that these experiences have given rise to further controversy, particularly the question of whether to play from the end of the wagon or from the side.

In large measure the complete, one-day production of the York Cycle on wagons has been broadly vindicated in practical terms and there is now no significant doubt that this could have been done, and that it was indeed the normal practice for many years.[5] If that can now be taken as axiomatic, further investigation and discussion of the practice at York, and by inference of practices elsewhere, are now possible. Since the streets of York are still more or less in their medieval configuration it has been possible to show in some detail where the wagons might have been placed at the individual playing stations.[6] It is now safe to assume therefore that the actors did have to use the acoustic of the streets and no doubt they would have found ways of exploiting it effectively. This could work in relation to the relatively small groups of onlookers which could gather at the rather compact playing places, a few hundred at most in contrast to the many thousands present at some of the French *Passions*. Such a mode of production might further the possibility of intimate scenes and it is clear that there are many of these, often involving only two or three characters onstage at the same time. Indeed it has been noted that often individual episodes in York as well as in Towneley were constructed around one or two main speakers.[7] It seems likely though that while one play was in progress the features and actions of another play or two could also be appreciated peripherally – just down the street, not quite out of sight or earshot. The modern experience of hearing the few episodes that have been done simultaneously at authentic playing stations has made this aspect quite clear and it raises the possibility of what we might call subliminal simultaneity. The arrival of each wagon would be a significant event at each playing place and there would be a tempting opportunity to make a strong immediate impact, a factor which may go some way to account for the oratorical force of many of the opening speeches, whether by God, by messengers or by tyrants, as happens so frequently in Towneley.

There is a still much disputed aspect of production regarding whether the action was confined to the wagons or whether the street was also used. Many modern productions have assumed that the action could descend to street level ad lib, thus providing more space, bringing the action into close proximity with the audience and also adding the advantage of having characters on more than one level alone. But this practice has been recently challenged by Margaret Rogerson,[8] and it is certainly true that keeping the action within the framework provided by the wagon can help to create and frame iconic effects. This last point is further strengthened by the fact that some plays contain passages where the dialogue is designed to further such iconic effects and where the action is deliberately static, as in God sitting or Christ hanging.[9] It is also true that scenes such as the Harrowing and the Last Judgement seem to require a vertical dimension and this may be achieved by building up to a higher level, where the action is visible to the spectators, rather than using the street, where sight lines may be poor for the audience standing at that level.[10]

But apart from wagon-based productions, whether processional or not, there is evidence in some of the original cycle texts for staging arrangements based upon permanent locations, with spaces for movement and action in between. The Cornish Cycle, for example, was performed in a circular acting space, the *plen-an-gwary*, which had fixed sites round the acting area. According to the diagrams in the manuscript some of the locations retained the same designation for the three days of production while others were reassigned as the dramatic necessity arose and the development of the narrative demanded.[11] Besides what happened on such fixed locations this arrangement made possible the significant use of the playing space between them, the practice being most clearly manifest in the Passion sequences of N Town. Such a mode of production thus attributes dramatic potential to places: the spectacle of characters going to a designated place for a known purpose is part of the dramatic intake for the audience, as in the driving of Christ towards Annas and Caiaphas at the beginning of *Buffeting* (T21). Not only is their motion towards the objective: there are also those waiting for them when they arrive. In such episodes there is absolutely no doubt that the text does require movement on ground level. Modern productions have made much of this, for example the use of the nave in the ruined Coventry Cathedral for processional movement within episodes treated as though it were a street.[12] But we should note that the wagon mode might offer a much less specific location if that were required.

In many ways the modern productions have created a new drama to meet the requirements of the twentieth and twenty-first centuries. These revivals have been going on for long enough for there to have been changes in the ways the plays were perceived. The work of Monck and Browne was predicated upon a specifically Christian purpose, one that sought in a reverential way to give expression to some characteristics of contemporary faith by drawing upon that of the medieval past. Browne was concerned to approximate his production to an act of worship.[13] But it is clear that this was crossed with a historical interest which was activated partly by a concept of medievalism and a desire to create pictorial effects answering to an idealized version of the earlier culture. Monck, in particular, wished to avoid buffoonery and his Nativity sequence was thought to contain too much gloom.[14] At the time of the first York Festival in 1951 there was a need to reassert a national identity in the aftermath of the Second World War and to reflect favourably on earlier roots.[15] Such considerations had a marked effect upon the way the plays were staged, and for a long while many of the values which now seem inherent in the original medieval productions were not taken account of.

But what emerges clearly was a strong desire to involve a large number of people in these York productions and this, I suggest, paved the way for the 'people's theatre' which had another, even stronger but also different manifestation in the National Theatre *Passion* in the 1970s and 1980s. Such a shift was most likely a reflection of increasing secularization even though there were still many ready to respond in spiritual or religious terms. By the time of this later sustained enterprise there had also been a change in the political climate. The Harrison-Bryden production was less dependent upon a religious priority and more upon an appreciation of the working world of craftsmen and the trade unions. The emphasis was distinctly upon a working community in as much as the first National production in 1977 constructed a fiction whereby the real actors played the part of workmen come to perform the plays. But it was found that in spite of the enormous popularity of this theatrical undertaking, the 'community' created at these performances was somewhat artificial, and one notably different from what might have been supposed to have existed in medieval York.[16] In York the continuity from year to year must have been fundamental, and this would presumably have manifested itself in conventional or inherited practices of staging and performance. Given the guild system of production in York it seems inevitable that individual guilds would evolve and sustain their own ways of doing things. Nevertheless, Benedict Nightingale, in his review, was able to identify a pertinent sense that the modern plays showed ordinary workmen committing horrors.[17]

The exploitation of Yorkshire accents has been a feature of some productions.[18] The Wakefield onlookers of Towneley in 1980 seemed acutely aware of the tone and humour of some of the Yorkshire Middle English. However Darryll Grantley suggested that the National *Mysteries* in their London context presented the Yorkshire dialect as something 'quaint'.[19]

It is striking that this sense of people becoming deeply involved in the performance, whether it be actors or audience, is ascertainable in much of the published writing about the cycle play productions. It is perhaps this factor more than anything else which has provided a driving force and has led critics to comment upon the remarkable strength of the plays in spite of the wide variety of production styles which have been manifested. Martial Rose, whose work on the practical performance of the Towneley Cycle has been fundamental to its modern interpretations, is said to have been interested by the crowd movement featured at York by Browne in 1954, but significantly he also saw a need to give scope for something more intimate.[20] Commenting upon the work of those creating and witnessing the 1957–8 production, Rose also noted that it was a deeply moving undertaking and that the ordinary people taking part (among whom he included himself) had an extraordinary experience.

But the methods of staging the Towneley Cycle at Bretton Hall (1958), at the Mermaid Theatre in London (1961 and 1965), in the town centre of Wakefield (1980) and in the courtyard of the Victoria College of the University of Toronto (1985), were all different and in the differences we can locate a reflection of the problem of deciding how far the cycle was coherent. Rose's initial production set a pattern for a static mode of staging. He used a fixed background for the twenty plays he chose.[21] But against this fixed background he introduced two pageant wagons which were used for episodes with small casts such as *Scourging* (22).

Perhaps the most noted effect of the two Mermaid productions was the presentation of violence even though only eighteen of the thirty-two plays were performed. Instead of the rather sanitized handling of the Passion as at the York Festival, the Crucifixion was now performed in grisly detail for the first time on the modern stage, in accordance with the strong prompting in the text. The production embraced extremes of levity and sublimity. But the presence of God on high added a sense of divine purpose in shaping the epic development of the history of salvation.[22]

For the whole cycle Jane Oakshott used three fixed stages in the town centre of Wakefield in 1980. There was also a procession which functioned as a means of moving the actors for each episode from one of the three fixed stages to another: the actors moved, but not the stages. By doing so the event undoubtedly attracted the attention of the potential audience, the weekend shoppers of Wakefield. Of itself the procession was not a formalized performance but it did help to define the strangeness of what was going on and created remarkable resonances between the performance and the onlookers.[23] Because of its location and time amongst the shoppers this production made one think of the relationship between the actors and those who surrounded them. It was brought home very strikingly that if one is to have a long performance in the middle of an urban centre the kinds of attention given by the onlookers are going to vary greatly.[24] Here and in other such performances with more than one playing place it was also possible for onlookers to move backwards and forwards in relation to the chronological order of the episodes. Exercising choice in this way undoubtedly gives the onlookers a distinctive potential for making their own way through a performance.

Since this production comprised the whole cycle it also gave rise to speculation about whether the plays were of a similar nature dramatically. The answer was emphatically to the contrary. It was palpable that the textures, pace and organization of the individual episodes varied greatly and it appeared that this unevenness was endemic in the text. It is notable that at York in earlier times there was some concern about maintaining standards of performance.[25] This arose almost inevitably because the individual episodes were distinct from one another and could therefore have quite different features and qualities. It has some bearing upon the possible unity of Towneley since it is apparent that cycle form can tolerate different performance values, objectives and modes. If the performance is to be managed by having many different groups take part and by using different locations for the individual episodes to be presented, it is inevitable that there will be variations of size and scope as well as variations in quality of performance. The text itself, whether it is put together before the event or after it, will reflect this unmistakably even if there is a relative coherence in composition as there does appear to be for the Chester Cycle. The 1980 production at Wakefield also reminded one that if the performance was processional there would be a significant impact as each new group of actors created a new impression on arrival at the place of performance. It also meant that there was a number of different actors playing the larger parts like that of Christ.

It ought be added here that in the 1980s the problem of the unity of the Towneley Cycle was only just beginning to be addressed. It was not then a significant doubt for many practitioners. Most assumed that the text is what it may appear to be: one intended for continuous playing on certain established occasions in parallel with its neighbour in York. Indeed this view can still be encountered today. Putting what we may call a revised understanding, Martin Stevens in his review of the Toronto production (May 1985) quotes from the organizers' brochure: 'Our hypothesis . . . is . . . that the sequence was performed in the round outside one of the parish churches, [and that] the production was shared by the parishes of the district.'[26] It was perhaps the 'York' assumption which led Peter MacDonald to suggest that, faced with a string of unrelated plays, the practitioners must strive to 'bring out continuities at the supra-episodic level'.[27] To this end he approved the presence of God on his scaffold as a witness to the whole cycle. On the other hand David Mills thought that the Toronto performance, which took place on an 'oval of scaffolds' and was performed by twenty-five companies of various provenance, put a kind of pressure upon the audience, requiring it react to a large variety of modes. He offers the persuasive idea that 'this production bonds to its setting', and he suggests that from the centrally placed throne of God an influence emanates through the rest of the acting areas. The audience were challenged to learn to use this configuration and to control their physical position and concentration accordingly. He implies that it is through this process that a coherent experience is generated for the audience.[28] His account makes it clear that the actors moved through the audience or sat among them and that the distances generated by the spread of the action were continually exploited for movement and for ways of shifting the attention of the audience around the whole area of the performance. One feature of the production was the hill on which some of the action took place, and this may well have acted as a unifying element as MacDonald has suggested, and indeed this effect was shared by some of the scaffolds.

In this production we are once again aware of the variety of modes created by having as many as twenty-five performing groups. It is apparent from the reports by MacDonald, Mills and Stevens that, although there was a measure of overall design, the initiatives of the different companies led to many different spectacular and theatrical effects. Stevens saw this as also having an effect in as much as the performances had differing levels of competence. However, he offers an interesting argument in support of his impression that the performance was 'remarkably unified'. Like Mills, he puts the process of unification into the minds of the audience, though he has a different basis for the attribution. He suggests that the expectation of the medieval audience would put in the right ingredients, based upon a common experience of cycle plays; such an experience, he specifies, would comprise the overall structure from Creation to Doomsday.[29] Within this there would be expectations for such familiar features as the tyrants' boasts, for the 'human perspective' of the Incarnation and disobedient wives. One could extrapolate this further to much smaller elements such as the likelihood that the Shepherds would prophesy and that they would sing. But one cannot help thinking that both these arguments about the audience, whilst they may be true in essence, do not finally show that the cycle itself was necessarily unified in production at its earliest manifestation; it would seem to me that we must fall back on to the position that cyclic form tolerated differences as part of its way of operating.

A further difficulty arises with the attempt to recreate the early performance, and it can be put very simply as Peter Meredith has done: we are not medieval people.[30] We may be able to get glimpses of what it was like to be present at a performance but a transition from modern times to medieval culture as a whole is impossible. This is especially acute in respect of the drama, which, by its intimate nature, demands a close interaction between the performers and the audience. Moreover, the ephemerality of performance is difficult enough to recover after only a few minutes, let alone half a millennium.

Apart from the occasions when the weather forced the actors to move indoors, and the special circumstances surrounding the National Theatre *Passion,* most of the modern productions have been in the open air. This has produced a variety of experiences and conclusions. We have noted that the York locations were often surprisingly intimate because of the configurations of the streets and crossings where the plays are known to have been performed. Nevertheless, there must have been a need to project above the background distractions and this must have been the case more especially with place and scaffold productions, and productions in the round. The characterization of some of the Towneley texts seems to bear this in mind: many of the speeches are declamatory and many episodes are constructed in such a way as to suggest the carrying of significance over some distance. The boasting tyrants come to mind here and there are speeches by God, Christ and the devils having a self-demonstrating element in them which seems appropriate for the open air. Meg Twycross has noted that when the Towneley plays had to be moved indoors at Toronto it was felt that there was a much greater scope for intimacy in the playing.[31]

Because several of the productions of Towneley have indeed been given essentially in a place and scaffold form there has been much discussion of how such arrangements can be matched to the surviving text.[32] Attention has been drawn to the ways in which a playing station set out as a hall could be used for a number of scenes, especially those like *Caesar* (9) involving the presence of rulers and judges. Alan Nelson has noted that bells are scripted on a number of occasions with the associated thought that the place of performance might have been near the church in Wakefield.[33] The complex text of *Conspiracy* (20) with its sequence of locations looks as though it might have benefited from a space with several fixed locations for Pilate's Court, Bethany, the room for the Last Supper, the Mount of Olives, Pilate's Court again and the Arrest. The juxtaposition of these items in the same episode is of interest because the central elements, those involving Christ, outside, inside and outside again, run in sequence. It would perhaps be possible to do each one separately, and it is clear that rapid transformations of a pageant wagon have been effective in modern times. But it is hard to resist the conclusion that the textual amalgamations of these items in Towneley require several locations and movement between them, the movement itself being of theatrical significance. We should not overlook the fact that in other cycles such movement was dramatically important, notably in the N Town Passion Play One and in some continental Passions, such as that of Arnoul Gréban.[34] On the other hand Martin Stevens has noted that at Toronto (1985) the decision was taken to use the same locus for the scene in Mak's cottage and that for the Nativity in *Second Shepherds*. Such an arrangement emphasized the parody implicit in the text.[35]

Three general matters arise from the experience of practitioners and those who have watched and commentated: the versification, the characterization and the extent to which the invention or insertion of modern methods and ideas have been compatible and acceptable. The Towneley

Cycle contains many varieties of versification and the modern performances of it in the open air have repeatedly been cause for comment. Whilst the modern auditor may not always be clearly conscious of which particular form and metre is being used at a specific moment, the alliterative effects and the presence of rhyme which has the effect of bringing words together and emphasizing repetitions and similarities between words are likely to be noticed. These effects are no doubt reinforced by features of the Yorkshire dialect which has so many strong sounds. The power of such effects has been noted by Atkinson, and it is notable that even when a degree of modernization has been carried out the use of alliteration and plentiful rhyming has been continued or adapted as by Bryden.[36] Our discussion of the Wakefield Master's high-powered language and versification suggests that there is much to hear and appreciate in the parts of the cycle where his work is present. In modern times, however, this intensity and even eccentricity have been treated with some caution, though most people who have heard the plays would probably agree that the sound is powerful and intriguing even if it is somewhat watered down. The Yorkshire dialect he wrote and its modern descendants embody one of the chief aspects of poetic language in the theatre: its power of concentration. To this we may add that these rhythmic and cohesive aspects have particular advantages in the open air. There may also have been some local characteristics in Towneley. Peter Meredith, commenting on performance of the Towneley *Pharaoh* (8) recalls that this is one of the plays taken over from York and suggests that the verbal changes of which there are many add a more colloquial tone.[37]

The characters are presented in a number of modes and I think it is important not to oversimplify the ways in which they are used. The fact that Towneley is divided into different episodes which are separate from one another and which are differently conceived, in the manner characteristic of the English cycle plays, means that different dramatists wanted different effects according to the nature of the incidents portrayed and their interpretation. Some characters have dilemmas, some are insistent and repetitive and some have a change of heart. Such a variety will be enhanced if several different actors play the same part in successive episodes, as at Wakefield in 1980. It has been argued that the effect of this is to make the characters, especially the divine ones, seem stronger precisely because of the many manifestations.[38] Some comment has arisen over the extent to which actors become the characters they present, and the consensus regarding Towneley seems to be that there is nearly always some distancing from the role by the actor and that this is closely related to the function of the role in the narrative. This last consideration needs further refinement because a character may have a series of different functions in the same play. The manipulation of these is fundamental to the way in which the plays work. The didactic and exegetical function of the plays, even though, as we have pointed out, it is not the only aspect of witnessing them, makes it inevitable that there is a strong pull towards a non-realistic presentation of character. This has led in the second half of the twentieth century to some parallels with Brecht whose work was particularly fashionable in British academic circles in the 1970s and 1980s when so much new and practical work was being done on the mystery cycles. The essence of this – to summarize with perilous brevity – is that the actor shows the character he enacts rather than being it. However, one may have some reservation about whether Brecht's theory was ever a complete account of what actually went on in his plays, and the same doubt applies to a Brechtian theory for the mystery cycles. In both there is indeed distancing and some evidence for it but there are also engaging details which involve one emotionally with the performance, as with the delicacy of the clumsy Shepherds in Towneley in the stable, for example.[39] I have been struck by a pertinent collection of medieval quotations made by John Elliott in which the commentators emphasize their impression of the truth of what they see. The following, translated from originals in Petit de Julleville, are revealing about what was appreciated in the sixteenth century.

> A young barber named Lyonard was a very beautiful boy resembling a beautiful young girl, and he played the part of Saint Barbara so discretely and so devoutly that many spectators wept with compassion.

> [The performers in *Acts of the Apostles*] were sage men who knew so well how to feign through signs and gestures the characters they were representing that most of the audience thought the whole thing was real and not feigned.[40]

These suggest that at the times of the original performances of medieval plays the expectation and the experience were that one became absorbed however the didactic function was managed. Indeed a deep emotional involvement might have been consonant with the devotional aspects.

Nevertheless, the distinctive ways of the presentation of character also have much value in manipulating the feelings of the audience. We can find in the Towneley productions evidence of several different types of speech in which the actors are at different phases in their approach to the audience. The divine presence of God can be manifested in his oratorical address to all men, and this is shared at times by Christ; at times, as in *Crucifixion*, Christ mixes this oratorical address with an emotional appeal, which in itself depends upon speaking from within as the man. However, with David Parry's playing of the role of Cain at Magdalene College, Cambridge in 1981, one had a sense of his being inside the role and yet that he was conscious of the wider implications of Cain's challenge to God as he enacted the part.[41] Some of his speeches seemed to be addressed to someone deep within himself and the audience were eavesdropping on what was said. In some other places the mode of performance has been more lyrical and the verse structure has been an important part of the process by which intense emotion has been expressed and contemplated. This is especially true of the lament by Mary, and that by Mary Magdalene. The boasts which begin a number of plays also present a challenge to realism even though they are so striking theatrically. The speeches of Caesar, Herod and Pilate are arrestingly addressed to the audience but the frenetic nature of these outbursts may indeed introduce a farcical element, one which increases our distance from them. For these characters one has a distinct sense that their realization for the audience depends upon a recognition of their embodiment of the grotesque. Though they are ostensibly human beings, their dramatic mode is closer to farce in its reduction to a few traits. We shall return to their shared evil characteristics below.[42]

The modernization of the cycles is an absorbing question, and it is in some ways encouraging that some discriminating critics have been much impressed by a modernized performance of medieval cycle plays when measured against attempts at reconstruction of the older practices or close fidelity to the original texts. This argues that the plays themselves are inherently dramatic and encourage inventive interpretation. But it is a delicate business and some modernizations are undoubtedly open to question. Looking back on the earlier revivals mentioned in this chapter, it now seems that the religious tone of the early revivals, as well as the patriotic decoration, was very much a reflection of the limited aspirations of the times concerned. Changing the religious tone is, after all, a modernization of a kind. Yet directors are often pressed to make the material apprehensible to their audiences and in doing so it is clear that some have imposed interpretations on the texts, sometimes in order to bring or increase order and unity, either of interpretation or perhaps staging.

York has always been more likely to be produced in its entirety and so it is no surprise that the whole-cycle presentations have been kept up in more recent times. One of the most interesting, and one very well received, was the millennium performance in the Minster. It is clear that this was a spectacular event and that much was gained in this respect from the exploitation of the building. But it was done on a fixed 'staircase' stage under the crossing, and it is clear that the effects were quite different from the original performances. Here there was apparently a loss of intimacy because of the scale of the spectacle.[43] The production continued to exploit the modern tendency to include large numbers of actors as a people or crowd, to the extent that even the principals reappeared wearing a brown dress as a kind of uniform for the crowd scenes.[44]

We can add to these matters which refer to the cycle as a whole some further details arising from the production of individual episodes. *Second Shepherds* has attracted a great deal of attention, and it is apparent that one of the chief aspects arising is the extent of the comic effects and what can be made of them. It is here that the inventiveness of practitioners has been plenteously manifested, but a contrasting effect may also be achieved. For example, J.-A. George writes that in her production she observed links between Mak and Christ as outlaws, an idea which may indeed help to set Christ apart from the society he was working in.[45] The Poculi Ludique Societas (PLS) production by Kathy Pearl at Perpignan (1986) also moved away from a comic mode. The text offers plenty of detail about suffering, whether it be in terms of work or the family, and the serious presentation of these difficulties was made to anticipate the Manger scene and how that could in some ways bring an alleviation. The serious tone was sustained in the presentation of gifts. The performance concentrated on showing that there was something deeply wrong with the world and emphasizing up the interjection of the Nativity into human suffering.[46] Michael West, reviewing a production at Duquesne in 2000, brings out some further ways in which this play can achieve power over its audience. The Holy Family was present in the acting area throughout the play and there was an attempt to suggest, by this anachronism, the timelessness of the central event. Indeed the device would have put the ultimate event, the Adoration, into a kind of reversal of time by showing the last first and throughout. However, this reviewer also felt that here the Shepherds' suffering was outweighed by the comic playing, and also by exaggerating the self-pity of Mak.[47] One striking aspect of another enterprise was the invention of a Jerry Springer format for a sequence containing *Annunciation, Salutation* and *Second Shepherds* at Cork. The purpose was to see the events as a flashback, and this is clearly an attempt to order the events according to an interpretation.[48] There was apparently a growth in confidence in the way these casts approached their tasks as a result of the familiar modern idiom.

The frequency of performances of *Abel* (2) has probably been the next highest to those of *Second Shepherds*. Cain has proved attractive to practitioners because like Mak he can be seen as an outcast and, also like Mak, the extent of sympathy playing around him can be exploited. Both parts have attracted resourceful actors who have been able to engage the audiences by the inherent ambiguity of the two characters. The other attraction of *Abel* has been the ways in which Abel himself can be seen to anticipate Christ, with perhaps also some side reference to Isaac.[49] Even in modern productions when one might suppose that such cross-references or prefigurations were rather out of mind and unfamiliar, they can be made to work; it is interesting that this appears to happen even when the plays are presented as isolated items.

The question of comedy has also arisen in relation to Herod, whose overbearing manner in Towneley is egregious. Even in the composite cycles he can be made to reveal a crafty menace which is grimly comic. Indeed the tone of his presence in the Coventry *Mysteries* in 1979 was a kind of 'horrific farce with masochistic overtones';[50] the final pose of the savage soldiers with bloodstained hands anticipated the Crucifixion. The staging within the ruined old cathedral was based upon three slightly elevated platforms and the director was able to use the spaces in between to good effect, producing a sense of street theatre. There was, however, an intriguing sense of division between performers and audience even though a large amount of intermingling was encouraged. It seems that in many productions of medieval plays where the actors deliberately work among the audience there is a paradoxical sense that there remains a palpable separation. It is also true that even in a modern secular environment directors feel able to rely upon or indeed to emphasize such cross-references.

The coherence of the Towneley Cycle can in part be reassessed through the consideration of modern productions discussed here. Whatever is inherent in the text the decisions about performance work in part to bring out what is there, and in part to impose interpretation upon what has been left to us out of a need to make the production respond to modern considerations which may be clearly far from the original. But the possibility of variation in interpretation and performance is inherent in cyclic form. It is not then surprising to find that in describing his work for a Chester play production, Edward Burns sets out deliberately to establish a variety of theatrical effects. He suggests that an eclectic production deliberately offers the possibility of continual redefinition.[51] The Chester Cycle is rather more uniform than the Towneley, but the scope he seeks to attain can also be reflected in Towneley as well. Perhaps we can only get close to these plays from Wakefield by accepting the advantages such redefinition offers. By working through such a process we may come to appreciate the theatrical versatility preserved in the texts and also the various preoccupations with the human predicament they offer.

# 2.3

# Special Features

In this section we shall consider a number of performance aspects of the Towneley Cycle which offer special or distinctive characteristics such as may help to illuminate the question of unity. Some of these may point rather to disunity, but we must consider such evidence as making a positive contribution to a consideration of the cycle's coherence. In the development of this section I shall make reference to many individual items in the plays which have already been mentioned for other purposes but I think it necessary to see them from many points of view and to give an account of the ways in which they function from different standpoints.

## Music

The most striking thing about the music in the Towneley manuscript is that it is relatively scarce. There is no musical notation in the whole manuscript and our discussion of the functions of music must therefore be based on the rather rare, explicit music cues and some internal references in the dialogue. We shall review the extent of both religious and secular music shortly but, first, it is clear that the absence of music might in fact be something which asserts a kind of coherence on these plays and helps to explain why the text is as it is. Three things are relevant here. First we need to be careful not to argue exclusively from the absence of music cues or references to music in the text: musical events may have taken place without such indications. The second issue is that it is apparent from the musical procedures surrounding other cycle plays that the amount of music might have varied from year to year. For example, the availability of musicians might not be constant and since, for *Purification* in the Chester Cycle at least, special provision had to be made to hire them, their presence could not be entirely guaranteed.[1] It is also apparent that in the circumstances of the urban centres at Chester, Coventry and York there would be resources available to meet a variety of musical requirements. In contrast Wakefield itself, lacking such urban development in the fifteenth century, might not have been able to provide the means to sustain as complex a musical framework or backing. Thirdly, the absence of music cues might be parallel to the absence of stage directions for many significant events on stage: a feature, indeed, of the copyist's practice or that of his exemplars.

However, where we can identify incontrovertible evidence that music occurs at some places in the text of Towneley, several of the instances correspond to their counterparts in the other cycles. Most of these instances are liturgical in type. They may be further determined by the requirements of the original sources in scripture or its exegesis. The following are liturgical items appearing in corresponding places in more than one cycle:

> *Gloria* in Towneley *First* and *Second Shepherds* (12/425 and 13/919sd):
> Chester (7/357) N Town (16/61sd) and probably York (15).
> *Te Deum* in Towneley *Harrowing* (25/415sd): Chester (17/276sd).[2]
> *Christus resurgens* in Towneley *Resurrection* (26/229sd): Chester
> (18/153sd) and York (38/186).
> *Ascendo ad Patrem meum* in Towneley *Ascension* (29/289sd): Chester
> (20/104sd) and York (43/178sd).

The *Magnificat* in the Towneley *Salutation* (11/48) might well be another example. This canticle, sung daily at Vespers, originates in Luke 1:46 and it was performed in Chester (6/63sd) and York (12/240sd). But, although its first line is present in the Towneley text, it is not marked for singing and there is an English paraphrase spoken by Mary (11/49–78).[3] The presence of such parallels may be a reflection of the process by which the Towneley manuscript was assembled.

There are, however, some examples of liturgical music in Towneley which do not find exact parallels in the other cycles. These are *Simeon Justus* in *Purification* (17/132) and the *Pax vobis* in *Thomas* (28/104 and 121, sung twice), both of which are marked for singing by Christ.[4] In *Harrowing* the first verse of *Salvator Mundi* is to be sung by the souls in limbo (25/44sd); it is also sung in the Chester *Judgement* (24/508) but at a different place. A further intriguing musical item occurs in the part of David in *Prophets* (7/103–59). There is no doubt that he sings since he says he will 'now syng you a fytt' and when the succeeding verses are over he concludes, 'Now have I songen you a fytt' (7/104, 157). He also refers to his harp and his minstrelsy. The intervening verses may owe something to the *lectio* for the Matins of Christmas but the style of the language has been likened to the Breton lays.[5] The absence of any Latin quotation may also suggest that the passage has no direct liturgical links.

In two other places one might also question whether highly charged words from the Bible might also be sung. In *Harrowing* Christ is given the words beginning *Attollite portas* (25/after 120 and after 188; from Psalm 23:7 and 9) as he breaks open hell. In the manuscript both these are copied as though they are speeches and accompanied by a speech heading. As there is no paraphrase, the Latin stands alone in each case. We cannot overlook the possibility that these are both music cues.[6] The second possibility, that some of Christ's last words were sung from the cross is perhaps more remote, though it is worth noticing that this happens in some German passion plays.[7]

A tally of these items works out as follows:

4 sung items correspond to those used in other cycles;
1 is possibly sung here as in others;
3 are sung here and not in corresponding places elsewhere;
3 items may be sung here and do not appear elsewhere;
11 items in all, therefore.

Such a total, even if all the speculative items were positive, shows that Towneley is much poorer in music having a distinctly religious provenance than the other three extant English mystery cycles.[8] One may also conclude from it that there is but a minimal observance of conventional practice in the places where music usually occurs and there is no sustained attempt to include the music in specific passages such as occurs in N Town for the Childhood (8 and 9) and *Assumption of Mary* (41), or for *Ascension* in Chester (20).

It has been demonstrated that in other cycle plays the musical interventions are often structural. They might be used to cover movement, to change the focus of the action or to assist with entrances and exits.[9] There is very little sign of these functions in Towneley; it is really only in the matter of underlining divine intervention in human affairs, as happens in the other cycles, that we find any consistency in the function of the musical items so far considered.

In one respect, however, we find that conventional practice is much exploited in that the Wakefield Master has extensively developed the musical elements in both his Shepherds plays. Because of the scriptural account, no doubt, the *Gloria* is a feature of these plays in the other cycles and commonly the interest in it is embedded in the action of the plays and it is made to function as part of the Shepherds' apprehension of their experience of the Nativity. In the two Towneley versions the music is used in very similar ways and it comprises both the excitement surrounding the Angel's *Gloria* as well as what may be described as secular singing. In *First Shepherds* there are four musical events. Three of them are set pieces and the fourth is a conclusion to the episode. The first accompanies some drinking at the end of the catalogue of foods the Shepherds are to eat. The Second Shepherd proposes that the one who sings best shall have the first draught from the bottle: 'Whoso can best syng / Shall have the beginning' (12/383–4). When they have all sung, however, the First Shepherd, without the consent of the others, usurps the bottle. In all probability the Second Shepherd finishes it off and the Third Shepherd is left to complain: 'I shrew the handys it drogh! / Ye be both knafys' (12/398–9). His remark is probably the key to this part of the play, a recognition of earthly folly and deviousness. It is followed up by the First Shepherd: 'Nay, we knaues all' (400). It is these imperfect men who must be transformed by what they are about to see. Once this fooling about is completed it is time to begin the change, and this is heralded by the Angel's intervention.[10] The next two music events are interlinked, a convention which appears in other Shepherds plays. There is no cue or stage direction for the Angel's speech which follows the spell but, as Stevens and Cawley put it, there can be no doubt that the *Gloria in excelsis* is sung at this point. There is a structural aspect here because the Angel's song marks a significant turning point in the play, away from the human and corrupt, and towards the manifestation of the divine. The message is delivered by the Angel in spoken words, but the Shepherds offer comments on the song, making it certain that it did occur and giving some clues as to the kind of music it was. The first speech after it by the First Shepherd gives clues about its strangeness and his own fears about its import; it also hints at the nature of the musical setting:

A, Godys dere Dominus,
What was that sang?
It was wonder curiose,
With small noytys emang.
I pray to God, save us
Now in this thrang!
I am ferd, by Jesus,

Somwhat be wrang.
Me thoght
Oone scremyd on lowde.
I suppose it was a clowde;
In myn erys it sowde,
By hym that me boght!    (12/439–51)

The 'small noytys' suggest an elaborate liturgical setting, and this is picked up a little later. After they have discussed the meaning of what they have heard they return to the quality of 'this song so fre / Of the angell' (12/589–90). The Second Shepherd adds that there were four and twenty notes to a long (12/598).[11] The First Shepherd adds a bit more detail suggesting the quantity of the small notes and the beauty of what they have heard:

So many he throng
On a heppe;
Thay were gentyll and small,
And well tonyd withall.    (12/602–5)

The quality of the music appears to be a factor in convincing the Shepherds of the truth of the Angel's message (12/591). Their appreciation also stimulates emulation. The Third Shepherd thinks he can do as well but he finds he needs the help of the others, probably, as Carpenter suggests, to undertake the three parts of the descant.[12] They all join in and at the end there is apparently some satisfaction (12/621–2). The Shepherds' appreciation of the Angel's song makes it likely that their musical competence is high and this has led to the assumption that their performance is effective and pleasing, and to the possibility that these roles were played by musically skilful actors.[13]

Unlike the Shepherds in all the other English versions these, and those in *Second Shepherds*, have no song on their way to Bethlehem but they do sing after their visit.[14] Once their visit is over they again turn to song, another convention for Shepherds plays. Their intention at this point is to 'recorde' what they have seen and to bring joy to everyone and praise to the lamb (12/719–24).

*Second Shepherds* is remarkably similar to its partner in its musical elements. It is also true that the music seems to function in much the same way in both plays. Once again there is an early song by the Shepherds – the *Gloria* is linked with a version by the Shepherds – and there is a concluding song. One important difference, however, is found in Mak's lullaby, as we shall see. The first song concludes the opening sequence in which the Shepherds have faced up to their misfortunes and found their sheep safely at pasture. The First Shepherd calls for a song and it quickly becomes one in three parts as for a descant: tenor, treble and mean (13/270–2). The details of the performance are not clear from the text but once it is over the mood changes to suspicion as Mak approaches. As his plot unfolds it becomes necessary for him to stimulate the belief among the Shepherds that his wife has given birth and his lullaby is apposite. Gyll is the prime mover of this scheme and it is she who suggests that while she groans and prays Mak should sing an appropriate lullaby. As they approach Mak's house the Shepherds hear the song and are quick to reveal or underline how unmusical it is.

| | |
|---|---|
| *3 Pastor* | Will ye here how thay hak? |
| | Oure syre lyst croyne. |
| *1 Pastor* | Hard I neuer none crak |
| | So clere out of toyne.   (13/686–9) |

These words in these few lines are packed with significance about what can be heard. There is a tone of sarcasm: false respect in 'Oure syre'; 'hak' used to mean breaking up the musical phrasing into short notes and the word again later in positive appreciation of the Angel's song (13/949); and 'crak' for making a loud noise, also used appreciatively later (13/946). Their poor opinion is further conveyed by the remark about being out of tune and by the word 'croyne' used for the noise made by bulls. The word 'thay' indicates that both Gyll and Mak are contributing to the cacophony: Gyll is presumably groaning or praying out loud.

The Angel's singing of the *Gloria* marks the end of the Mak story and the beginning of the revelation of the Nativity (13/919sd). The Shepherds are full of admiration for the music, using the words of praise we have noticed. They describe the rhythm, 'thre brefes to a long', and the 'crochetts' (13/948, 959) in what Rastall has characterized as 'very florid music indeed'.[15] Once again one of the Shepherds thinks he can imitate the song and in the following lines this is apparently done: 'For to syng us emong, / Right as he knakt it, / I can' (13/952–4). However, it seems that this particular attempt to do so is not quite successful or entirely approved. The Second Shepherd is sceptical: 'Can ye bark at the mone?' But the First Shepherd leads off: 'Hark after, than.' Whatever the sounds that are then made the conversation turns subsequently to the Messianic prophecies. But a few lines later there is still some noise going on for the Second Shepherd tries to quieten it: 'Let be youre dyn!' (13/956–73)

The last musical item in this play comes after the Adoration. As Mary prays for the Shepherds, she asks them to tell what they have seen and remember the day. The Shepherds acknowledge the grace they have found and they leave singing an unspecified song: 'To syng ar we bun' (13/1087). The implication is that the song reflects their need to spread the news of what they have seen.

There appears to be a significant range in the quality of the music in *Second Shepherds*, and this may well reflect the varying degrees of grace possessed by the three sets of singers. At one extreme is Mak's lullaby, indistinguishable from groaning and indicative of his fallen nature. At the other is the beautiful and technically sophisticated music of the Angel's song. The Shepherds themselves fall in between. They can appreciate both the awfulness of Mak's noise and the beauty of the divinely inspired music, and their musical knowledge is apparently good. But their performance here is questionable at least, and though they are impressed by what they have heard, what they produce may not be entirely successful. Unfortunately, we cannot now recover exactly how skilful the singers were originally, but the Wakefield Master shows that he was prepared to make dramatic effects out of such skills, and to portray contrasts within them that might have wider significance in defining both the human and the divine.[16] This does not necessarily argue for an exceptional knowledge of music in the Wakefield Master: rather it shows that in some of his plays he was prepared to make effective dramatic use of what he knew.

An overall view of the ways in which music is embodied in Towneley suggests that there was some attention from time to time to places where music was used in other English cycles, but that this practice was intermittent here. The Wakefield Master is hardly an exception to this in spite of his successful and enterprising management of music in the Shepherds plays. Besides this there are a few places where music appears in relatively unusual places. But on the whole there are extensive areas of the cycle where there is no sign of music. Virtually the whole of the Old Testament sequence comprising plays 1–9, except for *Prophets* (7) as noted above, has none. The Passion sequence, from *Conspiracy* (20) to *Dicing* (24), is similar but here we might notice that many of the speeches, aggressive and often in a mode of cruel caricature, hardly lend themselves to the kinds of music available at the time. What liturgical music there is seems to be concentrated largely in plays from *Harrowing* (25) onwards.

# Comedy

Comedy may be seen as one of the more limiting elements as it is spread through the plays in an irregular manner. Virtually all of it comes within the plays attributed to the Wakefield Master, and many of the comic details to interest him can be seen in more than one play. The effect of this and the virtual absence of comic elements in the rest of the cycle is to separate the work by this dramatist from the other writers, though there is one significant exception to this, as we shall see. The plays having comic elements of some size are *Abel* (2), *Noah* (3), *First Shepherds* (12), *Second Shepherds* (13), *Magi* (14), *Herod* (16) and *Judgement* (30); to these we should add *Annunciation* (10) on a smaller scale. In these plays comedy has a common function as a means of showing up human folly and portraying perversely foolish human ways which conflict with divine benevolence. The comedy is chiefly used to expose those who are in the wrong. This seems to be the intention with Cain whose language and deeds are poignantly foolish: he proceeds by insults, curses and scatological remarks, and often his sheer cheek, his boldness and his verbal ingenuity may inspire laughter. A case in point occurs when he calls God Hob over the wall and asks why he pipes so small when God's voice was presumably not so (2/299–300). This is developed further in the long sheaf-counting speech, an incident not unique to Towneley but much developed here. His assertiveness and his vacillation at this point are a comic contrast. There is another set piece of comedy in the proclamation of Cain's pardon as Garcio undercuts each of Cain's lines in what might be regarded as a comic stichomythia. The discordant relationship between Cain and Garcio is full of menace and mutual dislike, and the devices which make it plain are expressed with irony or even sarcasm. It is also a successful comic device to reverse the dominance-submission characteristics of the two characters by making Garcio speak the proclamation from up a tree and having Cain angry beneath it. We have to take these comic devices seriously in view of the darker purpose of showing why Cain was eventually exiled so comprehensively.

At the beginning of *Abel* the dramatist is concerned with what we might call the comedy of hardship, bringing out Cain's difficulties over his physical labours with the plough and over paying the tithe. Such a comic approach recurs with the burdens lamented by Noah's wife and much more fully with the Shepherds' opening speeches. In *Noah* the comedy is confined to two limited passages but there is no doubting the mockery and loss of dignity experienced by Noah through his participation in farcical combat with his wife. The sex comedy is underlined by the direct address by both parties to the audience about the predicament of both sexes. The listeners are invited to appreciate the sharpness of the discord and perhaps be mindful of the viewpoint of both sexes. There are also hints of sex comedy in the brief outburst of Joseph accusing Mary of infidelity in *Annunciation* (10). This has to be changed, even though it is a conventional trait, and the change helps to establish a different and more appropriate atmosphere ahead of the Nativity.

The most articulate voices in the comedy of hardship are the Shepherds. Their quasi-satirical lamentations are the extensive preliminary in both plays and they are backed up by the more explicitly funny episodes of the imaginary flock of sheep, the feast and the drinking song and the elaborate farcical treatment of Mak's 'baby'. These elements may excite our sympathy in some respects, except perhaps for Mak, and this is a means of generating an understanding of the fallen men that they are. There are also comic elements of sex comedy in both the Shepherds plays, but although there is some laughter in the treatment of women there is another more sympathetic edge to which we shall return in the next chapter. Because the comedy is partly satirical, there are also reflections upon the circumstances surrounding the Shepherds and this has a sharper edge, particularly towards the oppressors and those who represent them. The interpolations made by the Wakefield Master in *Judgement* are almost entirely confined to the lists of sins compiled by the devils. Here again the mockery of those who behave badly is given a satirical twist. Tutivillus also targets women for their self-decorating vanity (30/378–90) and also the conventional misdemeanour of chatting in church.[17]

These in turn link with the comedy surrounding the two manifestations of Herod the Great in *Magi* (14) and *Herod* (16). In these cases the folly is unredeemed and unredeemable, and Herod remains a grotesquely foolish tyrant whose ignorance and miscalculation are so egregious as to be laughable. He experiences a range of emotions but they all seem to make him the more ridiculous. He suffers from rage and frustration and even when he achieves a measure of satisfaction over the murder of the Innocents, it is seen to be laughable. Yet the paradox is that this ridiculous manner is also an embodiment of cruelty and terror. The underlying violence to be found in the portrayals of Herod may be linked to violence in Cain's treatment of Garcio in *Abel* and to that between Noah and his wife.

We can see, then, that the comedy in the cycle is largely mediated through these preoccupations of the Wakefield Master and there are links from play to play even though we should not regard the comic impact of

each as exactly congruent. Emphatically he uses comedy for a wider purpose and part of the richness of our response to his plays is attributable
to this comic dexterity. Such skill may also be manifest in the adaptation he has made, for it is true that the comic tyrants he presents are not
entirely his own invention. From the evidence of other cycles it is clear
that this particular character-type was of more general interest, and this
theatrical convention was taken over and exploited by the Wakefield
Master. In this he may well have been prompted by such characters in
the York Cycle. He added to the convention, but he also made sure that
his characterizations enriched the biblical stories he was trying to transmit,
often in a similar way.

## Spectacle

While we have expressed doubts in Chapter 1 about the nature of the
staging methods chosen for the cycle and pointed to the difficulty of
resolving them into one single comprehensive interpretation, it is plain
that there are many episodes which rely upon spectacle. The dramatists
exploit all sorts of traditional elements of this kind as found in other cycles;
indeed one of the characteristics of Towneley is its conformity to such
practices. The list of such items is very long and one should bear in mind
that many of them had a much longer history of representation in iconography, whether in churches or other visual contexts, such as illuminated
books. Besides their appearance on the actual stages, where they might
have been shown in the original productions, these spectacles are also
present in our minds when we read or remember the cycle and they would
be all the more so in the years when the cycle was evolved.

The spectacular elements include many of the great moments of
salvation history. Thus we have the creation of the world and the fall of
the angels, followed in the same play by the creation of Adam and Eve
and their being conducted into Paradise by the Angel (1/197sd). The
building of the Ark is enacted, and when it is built Noah and his family
are seen to go inside it. The spectacular drowning of Pharaoh's soldiers
is taken over from York. The New Testament stories give us the adoration
by the Shepherds and the Magi in which Christ and his mother are
presumably the centrepiece. One should also notice that in this cycle the
terrible incidents of the Passion are enacted, and in that particular sequence
Christ repeatedly appears as a victim of excessive human cruelty, especially
in *Buffeting* and *Scourging*. *Crucifixion* itself, independent as it is from

the remarkably cruel and detailed treatment of the York Cycle, enacts before the eyes of the audience the horrific details of Christ's suffering which have sometimes been suppressed in modern performances. These would also be very familiar from iconographical representation. Further highly powerful scenes follow with *Resurrection*, *Thomas*, where Christ is bloodstained, the miraculous appearances of Christ and his Ascension. *Judgement* adds to the York version, with its emotional appeal by the wounded Christ come down to judge, and the cruel taunting of the damned by the devils. Finally, and unique to Towneley, we note that if *Lazarus* really was placed at the end of the performance it leaves the cycle with a terrible image of a man speaking of death – wrapped in a shroud? – and his experience as one who has undergone it. Presumably his words might be complemented with his grim appearance as one who has died.

One particular feature which seems to be a frequent item in the cycle is the appearance of angels. Many of these have some basis in scripture, but it is clear that the dramatists saw in them a significant and visually effective way of making manifest the power of heaven exerted upon the earth. Angels make direct intervention in *Creation* and in *Abraham*. In the Nativity sequence God sends Gabriel to announce the coming of Christ to Mary, and there are further interventions by angels to the Shepherds, the Magi, to Simeon in *Purification* and to Joseph in *Flight*. Two angels instruct John the Baptist. At the crisis of the Passion it is the Trinity itself who appears to Christ at the Mount of Olives. But later angels again and again play a significant part in *Resurrection*, *Ascension* and *Judgement*. These occurrences make it clear that the composers of the Towneley plays made positive and frequent use of this particular motif, amounting to an effective device, embedded in the Christian story. In most cases, besides the spectacular effect, the purpose of the interventions is an explanatory one.

## Groups of Characters

It is one of the features of many of the individual Towneley plays that they have groups of three or four characters of the same status and often the same designation who work together and have an influence on events as a group. Very often they are but slightly differentiated among themselves and they usually operate as a unit. We can find plenty of instances of this dramatic device in other medieval plays, no doubt because it has a number of advantages. It allows close interaction and the dialogue can be very tightly written. Deliberation between the individual members can be a means of sparking one against another. They can indeed be given a sort of collective mind as though they were one person thinking aloud. The interaction can also be used in diegetic or heuristic ways, pointing towards ideas or attitudes which need to be gradually revealed or emphasized to the audience.

Such groups operate throughout much of Towneley. Some of them appear in plays taken over from York, as in *Pharaoh, Scourging* and *Resurrection*. For the last it is a common iconographical motif to show the soldiers sleeping at the tomb, and this may have influenced the development of the corresponding sequence in York. Whoever it was who adapted the play for the Towneley text, he decided to take over the York soldiers more or less verbatim. He used two sequences: the first in which the plot is set by Pilate's instructions to the soldiers, and the second showing their conspiracy to lie to Pilate about the miraculous details of what they claim to have seen and heard. In the *Pharaoh* adaptation much of the group dialogue is closely similar to York's, but in this case the names of the speakers are changed to make them more uniform.

The Towneley *Crucifixion* contains a passage of close interaction by the Torturers. It does not have direct verbal links with the York counterpart, but it seems likely that there was some influence as the versions are alike in conception. There is a similar close interaction between the Torturers as they carry out the moves necessary to fix Christ to the cross. This comprises both the dialogue with its broken lines and sharp expressions as well as the physical movements it implies. They show a very similar cooperative effort to overcome the difficulties of the task and they do it with similar grim satisfaction. We also find that the Passion sequence as a whole relies upon several examples of such interaction. Groups of Torturers are found in the Towneley *Buffeting, Scourging* and *Dicing*. The first of these is written in the Wakefield Master's stanza, and it looks as though the portrayal of the cruelty in the sequence by means of close group playing seemed effective to him. His interpolations in *Scourging* contain the passage where Christ is beaten and the verse, with its many short units, is wonderfully supple as a means of matching cruel words and actions:

| | |
|---|---|
| *2 Tortor.* | Now fall I the fyrst |
| | To flap on his hyde. |
| *3 Tortor.* | My hartt wold all to-bryst |
| | Bot I myght tyll hym glyde. |

| *1 Tortor.* | A swap, fayn if I durst, |
| | Wold I lene the this tyde. |
| *2 Tortor.* | War! lett me rub on the rust, |
| | That the bloode downe glyde |
| | As swythe. |
| *3 Tortor.* | Have att! |
| *1 Tortor.* | Take þou that! |
| *2 Tortor.* | I shall lene the a flap, |
| | My strengthe for to kythe.   (22/170–82) |

This dramatist extends group playing for different objectives in his managing of the Shepherds plays. Once again he may well be indebted to an established convention manifested at York, and perhaps at Chester, though for the latter considerations about the history and origin of the cycle may raise some doubts. The Towneley plays show the Shepherds quarrelling and rejoicing together, eating and drinking, offering sympathy, following up suggestions, acting in unison and using individual initiative. There is some distinctive character differentiation here – for example, Coll (First) is old and Daw (Third) is young (13/3 and 248–51) – but their effectiveness is predicated upon the dynamic of the group even where a device is twice employed whereby one is unaware of another's presence. Perhaps the chief advantage of the two groups of Shepherds lies in the way their dialogue and activities create sympathy for them. They have to put up with a good deal and they articulate their response emphatically, but their interaction also reveals their folly and selfishness as well as their generosity. This blend of vice and virtue makes them suitable recipients for the grace which eventually comes upon them.

The Wakefield Master uses groups of characters in other places, notably the Sons of Noah and the grotesquely cruel Soldiers at the massacre of the Innocents in *Herod*. But it is clear that such groups appear in plays other than those he contributed to the Towneley plays. Here we may cite the Kings in *Magi* and the Apostles in *Conspiracy*, *Thomas* and *Ascension*. To these we might add the Marys in *Resurrection* and the two groups of Souls in *Judgement*.

## Dialogue

Three kinds of dramatic speech occur plentifully in Towneley. They are all common enough in other mystery plays and their occurrence, as with the exploitation of groups of characters, indicates that there was a measure of conformity with established patterns. The use of monologue or soliloquy is widespread. Practically all the major characters have such speeches at some point. Apart from the boasts by Pharaoh, Herod and his Messenger, Caesar and Pilate, we can point to key speeches by Garcio in *Abel*, Noah, Abraham, Simeon in *Purification*, John the Baptist, Thomas, and Tutivillus in *Judgement*. Christ himself has several long speeches amounting to monologues, as when he recites the Ten Commandments and explains his coming to the Apostles in *Conspiracy*, and gives them their mission in *Ascension*. It is clear from this that these speech devices were widely used by both bad and good characters.

Also, there are many scenes where the dialogue between two people is a significant part of the dramatic effect. Examples can be found in the passages between Abraham and Isaac, Mary and Elizabeth, Joseph and Mary, Mary and John, Christ and Mary Magdalene, Christ and the Apostles in *Thomas*, and Lucas and Cleophas in *Pilgrims*. The evil relationship between Annas and Caiaphas is exploited in conversation in *Conspiracy* and by the Wakefield Master in *Buffeting*. In this last play a special development also appears in the fierce attempt by Caiaphas to make Christ reply to him. This passage, with its emphasis upon Christ's silence, is original to Towneley, but it may well be linked with a corresponding but different passage in York (29/191–395).

The third kind of speech is much used in a number of different plays and it is related directly to the emotional effects within the cycle. Such lyrical passages are often composed in strict prosodic forms and they make a striking contrast to the other forms of dialogue in which they are embedded. These passages include Gabriel's salutation of Mary and the adoration by both groups of Shepherds and the Magi. Mary's lamentation is another traditional feature present here and one occurring widely elsewhere within dramatic contexts and outside them. The same is perhaps true of Christ's address to the Daughters of Jerusalem and his words to the people from the cross. The latter is echoed in his speeches on his wounds: the one in *Resurrection* is apparently original to Towneley (26/230–350), and that in *Judgement* is found in a passage based on the York version (30/560–607). Thomas has a magnificent lyric as his plea for mercy after his recognition of Christ (28/569–616). The horrors experienced by Lazarus are also expressed in lyric form in a passage derived from a sermon, but here it is given a poetic structure.[18] It should be noted that among these passages only the speeches by the Shepherds are composed in the Wakefield Master's stanza. Even though a few of them derive from York it seems that other poets were working successfully at Wakefield and that their skills could be used dramatically.

The features discussed here offer a number of conclusions. The texture of Towneley is uneven in many respects but the policy of making it appear like other cycle plays is perceivable even if it is not comprehensive. The fact is that many aspects of performance, whether they are the result of conscious choice or are present because of conventional assumptions about the nature of cycle plays, are typical of comparable works. Many parts of Towneley are remarkably dramatic, and it is quite clear from our discussion of several aspects that much of the whole has material that was or is likely to be highly successful on the stage. There is little doubt from the information discussed in Chapter 2.2 that modern directors have been able to capitalize upon this and captivate modern audiences. We should note too that some of the items discussed here indicate that such elements are not confined to the work of the Wakefield Master. Perhaps indeed part of the difficulty in assessing the unity of the cycle is that his contributions are so distinctive and so successful in particular ways. But it is also true that all the cycles are inconsistent in some respects. York in particular presents us with much consistency in language but a great deal of variety in dramatic texture.[19] In York this may be in part the result of many changes of fortune among the guilds, bringing about differences in the texts, but there is little evidence that this was the case in Towneley.

# III

## IDEOLOGIES AND INTERPRETATIVE STRATEGIES

# 3

# Prologue:
# Interpretations

In the main sections of this part of the investigation we shall be concerned with several strategies for interpreting the Towneley Cycle, and
it is necessary to preface this by pointing out that the aspects discussed
here do interrelate to a considerable extent. In Part I we have examined
the complex problems the text presents in terms of regarding it as a unified
whole. The discussion of staging and performance in Part II has also given
rise to a sense of varied initiatives. This potential for incoherence is carried
forward when it comes to ideologies, for we shall find that for most of
the plays one interpretation will not suffice. There is one outstanding feature
in the conflict between conformity and dissent, whether it be a matter of
religious belief and experience or social attitudes. Similarly, when we
consider gender there also seems to be some conflict and it is apparent
that we should be prepared to contemplate not one structure of ideas but
an interactive process whereby such notions as conformity or coherence
have to take into account tensions and counteractions. This is also discernible in respect to the carnival aspect which we shall discuss in relation to
the section dealing with religion. In short the texts of individual plays
become sites for conflict within ideological structures. Nevertheless, the
consideration of the topics in this part helps to identify what is special
about the Towneley Cycle. Its independence of the other extant cycles
can be defined in terms of the treatment of the strategies and preoccupations
discussed here. This material is partly the result of individual initiative
on the part of the authors of the plays, but it is also sustained by the
process of selection which is fundamental to this cycle. There seems little
doubt that the distinctive elements in what follows help to draw the cycle
together and to support our appreciation of its coherence.

# 3.1

# Gender

The consideration of gender in Towneley leads us to look carefully at the frequency and the ways in which female characters are used and also to examine certain ambiguities in the treatment and characterization of Christ and some human characters. Indeed it seems that in certain respects that issues of gender were areas of conflict which ought to be acknowledged.[1] However, the conflict arises only in certain locations: the female characters may be roughly divided between the Virgin, Mary Magdalene and the other Marys on the one hand as virtuous characters, and the presentation of less admirable characters, especially Noah's wife and Mak's wife in *Second Shepherds*. But this broad division on moral grounds will be seen to be fruitfully inadequate when we come to consider the context and the dynamic of characters in each group. One of the facilities offered by dramatic form is its presentation of more than one perspective. To this we should add the ambiguity which surrounds Eve, which in itself might be seen as symbolic of something affecting most of the female characters. It will also be apparent that the treatment of Christ himself is less than simple in terms of gender. The ultimate judgement of these matters suggests both a reflection and an interrogation, however intermittent, from within the plays of the patriarchal society, which late medieval England presumably was. In observing this we have to recognize that the development or assembling of the cycle and its multiple authorship lead inevitably to a variety of emphases. A further subject presents itself when we come to compare the management of this broad topic with some aspects of its presentation in the other English cycle plays.

If we begin with a survey of the part played by women in the nine Old Testament plays, it is at once apparent that the only sizeable example is that by the Wakefield Master in *Noah*. For the rest, women's parts are completely absent or very limited, being concerned largely with what might be called family dimensions. There are no female characters in

*Abel, Abraham, Pharaoh* or *Caesar.* Abraham does mention Eve, remark-
ing upon how Adam assented to her and so hinting at an improper disorder
(4/13–15). As the emotional tension in this play rises, he also mentions
his own wife and the terrible task of telling her what might have happened to their son: 'What shal I to his moder say?' (4/225), and there is
an appealing anticipation of her actual words: 'For "Where is he?" tyte
will she spyr. / If I tell hir, "Ron away," / Hir answere bese belife, "Nay,
sir!"' (4/226–8) The vivacity of this quotation fits in well with the rigorous
emotional discipline of this play, which is clearly the work of an accom-
plished dramatist deeply interested in the emotional predicaments of his
characters. In this passage Abraham is more than a little apprehensive
of his wife as an outraged and formidable mother. His description of his
wife here may be in line with that appropriate for a stereotypic shrew, and
yet that 'Nay, sir!' is emotionally potent, suggesting a proper and deeply
felt unbelief on the wife's part.

Eve in *Creation*, Rebecca in *Isaac* and Rachel in *Jacob* are all small
parts and each of them speaks in a gendered way suited to their roles as
wives or mothers. Rebecca takes the initiative in sending away her son
Isaac to her brother Laban in Mesopotamia (5/41–63). Rachel expresses
her motherly concern about Jacob (6/75–8). Here too there is an emphasis
upon emotion. For Eve it is rather more difficult to evaluate the dramatist's
presentation because the main part of the Fall must have occurred in the
lost ending of this episode. Apart from a significant loss of two bifolia,
Stevens and Cawley suggest that the compiler substituted the Creation of
Adam and Eve for an earlier version.[2] In this extant text there is some
detail in Eve's part in so far as we can determine it. She speaks of paradise
as a place of joy and bliss (1/231). When Adam gives her a proleptic
warning about the tree, she accepts it meekly, but the audience must have
been conscious of the portentous events to follow. At this stage at least
the assumptions about her responsibility for them are muted.[3] Though the
Towneley text is fragmentary it would seem that Eve's part was more
restricted than her several interventions in York (plays 3, 4 and 5).

The characterization of Noah's wife by the Wakefield Master is altogether more complex, but I want to suggest that the traditional reliance
upon the rather grotesque, fabliau aspect of it has been overemphasized,
something which it is too easy to do. Though Noah mentions the Fall, he
does so without offering to blame Eve, indeed he rather puts the emphasis
upon the gluttony and pride attributed by a different common tradition to
Adam (3/53–4). The chief problem in what follows is to relate the quarrels
between Noah and his wife to their harmony once they are safely in the

Ark. The contrast could hardly be greater and it must have been an essential to the dramatic experience. Rosemary Woolf, who is somewhat preoccupied with realism here, sees the link as primarily allegorical, with the Wife as a sinner reluctant to enter the ark of salvation.[4] But her treatment of the contrast may rather be modified if we bring out the richness of the Wife's part during and after the storm.

The violence and hostility of the initial exchanges cannot be ignored, though from the point of view of the gender roles it is interesting that Noah's generic complaint about wives is countered and balanced by his wife's condemnation of husbands. However, as Ruth Evans has noted, there is some doubt about the 'voice' or intention here. It has also been noticed that the characterization of the Wife, dependent as it is upon caricature of female excesses embodied in fabliaux, has an inherent ambivalence.[5] It may well be that there is an implied sympathy for the Wife's being at the receiving end of Noah's temper:

> We women may wary
> All ill husbandys;
> . . .
> If he teyn, I must tary,
> Howsoeuer it standys,
> With seymland full sory,
> Wryngand both my handys
> For drede.   (3/300–8)

His assertion of her irascibility (3/270–1) is matched by hers of his and the parallel is a significant representation of the two attitudes. To this we must add that it is Noah who strikes the first blow. Noah's approach is predicated upon his own assumption that his wife will make trouble – possibly a similar expectation to that we noted in Abraham – but such an assumption is his responsibility as much as it may be the result of her behaviour. Jane Tolmie has pointed out that it was a husband's duty to chastize his wife.[6] The problem of interpretation arising from this is whether there is meant to be a degree of sympathy for her being beaten so fiercely (3/318–27). If the response was merely to mock her for her bruises then sympathy could hardly have been an issue. The dramatist has given himself ample space to portray the hostility between the two, to the extent of showing three rounds of fighting, in which no doubt Noah's physical superiority and readiness for violence are apparent (3/318, 553, 588). Towneley offers a different approach compared with the treatments of the quarrel in the other cycle plays on the subject of Noah. This one gives good scope for seeing the Wife as distinctly disadvantaged, and Noah as outstandingly aggressive.[7] By contrast the York version shows the Wife as more perverse, especially when Noah uses his sons to try to persuade her (Y9/49–50). In N Town (4) the issue does not arise, as the Wife is consistently complaisant. The Chester version is less a direct conflict between the two main characters, and the Sons and Daughters are more involved in preparing for the voyage. In this version the Sons carry their mother into the Ark and there she strikes a blow at Noah (Ch3/246).

Moreover, in spite of the undoubted sharpness of her tongue in the exchange of insults in Towneley, there is a range of emotion in her character, including a very understandable anxiety about what is to come (3/454–5, 536–8). Tolmie notes that her expressed wish for Noah's death and a desire to become a widow (560–3) remains a memorably unsolved part of the play.[8] Even if this is a reflection of the threat posed by women having independent power, the expression of such a wish articulates an important, if dangerous, tendency. But the chief aspect to be noted here is the nature and extent of the subsequent dialogue which ensues once they are all in the Ark. The episode begins when the three sons seek to calm their parents' dispute (3/599) – a significant event in itself because it implies blame for Noah as well as for his wife – and it lasts until the end of the play, a total of about two hundred lines out of eight hundred. The ensuing events are handled firmly by the dramatist, with no retrospect to the quarrel, and there is a significant shift of status in that Noah now defers to his wife in places, and her feelings of fear and wonder and her sense of revelation are carefully articulated. She is a means by which a new and better world is perceived. In this way she 'eludes the polarized roles assigned to women'.[9]

At the beginning of the voyage Noah calls for help from God 'As thou art stereman good' (3/618) and almost immediately he entrusts the rudder to his wife in a remarkable act of confidence. As the storm passes the Wife repeatedly is the means by which signs of mercy are perceived (3/671–2, 675–6, 681–2). Noah asks for her advice about which bird to send forth ('Dame, thou counsel me . . .' 683) and when the dove finally reappears, it is the Wife who first perceives her and the olive branch she carries. Immediately the Wife foresees the possibility of salvation: 'A trew tokyn ist / We shall be sauyd all' (3/748–9). This undoubtedly gives her a voice in the return of grace. The Towneley Wife's final question is about the salvation of those who are now drowned, and it leads to Noah's own prayer for grace (3/792–3). There is no doubt that the dramatist has given her a positive voice and the dynamic of his play is driven by the deliberately close dialogic interaction between Noah and his wife, even though the nature of the exchanges between them is altered radically as the play unfolds. In the York version the Sons and Daughters play a much larger part during the voyage and the Wife is less a medium for hope and Noah places little confidence in her. If Noah's wife is indeed suppressed in the earlier part of the play by means of her husband's (conventional) violence and even if her protests are to be controlled by the allowed rebellion in carnival, the woman's part has at least been stated.[10]

The only other woman in the Old Testament plays is the Sibilla in *Prophets*. She probably owes her presence here to St Augustine's inclusion of her in *The City of God*.[11] In fact her contribution is not given a gendered identity: she speaks grimly of the coming of Judgement Day and of how hell will gape and grin (7/205).

*Annunciation* (10) begins the New Testament episodes, and Mary the Virgin appears in twelve of those that follow. Often her appearances are restrained and her speeches limited, but there is no doubting the significance of her presence in many of them. She is presented in several forms: not one, but many Marys.[12] She appears traditionally quiet and complaisant and yet her ultimate destiny as queen of heaven, the consort of Christ consort and the challenger of Satan, argues an overwhelming importance. She also appears in the role of mother, with a mother's concern for her son, both before and after the Crucifixion. Moreover her somewhat ambiguous status as ordinary and humble, yet concurrently powerful and special, means that she is used to interrogate traditional structures, particularly the male-dominated hierarchy of power even if it be only in the context of the domestic sphere at times. Indeed it is here that her sexual ambiguity is most striking. *Annunciation*, her first appearance in the cycle, has two parts which conflict and are ultimately resolved. To begin with Deus emphasizes her purity in a prolonged description and it is continued by Gabriel. Following the biblical account, the latter makes clear the paradox of the Virgin's conceiving by the agency of the Holy Ghost: 'He shall vmshade and fulfyll / That thi madynhede shall neuer spyll, / Bot ay be new' (10/128–30).

Once this is firmly established it is challenged by Joseph. As in the case of Noah's wife and Mak's wife this episode, even though it had some scriptural basis in Matthew 1:19, had a fabliau background centring here upon the mismatch of an old husband with a young wife (10/170). Joseph's accusations on discovering the pregnancy are met with calm assurance from Mary, and without rancour. The managing of the episode takes an interesting turn once this is made clear. The interchange with Mary is suspended while Joseph gives a long account of the events leading to the marriage. The strength of her silence is sustained as he speaks of her in the third person. What is really happening is that Joseph is being allowed to condemn himself by his persistence over Mary's supposed betrayal. The Angel's intervention comes about when Joseph's position is manifest, and it doesn't take long for Joseph to accept the truth, which the audience, no doubt, had been invited to perceive for some time. Mary then returns to the dialogue and, significantly, she forgives Joseph for his mistake. In this play there is less ambiguity in the woman's role than in the play by the Wakefield Master we noticed above, and the traditional comedy is at Joseph's expense, as it is in York and N Town.[13] The 'good wyll' which Joseph sees in her is much developed in later episodes. However, in spite of the final resolution, the play does expose some disturbing aspects in the social context of gender relations. As Theresa Coletti has pointed out, Joseph raises a number of issues including adultery, cuckoldry and also illegitimacy: 'I wyll not fader it! She says amys; / For shame yit shuld she let / To excuse hir velany by me' (10/222–4). These may well reveal the difficulty of placing the central paradox of the virgin pregnancy within the medieval gender structures.[14]

In this episode and *Salutation*, which follows, the appearances of Mary generally show her as content and blessed. *Salutation* strikes a particularly tender note in her meeting with Elizabeth, also pregnant. Apart from the recitation of a translation of the *Magnificat* there is a delicate scene in which the two women talk in a family way about their state. The repetition of names enhances the quiet intimacy:

| | |
|---|---|
| *Elezabeth* | And Ioachym, thy fader, at hame, |
| | And Annas, my nese and thi dame, |
| | How standys it with hym and hir? |
| *Mary* | Dame, yit ar thay both on lyfe, |
| | Both Ioachym and Annas, his wyfe.   (11/22–6) |

There are no other voices here, and this particular tone seems quite deliberate and finished. Through the family concerns of the two pregnant mothers the links between generations are suggested by their enquiries, and the female nourishment of the unborn infants is emphasized.[15]

In the complexity of the Shepherds plays, Mary's role is strictly limited; in both she speaks only one stanza. Though the wording is different, the contents are broadly similar and her iconic status constant. In both she asks for a blessing upon the Shepherds, and perhaps the audience by implication; in the second version a phrase is included about the power of God's creating the child in her (13/1070). Nevertheless, apart from the treatment of Mary, in the main substance of these two plays the Wakefield Master calls upon a number of aspects of gender, as he does in *Abel*. In *First Shepherds*, apart from two mentions of the virgin birth, it is only a matter of referring to one woman, the notably foolish Moll who broke her pitcher (12/219–30). In *Second Shepherds* interest is focused explicitly upon the struggles within marriage. Although he again uses stereotypes for husbands and wives, his treatment of them is not straightforward and they reflect badly upon Mak, contributing in no small measure to the impact of his devious character. It is difficult to sympathize with the presentation of Mak's wife when he uses the fabliau material to mock her. This is especially the case when Mak refers to the frequency of the offspring she produces, completely ignoring the part he himself had played in their conception. This crude mockery is foreshadowed in the sustained misogynistic outburst by the Second Shepherd who details the sufferings of married men (13/105ff). His diatribe culminates in an abusive caricature, where restraint is abandoned in a carnivalesque manner:

> She is as greatt as a whall,          [*whale*]
> She has a galon of gall;
> By hym that dyed for vs all,
> I wald I had ryn to I had lost hyr!   (13/153–6)

However, as the plot develops the ground shifts. Mak's wife is given an opportunity of criticizing him and there is also a sense that her resourcefulness must be respected. She has a clear idea of the risks Mak is running and it is she who produces the idea of hiding the sheep in the cradle. The ambivalence of gender roles in this play is remarkable. Once again the stereotypes are present, as well as the sense of a male-oriented world, which in itself may not be surprising. But against this arise both the limitations of our sympathy with Mak, and also the part played by his wife. There is a remarkable difference between his earlier description of her:

> Lyys walteryng – by the roode –
> By the fyere, lo!
> And a howse full of brude.
> She drynkys well, to.   (13/341–4)

And her later articulation of the burdens carried by women:

> Why, who wanders, who wakys?          [*runs about*]
> Who commys, who gose?
> Who brewys, who bakys?
> What makys me thus hose?
> . . .
> Full wofull is the householde
> That wantys a woman.   (13/600–607)

It is important to note the dynamic here because the interaction between man and wife comes in two phases: the first occurs when he brings home the sheep (13/426–503), and the second when the Shepherds come to search his house (13/673–906). The former begins on a sour note by the Wife: 'Who makys sich dyn / This tyme of the nyght? / I am sett for to spyn' (13/428–30). By the time that we reach the second episode the misogynistic mockery has disappeared and we are presented with a competent fellow conspirator, and one who is both feminine and intelligent. This shift may lead us to recall the change in attitude towards Noah's wife, and in doing so we may notice particularly that the context for the two is contrasted. In *Noah* the issues of salvation are much more profound and the change may be seen as part of the revelation of this purpose. With Mak's wife we are concerned with a crime and the change in presentation effectively makes her an accessory. This disparity of objectives thus suggests that the reason for the change lies rather in the perception of the status of women than in the spiritual objective. This may well be reinforced by the repeated practice of initially referring pointedly to the gendered stereotypes and then departing from them.[16]

This argument may be taken a little further by considering *Herod* (16), a play which is largely concerned with the slaughter of the Innocents, and one attributed to the Wakefield Master. The framework of Herod's tyrannical boasting and his cruel decision may well underline the male-dominated values of power.[17] In Towneley the three mothers are responding to their plight through their grief and sorrow for their lost sons but also by vigorous challenge to the soldiers. Each of them offers violence to their assailants, the third one attacking the groin of the soldier (16/491, 510, 544). This is notably more aggressive than the corresponding passage in York. Notwithstanding the thematic or figurative references to vengeance recalling Abel and the torn body of Christ (16/532, 566, 564), we should note that these women speak with a passion which makes us keenly aware of their maternal sorrow:

Out, alas and waloway,
My chyld that was me lefe!          [*dear to me, beloved*]
My luf, my blood, my play,
That neuer dyd man grefe!   (16/523–6)

In spite of the very loaded significance of this episode, which anticipates
the laments of the Virgin, there is no doubt that the Wakefield Master
again articulates the feelings of women in a way which implies an understanding of their difficulties in a hostile and destructive environment. In
her study of the Innocents plays Theresa Coletti has suggested that the
women's response tends to destabilize male power structures, and also to
imply alternatives.[18]

To return to Mary, she has two other appearances in Towneley before
the beginning of the Passion. In *Purification* she confirms that through her
the law is fulfilled (17/127–32). There is, however, a lacuna in the text
here, comprising the end of this play and the start of the next, which is
*Doctors*. The lost material may very well have given further scope to Mary,
and its removal is probably the result of Protestant anti-Marian sentiment.
*Doctors*, as we have noted in Chapter 1.2, is one of the borrowings from
York. At the beginning there has been a change in Towneley whereby
three Magistri are substituted for Mary and Joseph, but in the main episode
the text is very close to York, except that linguistically it has been aligned
by the scribe with the dialect nearer Wakefield. Mary's part is written
in such a way as to show a mixture of boldness and meekness. Joseph is
rather reluctant to break in upon the learned clerics but Mary insists that
they should, and it is she who takes the lead in doing so. But the scene is
delicately managed by the York dramatist, as she seems reluctant to take
on her husband's conventional role:

Go we togeder, I hold it best,
Vnto yond worthy wyghtys in wede;
And if I se, as haue I rest,
That ye will not, then must I nede.   (18/233–6; cf Y20/241–4)

By tradition Mary's participation in the Passion is extensive and it
inevitably brings about a fundamental change in her role, as can be seen
from many iconographical treatments.[19] Such treatments offer a wide range
of emotional effects, as well as often suggesting that she has a continuing
presence as the events unfold.[20] In the Towneley narratives she has but
a limited part and her appearances are constrained by the scriptural

framework, but in various ways she articulates emotional responses to the events contained in these episodes.

The latter part of *Scourging* (22) shows Mary's encounter with Christ as he carries the cross. This play owes something to York 34 in that some lines are the same but the extent to which Mary's part is unique to Towneley is somewhat masked because of a lacuna in the York text. St John's speech in which he laments that he must tell Mary is the same in both plays and this suggests that the part of Mary may well have been similar.[21] The Towneley version is constructed to highlight the shock to the Virgin and the support given to her by Mary Magdalene and Mary Jacobi who try to shield her from the terrible news. But John says that he must tell what has happened if they are to speak to Christ before he dies. The emotional pitch of the scenes is further heightened as they meet Christ with the cross. In fact there are conflicting emotions here in as much as Christ says he must die in order to redeem 'mans saull' even though Mary begs him to have pity on himself (22/440). In spite of the intensity of Mary's sorrow, which in itself perhaps anticipates the deposition from the cross, the climax of the scene is Christ's warning to the Daughters of Jerusalem, based upon Luke 23:28–31. The wording in the play draws attention to the plight of mothers who will bring forth children, and the threat seems to point directly to the Virgin as mother in a passage which has no direct counterpart in the York text: 'Childer, certys, thay shall blys / Women baren that neuer child bare, / And pappes that neuer gaf sowke, iwys; / Thus shall thare hartys for sorow be sare' (22/474–7). There is an underlying reference here to the Second Coming and the Day of Judgement,[22] and Mary is silent here as the Torturers force the pace to Calvary.

In the following play, *Crucifixion* (23), Mary's part is more extensive than in the corresponding play at York, *The Death of Christ* (36). It consists largely of an elaborate lament in lyric form, set out in three stanzaic forms and heavily alliterated throughout (23/311–44, 367–82, 396–423, 435–52, 461–502). This assumption of a consciously poetic form is no doubt related to Christ's speeches from the cross although they are in a different metre, arranged in eleven-line stanzas (23/234–96, 505–35). These speeches form the core of the play while the other episodes are concerned with Pilate's boast, the preparations of the Torturers including the nailing and lifting of the cross, and then, later, the death of Christ, the deposition and intervention by Joseph of Arimathea. Thus the play is full of incident except for the lyrical passages noted above. The addition of such lyrical episodes is a feature of Towneley.[23]

Though there are no speeches or actions assigned to her at the beginning of this play, it is likely that Mary is supported by the other Marys in the traditional manner. She is a melancholy figure in the central episode, though it is surprising that she remains silent until Christ is actually hanging on the cross and that she is given no words at the deposition. No doubt there was an opportunity for iconic moments as the action unfolded and the dramatic impact of the scene depends upon such features, as well as upon the imagery given by Mary's words. From the aspect of gender, however, Mary's words are significant. Her role as mother is much emphasized through images of blood (315), food (319), the baby (barne, 332), tears (341) and nakedness (342). In the following lines the 'robe' may be a deliberate double image for a garment she made for Christ and his flesh, shaped in her womb: 'His robe is all to-ryffen, / That of me was hym gyffen, / And shapen with my sydys' (23/405–7). In the rest of her speeches there are frequent references to 'child' and 'son', and the imagery referring to birth and motherhood is sustained throughout. Addressing Death, she asks 'Who kend the to my childe to gang?' (463), and at a later moment she says, 'sen I had childer none bot oone' (474). Lamenting her lonely life now that he is gone at the end of her speech she begs, 'Mi dere sone, haue mercy!' (502).

These features are characteristic of the conventions in early liturgical Passion plays for the lamentation of Mary, especially in her repeated attention to the physical wounds inflicted upon her son (316, 329, 337, 370, 464) and to the destruction of his beauty (face, 329; eyes, 367), but the concentration in this dramatic context is striking. She sees him as a lamb among wolves (410–13). Conscious of her sex, she exhorts other women to join in her lamentation. This may be addressed to other characters on the stage or indeed to women in the audience:

> Madyns, make youre mone,
> And wepe, ye wyfes euerichon,
> With me, most wrich in wone,    [*wretched everywhere*]
> The childe that borne was best!'   (23/418–21)

Once again it introduces a certain ambivalence.[24] The elaborate exploration of the emotions of the forlorn mother actually stimulates a response from Christ on the cross: 'My moder mylde, thou chaunge thi chere! / Sease of thi sorow and sighyng sere; / It syttys vnto my hart full sore' (23/503–5). His explanation, that he suffers for a good reason, to redeem mankind, ought to satisfy her, and the reminder that this was the primary cause of

GENDER                                                        149

his coming is meant to assuage her grief. However, he points to a new
role for her, one which allows her to continue as a mother: 'Take ther
Iohn vnto thi chylde' (521).

Christ's speech brings to an end Mary's part in the dialogue. Her spoken
role is apparently now completed but the treatment of her in *Crucifixion*
is clearly coherent and consistent and it enables a number of significant
links to be explored, particularly those with Christ, St John and the other
women. Some of this depends upon traditional material or elements from
the scriptural narrative, but Mary's role as a woman is dependent upon
the need to sustain these relationships. Her femininity is perceived in a
context involving that of others. In *Ascension* (29) her part is less central
to the action, though the loss of some pages at the end of the play makes
conclusions about her role difficult. If it is true that the lost passages contained such items as Mary's death, assumption and coronation, as suggested
by Stevens and Cawley (*Plays*, vol. 2, pp. 632–3), the last part of the cycle
would have had a very different effect. Perhaps we should note, however,
that the Chester Cycle as it approaches the Judgement play is much concerned with the Coming of the Antichrist. However, she seems to be a
witness through much, if not all, of the surviving fragments of the play.
The main action concerns Christ's relationship with the Disciples and
his setting out a new preaching role for them. Mary is used to reassure
the continuing uncertainty felt by Thomas, by asserting that her son has
always spoken the truth and fulfilled his promises. When Christ appears
he reaffirms the mother–child link between Mary and St John which he
had set up at the Crucifixion (29/261). The effect of this is to sustain her
maternal role and also to offer increasing comfort to her. Her vulnerability
is emphasized by a further motif of a physical danger to her: at first this
is unspecified as coming from 'foes', but later she particularizes it by saying
that she fears destruction by the Jews who had demanded the death of her
son (29/395–9). She ends the fragment, however, in a positive way by
encouraging the Disciples to sustain the truth of her son's teaching and
she urges them to preach, particularly to the inhabitants of the city of Jerusalem (29/44–9). Through all the play her witness, including support for the
mission of the Disciples, is always linked to her role as a mother.

Summing up Mary's role in the Passion in Towneley we may say that
it intensifies the emotional content by drawing upon her role as a suffering and loyal mother. Though this may be regarded as a sexual stereotype,
it does operate as a powerful dramatic technique on a number of key occasions, and it probably opened the way for emotional responses in the

audiences. A similar process may be found in the effect of Mary Magdalene and the other Marys who appear several times in the Passion. The former is a useful antithesis to the Virgin because her starting point was thought to be a sinful life, and though she was held to have reformed, her dramatic role might imply a kind of opposition, or at least in Towneley it is made to be ideologically oppositional.[25] Traditionally she had done things which the Virgin as an idealized wife and mother could not possibly have done. Admittedly this is not true in the episode where she comforts the Virgin in *Scourging* (22/390–4, 412–14), matching her in amenable and complaisant sexual behaviour. But shortly afterwards there comes a passage charged with sexual hostility where her more aggressive character comes into play. The Torturers abuse Christ for his warning to the daughters of Jerusalem and seek to dismiss the women as irrelevant. The Second Torturer particularly calls up a stereotype arising from the fear of ungoverned female tongues: 'Thise qwenes with scremyng and with showte, / May no man thare wordys stere?' (22/487–8). Upon this Mary Magdalene defiantly calls for vengeance: 'This thyng shall venyance call / On you holly in fere' (22/492–3). It should be noted here that all these lines (487–93) are part of the borrowing from York. However, York does not attribute 492–3 to Mary Magdalene but to the Third Mary: see Y34/196–7.

In a similar vein she is again challenged by Peter and Paul in *Thomas* (28/1–73). Here she brings to the Disciples the news of the Resurrection, but her account is dismissed in sharply misogynistic language by these two Apostles. Paul is especially fluent in his condemnation of the unreliability of women: he cites 'bookes' warning of their deception, but the law he quotes is probably based upon contemporary commonplaces rather than the anti-feminist nature of some of his writings in scripture.[26] His anti-feminist phraseology is intense, and it may well have been designed to produce a contrary reaction from the audience:

> For with thare quayntyse and thare gyle
> Can thay laghe and wepe somwhile,
> And yit nothyng theym grefe.   (28/32–4)
> . . .
> 'Till an appyll she is lyke;
> Withoutten faill ther is none slyke
> In horde ther it lyse.
> Bot if a man assay it wittely
> It is full roten inwardly
> At the colke within.   (28/38–43)

In spite of Mary's affirmation Peter sides with Paul until a moment of miraculous conversion when he finds himself weeping at the news and then he recalls that he had denied and betrayed Christ, 'For drede of womans myght' (28/78). Stevens and Cawley attribute this change to 'careless editing' (*Plays*, vol. 2, p. 619), but their view may be questioned in the context of a play where belief and changes to it are very much in question during the bulk of the action concerning the incredulity of Thomas. Mary Magdalene's speeches here are not vituperative: she calmly holds her ground and she is vindicated firstly by Peter's change of heart and shortly afterwards by the appearance of the risen Christ to the Disciples. Her position is made the stronger because of Peter's impulsive nature as repeatedly indicated in the Gospel narratives. The thematic link between the incredulity of Peter and Paul and that of Thomas is a feature which helps to hold this play together.[27]

In her other appearances in the cycle the tone is less tense but it should be remembered that the selection of episodes here has not included details of the Ministry, and the meal at the house of Simon, in which she appears in other versions, is much shortened by the omission of the establishment of the Eucharist.[28] In *Lazarus* she has two brief speeches welcoming Christ and she asserts that he would have saved Lazarus before his death had he been there. In *Resurrection* she plays her scriptural role, at first mistaking the risen Christ as a gardener and then, on his prompting she rejoices: 'I am as light as leyfe on tre / For ioyfull sight that I can se' (26/648–9). Earlier in this play, in a much more sombre state, she expressed her grief that Christ had suffered for her sake. At the moment of recognition, however, her response has a distinctly physical dimension in that she wishes to draw near to Christ and kiss his feet (26/609–10) and she speaks of being 'blyth in bloode and bone' (26/644).[29] Though her role is not as extended in Towneley as it is in other cycles, particularly N Town, she does have a role here complementary to the Virgin in her truth telling and her love for Christ, which has at times a physical aspect.

The aspects of gender we have been discussing here range through a considerably variety of female characters. While it may not be true to say that the presentation of them is uniform, we can be confident that while the treatment of gender pays considerable attention to stereotypical female behaviour, the different contexts give rise to varying ways of manipulating this material. No doubt the examples we have discussed come from work by different authors, amongst whom the Wakefield Master's is a distinctive voice, but I think it is clear that at times women are given powerful voices and significant roles in the unfolding of events. In some of these they articulate their own position very strongly, expressing shifting attitudes towards women in the fifteenth and sixteenth centuries, and to some extent undermining assumptions about male superiority. It is striking that their place in society, albeit underprivileged, is given some recognition. We should also not lose sight of the fact that these women are very effective parts of the dramatic experience embodied in many of the episodes we have been discussing. Particularly in well-established narrative segments their participation is indispensable, and their conflict with male assumptions enriching of the theatricality of the plays.

Gender issues have also been raised in the consideration of Christ's body, particularly at the Passion. There are undoubtedly sacramental aspects here as well as some implications for the function of the Towneley Cycle in terms of social symbolism. We shall return to these in a later discussion. But Christ's body as a resonant feature of these plays has been perceived as a place for controversy and it also has a double function in terms of gender.[30] The most significant aspect of this is a product of the sustained violence through which Christ is perceived in the Passion sequence. This has extensive precedents in other cycle plays, especially and most pointedly in the York *Crucifixion* (35), whose action is confined almost entirely to the process of nailing Christ to the cross, as well as in iconography.[31] It is probably the intensity of the violence together with Christ's submission to it which has given rise to the perception that this orientates him towards a feminine role, though it must be admitted that there is no conscious acknowledgement of this in the text. The justification for raising the matter must come from critical and ideological approaches not familiar to those who created the plays in the first place. To some extent the sexual symbolism may be attributed to the concept that Christ's body offered a number of paradigms which may be identified in other works, verbal or visual. These may be related to the feast of Corpus Christi and they include its representing the whole Christian community, which has attributes of both genders and also the symbolic union of Christ as male, united with the Church as his bride.[32] Another important thread relating to the concept of Christ's body comes in the emotional responses to his role as the Man of Sorrows, a point to which we shall return in the next chapter.

The Passion sequence in Towneley contains a good deal of work by the Wakefield Master, though the contribution of other authors is also apparent. In this part of the cycle he seems to have made sure that his own passages matched the violence presented by others. For example, the repeated threats of violence from Caiaphas in his *Buffeting* (21/275, 280, 289 and many more) complement the mockery and exposure of Christ in *Scourging* by the Torturers who strip Christ, bind him and carry out the beating (22/157–82). In the latter they also anticipate what is about to happen to Christ at the Crucifixion, which the following play duly enacts (22/322–34). During these events Christ is passive, naked and vulnerable, and they portray how he staggers and swoons (21/595, 21/601, 22/300). The visual aspects of the dramatization must have been overwhelming. In these episodes the body of Christ may be seen as feminized.[33] The Torturers repeatedly take a physically dominating role in their contact with Christ: they make him sit down in order to mock him; they bind him to a pillar; they lie him down to nail him to the cross; and in the same sequence he must be prone while they draw upon his arms and legs with ropes. Though Christ is not entirely silent through the Passion, he speaks very little and, apart perhaps from the threat to the daughters of Jerusalem noticed above, he shows complaisance rather than resentment or aggression. Such complaisance would accord with the notion of his willingness to undergo torment and death. This would contrast with his more dominating, masculine manifestations in *Harrowing* with its martial imagery and in *Judgement*, and it brings into question the double nature of Christ's sexuality. It has been suggested that this was an essential in that Christ had to be completely human, sexually whole, and a representation of all people of both sexes.[34] The treatment of these aspects of Christ's sexuality in Towneley is undoubtedly similar to other versions, including that of York, yet it does appear to be an independent presentation which has some coherence in the Passion sequence. In discussing the Virgin we noted that patriarchal stereotypes were present but that they came under pressure as the narrative developed. Male stereotypes of this kind may be found in the Torturers at the Passion, but it is likely that Christ's body was treated by the dramatists in such a way so as to humanize it by means of gender characteristics. It does seem that by reading these plays in terms of gender their rich symbolism is enhanced.

# 3.2

# Religion and Popular Culture

I n this chapter I should like first to discuss a range of religious aspects in Towneley and then to consider complementary aspects of popular culture which I suggest cannot be entirely separated from them. These need to be treated together because of the ambiguity inherent in many of the individual plays. It will be perceived that on the one hand there is a good deal of orthodox material in the work of the contributing playwrights; on the other hand the presence of subversive material raises questions about the extent of dissent within the plays and the possible responses designed to contain it.

## 3.2.1 Religion

It may seem strange to attempt to address a topic which is so clearly fundamental to the Towneley Cycle, as indeed it is to all the cycle plays, and yet if we are to consider the unity of the work adequately it seems appropriate to review the nature of the religious experience it offers to see how far it is coherent. It has been suggested that the cycle plays contained the collective voice of the Church.[1] But although Towneley may have much in common with the other surviving plays of this type, we need to be concerned here with its individuality. In spite of the common inheritance of the cycles in religious terms, there will be some features which are more emphatically treated or even found to be unique in Towneley. These may help to give it its individuality and at the same time they may point to the preoccupations the compiler or authors might have had in setting out the cycle in the form in which it has come down to us. Among such characteristics is the polarization of good and evil in some parts of the cycle, which is treated in Chapters 3.4 and 3.5, and this will need to be seen against the consideration of religion in this section.

The common inheritance of the cycles is partly a matter of chronology in as much as the beginnings of cycle form late in the fourteenth century and its much more extensive development in the fifteenth century, in England as well as on the continent, are contingent upon significant events in the history of the Church. The later medieval period saw a great crisis in matters of faith. From the twelfth century there were shifts in the attitudes to Christ as he came to be perceived more and more as a figure of suffering.[2] This increased the element of personal tenderness in devotion under the influence of St Anselm and St Bonaventura, and must have increased the intense emotional contemplation of the Passion.[3] Along with this came a criticism of the wealth of the Church which manifested itself in some aspects of the work of St Francis and his followers who were conscious of the life of Christ himself and also paid attention to the poverty of the Apostles.[4] Some of the feelings of these times were so intense that their apparent confrontation with the Church authorities and practices caused them to be regarded as heretical. The twelfth century is characterized by the Lateran Councils of 1139 and 1179 where there was both an interest in reform and a desire to combat the unorthodox, now regarded as heresy. In the thirteenth century Innocent III moved to counter such irregularities and also to sustain the faith more positively. The Fourth Lateran Council (1215) concerned itself with the need to attend to the laity, and in order to do this more effectively it made moves to improve the education of priests.[5] From it came the requirement of annual confession and insistence upon attendance at Easter Mass by all Christians. It is apparent that the bishops were an important means by which this greater awareness was to be promoted. Innocent also approved the formation of the order of friars by St Francis (1210). A. C. Cawley suggested that the instructions issued by Archbishop Thoresby of York in 1357 might have influenced Towneley regarding a number of doctrinal matters.[6] We should notice the issue of the Constitutions Archbishop Arundel of Canterbury (1407, promulgated 1409) against Wycliffite books and Bible translation, and imposing controls on preaching.[7]

In England these changes of emphasis were accompanied by, and indeed promoted through, many written works, such as *The Lay Folk's Catechism*, which was an English verse translation of the instructions of Archbishop John Thoresby of York. It was written in 1357 by John Gaytrick, a Benedictine monk of St Mary's Abbey within the city. The corpus of such writings, often conceived as aids to preaching and now deliberately presented in the vernacular, is large and they form the inheritance of the authors of the cycle plays. They included such works as Robert Manning,

*Handling Sin* (1303), *The Azenbite of Inwit* (1340), *The Book of Vices and Virtues* (c.1375); John Mirk, *Instructions for Parish Priests* (c.1400); and the anonymous *Mirour of Mans Saluacioun*, which has survived in nearly four hundred manuscripts from the fourteenth and fifteenth centuries.[8] Though *The Lay Folk's Catechism* is only one of many such works of devotion and instruction following the increased urgency, it is suggestive of an influence and state of mind in the region of York at a time just before the inception of the York Cycle which can be traced at its earliest in 1376.[9] Even though the Towneley Cycle did not appear until much later, its close relationship with parts of the York text suggests that it owes a good deal to this earlier period of spiritual development. Another likely contributor to the process of instruction and one with a remarkably wide distribution was Nicholas Love's *The Mirrour of the blessyd lyf of Jesu Christ* (c.1410) which was specifically designed to be a counter to Lollardry.[10] His emphasis upon miraculous aspects of the Christian narrative is a contrast to the Lollards' concern with the understanding of the Ministry. However, the suggestion that the English cycle plays were specifically designed as counter-Lollard enterprises advocated by Ruth Nissé in the case of York and Lauren Lepow for Towneley is not entirely convincing. There is a great deal in these plays which does assert fundamentals of Catholic belief and doctrine but that there was an overriding priority to defeat Lollardry in specific ways remains open to question. Nevertheless we can agree that some aspects noted by these critics emphasize the nature of orthodoxy, and that the value of a sustained effort in the vernacular is high.[11] It is important that we should not lose sight of the wider European perspective here. The development of cycle plays in France and some German-speaking states based upon the scriptural narratives and aimed at the spiritual health of the community does seem to follow widespread religious concerns. To an extent these were centrally motivated even though they may have worked out differently in various communities.

Other historical circumstances also played a part in the increasing spiritual preoccupations and these were not necessarily prompted by Lollardry. Besides the growth of greater missionary activities, complementary to the increase in individual heretical beliefs, there was also the Black Death. This struck western Europe in the middle of the fourteenth century and its impact was devastating physically as well as contributing to many changes in religious consciousness. Not only did it make the awfulness of mortality acutely perceptible, it also produced in some scepticism about the efficacy of the Church as a means of protecting the faithful against it. The impact of such scepticism was partly to increase dissent but this also led to great concern to establish and consolidate orthodoxy in society in general. It is therefore not surprising to find that the cycle plays, in France as well as in England, were civic affairs. The Church may have held, or attempted to hold, control over doctrinal matters but it is clear that in very many places the actual management was in the hand of lay authorities and answered to their requirements. Such a position did have evangelical benefits from the Church's point of view, but it was also potentially a source of some religious difficulties as the fragmentation of central authority became more general in the sixteenth century.[12]

We may not be able to say that there is one centralized belief structure manifested in the Towneley Cycle to which everything refers. Nevertheless, there are some features which point to emphases and recurrent concerns, and taken together they may well be seen as distinctive. One should note, to begin with, that a very high proportion of the stage action is concerned directly with the presentation of narrative. The dramatists are interested in showing the events which matter and in the unfolding of lesser parts of the narrative within the greater. Many of these narrative elements are directly derived from the Bible, but they can also be affected by narrative conventions, as in the gifts given to the infant Christ in both the Shepherds plays (12 and 13). Similarly the details of *Crucifixion* (23) follow the established pattern of the grief of Mary, the role of St John caring for Mary, the breaking of the temple, Pilate's labelling of the King of the Jews, the affirmation of divinity through the restoration of Longinus's sight when he pierces Christ's side and the words of Christ on the cross. It is notable that many of the episodes not composed by the Wakefield Master show strong narrative interest, as in *Isaac* (5), *Jacob* (6) and *Conspiracy* (20).

However, we should add to this that many details of the narrative are referred to in advance or in retrospect, and that the scope of such references varies greatly. This, I believe, is one of the basic characteristics of cyclic form, and the Towneley Cycle provides many examples of it. The Wakefield Master's *Scourging* (22), for example, shows the Torturers recalling many of Christ's deeds as they carry out their cruel work. They recall his changing the water into wine at the wedding, healing the leper, reviving the Centurion's son, restoring the sight of the blind man, his alleged breach of the Sabbath and the possible rebuilding of the temple in three days. The context of these is that the Torturers mean to abuse

Christ by implying that they are outrageous indications of his guilt and deserving of their retribution, but they all serve to make the audience think the contrary. In *Pilgrims* (27), an episode not attributable to the Wakefield Master and one which has considerable significance regarding the religious aspects in the cycle, there is an extensive retrospect based upon the account in St Luke (24:13): before Christ appears to them, Lucas and Cleophas lament the details of the Crucifixion in an emotional passage which is clearly meant to summon up the picture of the Man of Sorrows. Some of the detail is compressed:

> Blo thou bett hym bare,
> His brest thou maide all blak,
> His woundes all wete thay ware,
> Alas, withoutten lak!   (27/15–18)

They go on to recall the Betrayal by Judas (46), Christ's silence (60), the swoon of Mary (75), the drink of eisel and gall (90) and the nails used on the cross (100). The lament is centred on the death of Christ, the pilgrims being unaware of the Resurrection even though in a performance the audience would be by way of the preceding play (26) which ended with the rejoicing of Mary Magdalene.

We are somewhat hampered by the probability that this cycle was never performed in the way the text implies, but to read it through cannot but reveal that the processes of anticipation and recapitulation are extensive and this has the effect of causing the reader to have many narrative details constantly in mind. This particularly reflects upon the incidents of the Passion, as we have noted, but there are also other recurring elements like the Virgin birth or the anticipation of the Resurrection. Much of this conforms with the optimistic aspect of the cycle in which it is perceived that the sacrifice made by Christ was effective for the redemption, and a good deal of the details look forward to the ultimately reassuring prospect of heaven, but there is also an effect by which the intensity of Christ's suffering and the pain felt by his mother have a repetitive emotional impact upon the audience (or the readers, if one supposes there never was an audience). Added to this are the improbability and contradiction, which are endemic to the dramatic process employed here. As we have seen, the misery of Lucas and Cleophas occurs even though the audience know of the Resurrection. Similarly, Mary Magdalene in *Resurrection* (26) approaches the tomb lamenting even though earlier in the same play Caiaphas has reported that Christ has 'openly' told his listeners 'That he shuld ryse up bodely / Within the thryde day' (26/168–9). But these are not really contradictions and to apply stringent probability is no doubt inappropriate. The purpose of such cross-references is really mnemonic recalling known elements in the narrative. The dramatists have to present each narrative segment with its own inherent authority, based upon scriptural precedent if possible, together with an independent dynamic of its own so that the effect of each particular segment can be made. This occurs even though at times the individual incidents may refer to overriding common themes such as the Man of Sorrows or the sufferings of Mary.

The emotional impact of religious details has two contrasting aspects even though they do not necessarily contradict one another. On the one hand there is the guilt which requires vengeance, as expressed by the Bad Souls near the beginning of *Judgement* (30). They foresee that justice is inevitable, especially in the light of their having broken so many commandments. Even Christ himself at the Ascension promises vengeance upon those who do not trust in him (29/158–61). But on the other hand there is the prospect of reconciliation. The action of both the Shepherds plays works from a poignant sense of earthly suffering and discomfort, whether it be the plague affecting the sheep, oppression by landlords or marital disaffection, towards a perception of grace and a new start. The presentation of the Shepherds has indeed a particular emphasis in Towneley. In contrast to the Shepherds in Chester (7) who are transformed spiritually and adopt new roles with religious purposes, the Towneley Shepherds remain common men and shepherds, even though they exhibit tenderness and grace towards the end of the play in the way they treat Mak, his baby and the Christ-child. It has been pointed out that the Shepherds show a pattern of charity. The plots of both Shepherds plays bring some comfort to hardships and this is reinforced in *Second Shepherds* by the kindness shown to Mak's baby, and also in the mild punishment inflicted. Perhaps this sweetness of temper late in the play is a reflection of the benefit of good works.[13]

We have seen how the manipulation of the narrative involves the recurring hope and anticipation of salvation and underlines the necessary suffering of Christ to effect redemption. Along with this there goes a series of themes or leading ideas running through the plays intermittently and supporting the reassuring outcome. One of these is the repeated emphasis upon the Trinity: there is no doubt that this was represented frequently in iconic terms outside the plays. For example, there is a roof boss in the nave of Norwich Cathedral showing the Trinity in the cluster of carvings surrounding the Last Judgement and there are two stained glass representations in York Minster.[14] But it also appears as part of the dramatic experience. In the first stanza of the cycle, Deus proclaims his unity which contains the three aspects of the godhead, 'Fader, and son, and holy goost, / On God in Trinyté' (1/5–6), and again 'Oone God in persons thre / Which may neuer twynnyd be' (1/10–11). This being established at the beginning there are many later references, often at critical moments in individual plays. Lucifer's pride is a challenge to the Trinity as he seeks their seat (1/105). Noah, in his opening prayer, refers to 'Thre persons withoutten nay, / Oone God in endless blis' (3/3–4). In part the emphasis may well have been inherited through the York plays: Moses concludes the *Pharaoh* by honouring the Trinity in a play copied from York (8/428). However, the concept of the Trinity is adapted to a number of different circumstances, apart from the occasional shorter references like that of Noah (3/4), and of 2 Rex in *Magi* (14/613). Noah also makes the point in his narrative recapitulation that the decision to make man to be a replacement for the fallen Lucifer was taken 'Of the Trinité bi accord' (3/44). The configuration is perhaps even more important in *Baptist* in which there is a distinctly ritualistic and symbolic framework. Here John uses the traditional formula for baptism referring to the Trinity (19/185–90), and when Christ blesses him in return he does so in the name of the Trinity. John then thanks 'Almyghty God in persons thre, / all in oone substance ay ingroost' (19/249–50). During the Passion the dramatist meets the challenge of Christ's anxiety on the Mount of Olives by inventing a dialogue with the figure called Trinitas. The purpose is to pinpoint the complex symbolism of Christ's incarnation and death. Speaking as the Father, Trinitas reminds Christ of the latter's life as a man and that he must die as men do, and go to hell. Yet this must ultimately lead to the redemption of all sinners:

> Sen thou art man and nedys must dee,
> And go to hell as othere done –
> Bot that were wrong, withoutten lee,
> That Godys son there shuld won
>
> In payn with his vnderlowte –
> Wytt ye well withoutten weyn,
> When oone is borod, all shall owtt
> And borod be from teyn.   (20/572–9)

It is clear that here the dramatist is presenting an interplay between two figures of the Trinity. The dramatic and religious functions of this figure are to link Christ's uncertainty teleologically with specific elements in salvation history, such as man's sin and the need for the Redemption. The power of the Trinity is invoked by the suffering Christ in one of his few speeches during *Scourging* (22/147). In *Resurrection* Christ promises Mary Magdalene that he will appear before the Disciples in the form of the Trinity (26/617). When he does appear to them later in *Thomas* it is not clear that this is a visual effect in the play, but he does invoke the Trinity in blessing the honey and fish brought for him to eat (28/193–8). Later, the Seventh Apostle appeals to Christ in Trinity (28/247). These references thus function in a variety of ways but it is clear that the dramatists use them repeatedly to suggest the threefold power of which Christ himself is an integral part. They sustain an interest in the mysterious nature of the godhead, which it was necessary, from an orthodox point of view, to offer the faithful, not least because in this mystery faith could be made apparent.[15] The advantage of dramatization is that the splitting of the three members deepens the mystery and in places Towneley shows clear steps to exhibit this.

Such a process is also sustained by other devices. One which operates structurally, appearing in several Towneley plays, is the legend of the oil of mercy. In the first instance the appropriate place for this would be at the end of the narrative of Adam's life when Seth, his son, brings back from Paradise three seeds from the Tree of Life. These form the oil of mercy and are a promise that eventually Adam's sin and all that flowed from it will be redeemed. The concept of promise is important structurally because it is an anticipation of what will later be fulfilled. Ultimately they connect the Tree of Life with the wood from which the cross is made.[16] Unfortunately the lacuna at the conclusion of the Creation prevents us from knowing whether the initial phase was ever present in Towneley, but it is clear from a number of references that the dramatists knew the legend and made use of it in a number of places. As he describes the pains that people now suffer, Noah unmistakably recalls the promise, whether or not it was once present in the earlier episode:

Oyle of mercy he hus hight,
As I haue hard red,
To euery lifyng wight
That wold hym luf and dred.   (3/66–9)

Abraham, in a brief reference at the beginning of the next play, also mentions it as part of his impatience for God's intervention (4/6). But the salient reference is by Deus himself at one of the key points in the cycle, the preparation for the Annunciation. This would be the appropriate place to recall the legend, and Deus does so in a way which points directly to the Redemption. He says he had promised the oil of mercy and now the time has come to bring mankind 'Outt of payn' (10/15). It should be noticed that this reference comes in a momentous speech which recalls the past and gives promise for the future and ends with the instruction to Gabriel to inform Mary of the Incarnation (10/1–76).

Such material used intermittently was no doubt part of the general spiritual inheritance of the period and we can see other ideas running through the plays in similar fashion. We may notice here the use of the title Emanuel and the frequent figure of healing which appears in several verbal formulae. The meaning of 'Emanuel' is given in Matthew 1:23, 'God with us', and the reference there recalls the prophecy in Isaiah 7:14 which uses the same title for the child to be conceived by a virgin. In Towneley it is used by the Boy with Moses after the escape from the Red Sea (8/421), by the First Consultus informing Herod of the threat posed to him by the child in the same prophecy of Isaiah (14/425, and repeated at 16/311), and by the First Magister at the beginning of the surviving text of *Doctors* (18/4).[17] The first of these is in one of the plays borrowed entirely from York and the third is part of an interpolation not found in the original York text from which the bulk of *Doctors* was also copied.[18] The second reference comes in one of the plays attributable to the Wakefield Master.

The concept of healing centres around two words which appear with surprising frequency: 'boytt' or 'beytt' refers chiefly to a remedy for ills and it is associated in several places with 'bail' (bale) meaning suffering; 'leche' refers more specifically to the healer.[19] The referent is almost always God or Christ, and especially in his role as the one who alleviates human suffering. These words are spread through the cycle and they appear in eleven plays altogether. The images are used by divine characters as well as by human beings, and in most cases the speakers are virtuous. Abel in urging sacrifice, itself an important reflection of the recurring concern for sacraments, speaks of God as 'oure saulis leche' (2/85). Abel is one of a number of figures who have priest-like qualities, and it is pertinent that Cain responds to this prompting by using a proverb about the fox preaching to geese, a commonplace for abusing the clergy.[20] Noah, another priest-like figure for part of the play, prepares his family to take refuge in the Ark and in doing so refers to God, who has been instructing him, as the 'Beytter of bayll' (3/451). Deus at the Annunciation, referring to the oil of mercy, as we have noted speaks of the need to relieve the sufferings of those in hell (10/10), and the same phrase is used by Mary the Virgin, in grief at the Crucifixion when she recalls the incarnation: 'A childe our baill shuld bete' (23/488). Deus also refers to himself as healer in his introductory speech at the Annunciation: 'For I am Lord and lech of heyle' (10/45).[21] Thus the references to this formulation operate partly in anticipation of the incarnation and partly as a concentration in later phases of the cycle. During *Resurrection* Mary Magdalene has two such allusions. In the first the link with medicine is explicit: 'For to ich sore he was medecyne / And bote of all' (26/359–60), and later she uses the alliterative formula 'Lord and leche', as expressed by Deus at the Annunciation (26/420: cf. 10/450). Christ makes direct reference to himself in this form at what may be seen as key moments in the overall narrative. In *Baptist* he asserts that, having given the symbolic lamb to John the Baptist, for those who trust in his sacrifice 'I shal be boytt of all thare bayll / And send them socoure on euery syde' (19/212sd and 229–30). Here the phrase is associated with symbolism.

Further witnesses making use of this figure of healing are to be found in the First and Third Kings who use identical words: 'boytt of bayll' (*Magi*, 14/539 and 542), and in Lucas, again making use of the alliterative formula, 'That lord, alas, that leche' (*Pilgrims*, 27/19). Even unsympathetic witnesses are also used in a way which underlines the concept. Thus the First Torturer in *Crucifixion* alleges Christ's claim as healer (23/36), and in *Conspiracy* Judas refers to Mary Magdalene and the ointment in similar terms: 'This fare ointment, hir bale to beytt, / Apon his hede she put it thare' (20/284–5). All these references would seem to sustain one another and their occurrences are spread through plays coming from different provenances. They are of course not necessarily confined to Towneley, and they may be thought of as being part of an inheritance common to all the authors participating in this text. However, we also find that the Wakefield Master was able to turn the figure to comic effect at one point. In *First Shepherds* as the feast begins with the 'good ayll of Hely' the First Shepherd praises their drink with the familiar words; 'This is boyte of our bayll, / Good holsom ayll' (12/357–8). Perhaps one shouldn't labour the joke too much but this may hint at the fascinating mixture of innocence and worldliness characteristic of these particular shepherds, and it could be a very small hint, along with other substantial ones noticed elsewhere, of the sanctity embodied in the Shepherds. It is not the only place where the Wakefield Master picks up on ideas of his predecessors.

We have discussed some of the anomalies in the structure of the cycle in Chapters 1.1 and 1.3 where the main concern was to show discontinuities in texture and also the omission of some episodes which might have been expected on the analogy of the other cycles in English. Here, taking a slightly different perspective, we may look at the way some of the individual plays may be seen to contribute material essential to the religious experience of the cycle as a whole. So, setting aside what might be termed apparent discontinuities, we shall look at some pivotal episodes where the resonance of individual details might transcend the separate episodes. The importance of this process will depend upon the way in which the compiler might have appreciated the wider significance of such aspects.

In discussing thematic features we have noted that these appear in *Annunciation*. The play's significance is enhanced because for the first instance since *Creation* Deus has the opening speech. Such a decision suggests a new start to unfolding events and points up the beginning of the episodes dealing with the life of Christ. This first speech is characterized by an account of the current predicament of mankind following Adam's fall and the necessity for help and restoration. The solution decided upon by Deus is that his son should take manhood and, in figuratively resonant lines, he links Adam and Christ, the Tree of Life and the cross, and Eve and Mary the Virgin:

> For reson wyll that ther be thre –
> A man, a madyn, and a tre.
> Man for man, tre for tre,
> Madyn for madyn; thus shal it be.  (10/31–4)

He mentions the virgin birth and explains that this will be the fulfilment of the Prophets. He then instructs Gabriel to hasten to tell Mary of his decision. The way this is presented leaves Deus very much as the defining presence: there is no reference to the Debate of the Four Daughters which is sometimes used in continental cycles to initiate Christ's mission. Nevertheless, the themes he does raise are entirely consonant with what happens in some other cycles at this point in the salvation narrative, as for example Dieu in Gréban's *Passion* (3267–308; 3333–56).[22] In his message Gabriel emphasizes that God's grace will cause her to conceive, and that he shall be circumcised. In the rest of the play Joseph's shock over Mary's pregnancy is used as a means of telling the story of how he was chosen as Mary's husband, an episode not found elsewhere in this cycle. So overwhelmed is he by the turn of events that he decides to go to the wilderness but an Angel intervenes with the truth. Once he is made aware of it, Joseph is apparently very willing to ask forgiveness for his folly. This episode showing his doubts is very mild in tone compared with the comedy found in some of the other dramatizations of the episode, as in York (Y13/93–255). Instead it is turned towards portraying the influence of divine power and authority, a dominant theme shown here working successively on Mary and Joseph.

*Baptist* (19) stands at a key position rather similar to that occupied by *Annunciation*: in this case the beginning of Christ's adult life, leading quickly to the events of the Passion. Its opening speech by St John is addressed to the audience (1–64). Besides giving a brief account of his family, he follows scriptural precedent in explaining that he is a forerunner, but he puts a significant doctrinal gloss upon his mission in his anticipation of Christ hanging upon the cross and shedding his blood. It is this blood which will make possible the new baptism through the Holy Ghost, bringing the remission of sins (19/43–6). There is further doctrinal matter later in the play. Though reluctant to baptize Christ because he feels himself to be unworthy, John follows the instructions of the Angels. Christ emphasizes that baptism is a worthy sacrament and he requires the ritual anointing with oil and cream in accordance with Catholic practice. John obediently anoints Christ after the immersion (19/193–4). This part of the play is redolent with significant material. Apart from the symbolism of the Lamb and the references to the Trinity, we also find the idea that Christ comes to fulfil the law (19/169–7). The action of the play draws to an end with an extended anaphora based upon 'farewell' addressed to Christ. This formal lyrical device allows John in an emotional sequence to rehearse many attributes concerning Christ's beauty (19/257–72).[23] The passage is followed by John's resolution to go forth and preach. He begins by urging his present audience to forsake the deadly sins, and reminds them that baptism brings the obligation of obedience. The urgency of the need to preach is a theme urged by Mary Magdalene at the end of *Ascension* (29/445–7).

The latter part of the Towneley Cycle has come down to us in a somewhat distorted form because of the loss of some twelve leaves. This involves the loss of the end of *Ascension* (29) and the beginning of *Judgement* (30) and whatever lay between them. In all probability the lost sheets also contained episodes concerning Mary the Virgin on a parallel with those extant from York and it may also have shown the coming of the Holy Ghost at Pentecost, as we shall see. However the surviving plays following *Crucifixion* (23) up to *Judgement* (30) do offer us a number of religious themes in a part of the cycle where, in the inevitable absence of scriptural detail, there is less pressure to be concerned with the presentation of narrative. Indeed I want to suggest that this might be regarded as an area concentrating upon a range of doctrinal matters.[24] Among these it seems that there is a persistent interest in portraying Christ in a positive manner and this is manifest in a number of episodes, especially *Harrowing* (25), *Resurrection* (26), *Pilgrims* (27), *Thomas* (28), *Ascension* (29) and *Judgement* (30). It may well be that the compiler sought deliberately to include such characterizations. It should be noted that these episodes show very little sign of the work of the Wakefield Master.

*Harrowing* owes a good deal to York (37) and this includes some of the most compelling doctrine. The dispute between Christ and Satan offers an opportunity to lay down some fundamental truths. For one thing Christ brings to an end Satan's doubts about Christ as the Son of God; he also recalls that his coming now to release the souls was anticipated by the Prophets and had a legal backing. In this he outwits Satan's attempt to juggle with the law, as well as latching on to the prophetic strain we have noticed elsewhere. But the climax of the dispute, which comes before Christ binds Satan to remain in hell, is reached when Christ pulls together the new law, the need for obedience, the importance of the sacraments, his death and resurrection and the coming judgement:

> And all that will not lere my law
> That I haue left in land for new,
> That makys my commyng knaw
> And all my sacramentys persew –
> My deth, my rysyng red by raw,
> Who trow thaym not, thay ar vntrewe –
> Vnto my dome I shall theym draw,
> And iuge theym wars then any Iew.   (25/341–8) [This particular
>         stanza is closely copied from its York original (Y37/313–20).]

The Towneley *Resurrection* (26) by contrast has significant doctrinal passages added to the York original. The Centurio is given a passage in which he asserts the true divinity of Christ having been impressed by the wonders accompanying his death. His entry is perhaps made more sensational by his having come in on horseback, a detail not marked in the York version (T26/44sd). But the chief doctrinal addition is in the long speech by Christ himself (26/230–350). This makes the spectacle of Christ showing his wounds an integral part of the Towneley version: 'Behold how dere I wold the by! / My woundys ar weytt and all blody' (26/236–7). The visual impact continues as the affective aspect of the scene develops:

Behold my body, in ilka place
How it was dight –
All to-rent
And all to-shentt
Man, for thi plight.   (26/250–4)

In this critical passage he continues through the scourging and the drink of gall and the 5400 wounds.[25] These sufferings were undergone for love and so love is required in return. The point is reinforced visually as he spreads his arms (26/325). The practice of the dramatist here may be paralleled in York and Chester, but we should also bear in mind that this assertion of an image may be directed by a need to counter Lollard emphasis upon biblical exegesis by means of an unmistakable visual image.[26] The contemplation of such images is one of the imperatives of the orthodox dramatization of sacred history and this is an emphatic addition in Towneley. Linked with the appeal for the return of his love is the reassurance that mercy awaits all those who are not afraid to ask for it; even Judas might have received it, had he but asked. Christ offers those seeking release from sin his own body as a meal ('measse', 26/343): those who take it righteously will never die, but those who take it in sin are damned. Not only is the speech powerful in dramatic and iconic aspects, it is also composed in a lyric mode which sustains the emotional intensity of the scene.[27] Yet we also see that the ideas here are fundamental to orthodox devotion, especially those dealing with the sacrament of the Mass.

Besides the extensive retrospect by Lucas and Cleophas noted earlier, *Pilgrims* places great emphasis upon the act of breaking bread. This is the kernel of the gospel account (Luke 24:30), but here it is dramatized in visual terms for we see Christ break the bread in three (27/296sd) and then the two pilgrims describe and recall the action in several ways after Christ has miraculously disappeared. The doctrinal elements are less emphatic in this play but this presentation of the breaking of the bread has obvious links with the Mass.

The broad concern for doctrinal matters and the interest in the missionary dissemination of the faith continues in *Thomas* (28) and *Ascension* (29). The former begins with a vindication of Mary Magdalene who brings news of her meeting with the risen Christ. At first she is scathingly doubted by Peter and Paul but there comes a moment when Peter bitterly recalls his own former denial of Christ before the Crucifixion (28/85–8). The change of mood is marked by the entrance of Christ, singing a triumphant Latin song.[28] His outward appearance is spectacular as he wears red clothing and draws attention to his wounds. His main speech (28/ 129–76) is a concentrated summary of elements of faith: the Redemption (132); the Resurrection and the palpable evidence that this is the resurrection of a human body: 'Grope and fele flesh and bone / And fourme of man well-wroght; / Sich thyng has goost none' (28/133–5). The imagery is intense: 'Luf makys me, as ye may se, / Strenkyllid with blood so red' (28/153–4). The physicality is stressed no doubt in anticipation of the testing of the belief of Thomas to come later in the episode:

> Mi dere freyndys, now may ye se
> Forsoth that is I,
> That dyed apon the roode-tre
> And sythen rose *bodely.*   (28/169–72; my emphasis)

After Christ has eaten honey and fish, to prove his corporeal existence, he reminds the Disciples that he had forewarned them about the cruelty of his death. He offers them forgiveness for deserting him and urges them to their new task, which is to preach repentance to those who are lame through sin (28/229–30).

When Thomas appears he begins with a lament for Christ's death which dwells upon the cruelty of the nails and the shedding of blood (28/284–6). The long process by which he is convinced that Christ really has risen, the chief purpose of the whole episode, is rich with recollected detail of such things as the establishment of the Eucharist and the Passion, together with the grief of Mary Magdalene. Indeed although the reversal of the incredulity of Thomas is the avowed purpose of the sequence, it is apparent that the dramatist has addressed with close attention the religious themes we have been discussing. When Christ has accepted the submission of Thomas, he then looks forward to Doomsday and reminds everyone, presumably including the audience, of the division to be made between those who believe and trust correctly in him and those who do not. He even anticipates the need to give alms, a theme which returns in *Judgement*, a play which is substantially taken over from York. It seems as though in these plays near the end of the cycle the need to prepare the faithful for Judgement becomes more urgent: though we should notice that this may be something eagerly awaited by those in the right state of mind. The emphasis we have noted on the figure of Christ late in the cycle reaches an important climax here.

In *Ascension* Christ resumes themes in the previous play, though there is less of the Passion imagery. He raises particularly the need for faith and rebukes the disciples for not having believed in the Resurrection. From there he sets out their mission:

> Therfor ye shall go tech
> In all this warld so wyde,
> And to all the people preche,
> Who baptym will abyde
> And trow truly
> Mi dethe and rysyng.   (29/149–54)

For the sacrament of baptism he stresses the importance of the Holy Ghost, and in doing so he anticipates Pentecost. But the latter is not present in the surviving text and it may have been lost in the lacuna which cuts off the end of this episode and the beginning of the next play, *Judgement*. As Christ ascends the angels sing an antiphon, *Ascendo ad Patrem meum* (29/289sd), which is also sung in the York version, though it should be borne in mind that the text of Towneley is independent of York in this episode. Indeed, Stevens and Cawley point out that this version is the most elaborate of all the surviving Ascension texts.[29] The presence of liturgical music is clearly meant to be an integral part of the performance in this part in the cycle. It must have added a great deal to the sense of worship present in these late episodes.[30] After Christ has ascended, an angel prophesies the Judgement and then the main dramatic initiative passes to the Virgin Mary. She longs to be reunited with her son but she makes the point that this is the fourth of her Joys, thus drawing attention to a devotional commonplace which is only rarely observed elsewhere in Towneley.[31] She speaks the last words in the surviving fragment and in them she repeats the obligation on the Disciples to preach to the people and to speak of her son's works, lest those who will not follow be damned (29/444–51).

*Judgement* provides a culmination of the nexus of themes in the last plays but in the interpolation attributed to the Wakefield Master a good deal of new material is added. Textually the play is interesting because it is largely a direct borrowing from York 48, yet there are close links with sections of the late episodes in Towneley. For example the inevitability of Judgement is emphasized by the Bad Souls following the breaking of Commandments; Christ makes a powerful visual moment when he again exhibits the wounds he suffered for human misdeeds (30/576–7). This image of pity is a vision of mercy for those who trust and believe, and one of reproach and condemnation for those who do not.[32] The play also elaborates the deeds of mercy as the chief means of separating the Good Souls from the Bad.

The fact that several episodes before *Judgement*, among them plays not demonstrably borrowed from York, have such a strong interrelationship with this play may be due to their being composed so as to link with the York borrowing, but the uncertainty about the date of the compilation of Towneley means that this must remain speculative. However, there is no doubting that the passages attributed to the Wakefield Master were added to the York text rather than the York being adapted by shortening the Towneley version.

These additions are critical for an assessment of the religious mode of Towneley even if they are not replicated throughout the cycle. They are complementary to the Shepherds plays, for example, where the innovation by the Wakefield Master is comprehensive. In *Judgement* the additions in his characteristic stanzas are confined to the roles of the Demons, which are transformed by them. However, the Towneley text, as Stevens and Cawley note, is closely faithful to the York text in respect of the role of Jesus. The first interpolation in Towneley is a dialogue between the First and Second Demons. The writing here offers a sharp and tangy virtuosity to the actors, as they express their anxiety as well as their hopes. They know they can not escape judgement but they expect to capture many souls and to do so they must use their records – 'rentals' as they call them (30/196). The performance element comes in strongly as they recite a list of evil doers who are guilty of pride and lust, both deadly sins. The alliteration and the characteristically gnarled language make the sins and sinners seem grotesque, and the intention of the poet is clearly to make the list seem appallingly long as the two Demons twist and turn reciting so many sins. One claims that if the world had gone on longer they would have been able to build hell even larger (30/261–4). The predicament of the poor, who must always pay (30/276), is also an issue; an instance of the Wakefield Master's interest in social aspects, to which we shall return.

But even if he does have some concern for such social matters the author of this interpolation is orthodox when he comes to introduce his devil Tutivillus. Though this character had a long past it is perhaps significant for our purposes that that there is a deliberate association with Lollardry (30/311). Here, however, this aspect does not seem much developed for Tutivillus also stresses the presence of the deadly sins, adding graphic circumstantial detail. He rejoices in the grotesque punishments the damned are to suffer: 'Ye shall clym on hell-crokkys / With a halpeny heltere' (30/467–8).[33]

The second part of the interpolation of devils, which follows the judgement of the Good and Bad Souls by Christ (30/705), elaborates the monstrous sins and the joy of the Devils at the torments to come. It adds little to the narrative, but it does much to change the tone from the York original. Instead of the speech by God which puts a triumphant ending to history, the Towneley version has the Devils gloating until the penultimate speech and gives the last words to a loyal Good Soul. In spite of the latter, the grimmer tone inserted by the Wakefield Master is a significant change in the religious impact of this episode and perhaps of the cycle as a whole. This brings us back to the problems about the ambiguity at the end of the cycle because there are still two more plays after *Judgement* in the manuscript, and it is not clear exactly how the cycle was meant to conclude. We shall probably never find conclusive proof about this and we have to accept that the manuscript at this point is teasingly ambiguous.

In *Lazarus* (31) we can see some doctrinal points are made. Martha foresees the resurrection of the dead and the coming to judgement, a detail which in itself may argue that this play is misplaced. But then Christ emphasizes the need for belief in his resurrection and in his lasting essence in a memorable passage:

> I warne you, both man and wyfe,
> That I am rysyng and I am life;
> And whoso truly trowys in me,
> That I was euer and ay shall be,
> Oone thyng I shall hym gif:
> Though he be dede, yit shall he lif. (31/51–6)

Coming so near the end of the cycle this passage gives an appropriate emphasis to the message of salvation. Lazarus, once revived, gives a terrible picture of the pains of hell in a lyric passage expressed by means of complex prosody. Besides recounting the horrors, he warns that at the time he is speaking of the remedies offered by the Church – singing mass and giving alms (31/177–8), and confession (31/187–8) – will no longer be available. There is much urgency: 'Wit thou well, acounntys gif thou shall; / Therfor amende the whils thou may' (31/216–17). The placing of *Lazarus* at the end of the cycle (ignoring *Judas* which was copied by a different and later hand) was seen by J. W. Earl as a fitting conclusion of the cycle precisely because it may offer an appropriate final sermon on the horrors of hell which the message of the cycle as a whole urges everyone to avoid. He suggests that the use of commonplaces about suffering in hell enhances this.[34] The emotional impact of this putative ending, however, is a blend of the brilliant hope of the resurrection and the grim fear of hell.

The general conclusion to be drawn from this review of the religious elements in Towneley suggests that some themes and ideas recur and that there is some continuity between them. This may be occasioned in part because some of them are commonplaces, such as the idea of Christ as healer. Nevertheless, we cannot ignore that the cycle is in part a process of selection and these items form part of that process in action. They reflect positive devotional and exegetical choices. It is an interesting demonstration of that aspect of medieval authorship which brings together material from different sources. In this case one of the principal resources is the York Cycle, but the differences in original composition and in selection we have noticed help to make Towneley distinctive.

### 3.2.2  Popular Culture

In addition to this consideration of orthodox religious material and departures and variations from it, we also need to take account of some other elements in the cycle which may represent survivals of other cultural activities, practices and beliefs. The terminology of this material has been the object of much dissent. To some extent it may be a matter of pre-Christian beliefs or embody in rituals a parallel system of beliefs which are essentially pre-Christian but survive into the time of predominantly Christian faith. Closely related to these so-called folk elements there is also the material adduced by the theorists of carnival or festive celebrations. These gave an opportunity for licence or subversion of established authorities or practices and their relationship to normally conforming behaviour can be problematic.[1]

The theoretical approaches to folk practices and carnival have been much discussed in recent years and it is apparent that much of the material proposals that both views were concerned with will hardly lend themselves to a coherent anti- or counter-religion. Nevertheless, we should pick out a certain number of items which may embody folk elements or be allied to the spirit of carnival. Instead of being a coherent whole they are best considered as a series of traces which at most suggest a divergence of attitude in certain places in the cycle, and there is also ground for supposing that they were incorporated as a result of a reaction showing itself in individual episodes or incidents, rather than being in question over the whole cycle. The term 'popular culture' is convenient here as suggested by Peter Burke.[2] By using it we may underline that we are not dealing with an organized phenomenon so much as with a variety of impulses.

Many of the items we discuss here have a scent of subversion about them. We shall have to consider later whether this is wholehearted dissent or an attempt to control dissent by incorporation and by allowing such elements to be circumscribed by the religious structures we have been discussing earlier in this section.

The survivals of Christian beliefs have been reviewed many times, and there is really no need to attempt another survey here.[3] In Towneley subversion may be observed in the impertinent servant Garcio (Pikeharnes) in *Abel* (2) and in Slawpase in *First Shepherds* (12). The Shepherds' feast in midwinter in the latter play is an example of mysterious midwinter fecundity, itself probably related to the rituals associated with the renewal of natural plenty. At the same time this motif might also be held to reflect carnival in the inversion of orderly subordinates. This might show itself further in the ridiculous figures of authority which can be found in the characterizations of Pharaoh, Caesar, Herod and Pilate. But perhaps the richest vein for this cultic material may be found in linguistic aspects: the use of jests and equivocations, and the presence of folk tales which may be told for themselves or which may be used to reflect upon the orthodox biblical narratives.

There is no doubt that the medieval Christian drama, from its earliest manifestations until its disappearance late in the sixteenth century, embodied various kinds of antibodies which it had to contain because it could not comprehensively eradicate them. To put this another way the medieval dramatists we are concerned with in Towneley had a range of resources which they might draw upon from sub-literate cultures, and these continued to speak through the drama which was officially recognized and in some cases blessed as the official voice of the Church for a substantial period of time. That this embodiment was at times a deliberate strategy, even though the Church also carried within it a deep anti-theatrical prejudice for many years before the creation of the cycle plays, may be illustrated by the passage attributed to Pope Gregory by Bede requiring that missionaries to Britain should at the beginning build altars on the temples of idols 'that the people . . . flocking more readily to their accustomed resorts, may come to know and adore the true God'.[4] But we may find in Towneley that this questionable material actually enhances what is going on in many cases both in terms of the religious truths the writers were seeking to reveal and support and in terms of the theatricality of the plays and their capacity to grasp the attention of an audience.

In the following account of this material it will become apparent in the first place that the majority of it appears in the plays attributed wholly to the Wakefield Master, and it is also true that even in some cases where he is not entirely responsible for the original design of individual plays his contribution may contain folk or carnival elements. But having discussed his characteristic contributions in this respect we shall also take account of another: there are some plays which do not show any sign of his influence and yet some similar material is present. This is particularly true for some of the plays taken over from York.

The Wakefield Master's treatment of Cain is largely orthodox, as we have seen, especially in regard to his final condemnation as one who refuses to ask for forgiveness and who turns his back upon God. Yet he does not go without defiance and his abuse of God, together with the proclamation of his own pardon, give an edge to the play which is not entirely comfortable. This is enhanced, no doubt, by his foul-mouthed obscenities, his verbal adherence to the devil and his abusive relationship with his servant. The intensity of Cain's rebellion is further underlined by the boy's reaction against him as it makes a structural parallel within the play and intensifies the difficulty of controlling Cain. The idea of an impudent servant for Cain may have been anticipated at York in the character of Brewbarret (Y7/73–81).[5] Moreover, it has been noticed that carnival often stresses the material life, the actual harsh detail of existence, as a part of its departure from it. This materiality reacts against attempts at abstract harmony.[6] Such detail is undoubtedly present in this version for a great deal has been added to the biblical narrative about the hardship of the labour and the difficulties encountered. Another significant aspect is that the action involves bringing on a plough which is the subject of some stage business, and it is possible that this evokes the practice of the plough Monday rituals noted by Mills. In practice such activities were a way of stimulating fertility; as Cain's activities are barren here, the effect might have been ironic. Along with this goes his parody of pardons and his resistance to them, as noticed by Gash.[7] Tithing was unpopular and much resented, and objections to it were part of the Lollard outlook, yet the practice was determined and supported by the Church hierarchy, and even though the irregular tithing shown here is rather similar to comparable episodes in other cycle plays, it is clear that this particular Cain is to be blamed for his behaviour over it and that it is part of his evil nature however much it may reflect popular culture.

There is also a challenge to authority by Noah's wife, as we have seen. We should note though that this is not a challenge against divine authority so much as against Noah as husband and powerful master. Much of the dramatic interest of this play is concerned with the confrontation between them and we find this motif in other cycles, particularly York, which presumably precedes Towneley and Chester. It is no doubt partially dependent upon a fabliau theme concerned with the excesses of female behaviour presented as both grotesque and threatening. It recurs in both the Towneley Shepherds plays.[8] It may be worth recalling that the dramatist in this episode has not made Noah entirely innocent or admirable in his treatment of his wife even though in other parts of the play he exhibits a priest-like sanctity and an appreciation of the divine purposes. But the ending of this play reconciles all elements albeit without the rainbow, the sign of God's mercy in the Chester version.

Before we leave *Noah* we should notice that the outline of this story is essentially biblical, with the exception of the conflict between Noah and his wife and her submission. Stevens and Cawley identify three different traditions for Noah's wife, all of them non-scriptural. They point out that the one chosen here, essentially that of the shrew, contrasts with the complaisant one of N Town and the devilish one of the Newcastle *Noah's Ark Plays*.[9] In the Shepherds plays the practice is somewhat similar though the introduction of non-scriptural material is more substantial. There seems little doubt from our discussion of performance in Chapter 2 that these non-scriptural activities of the Shepherds together with the attraction of Mak as a theatrical device have been strong features of the response to the plays in more recent times and this is no doubt a recognition of their dramatic vitality. In both plays the design embodies a structure which draws upon folk and carnival motifs and at the same time seems to direct them in such a way that they reflect upon the orthodox Christian narrative which derives from the small amount of detail in the original biblical accounts.

Perhaps the most outstanding aspect is the use of parody, though often it is parody which enhances the model upon which it is based. The *First Shepherds* gives us a feast in midwinter and in doing so suggests the Eucharist itself. All the Shepherds participate in it and though there are cross-currents about the kind of feast, the effect within the play is to prepare the Shepherds for the spiritual harmony coming with the Nativity. The nature of performance already noted gives rise to further effects and I am inclined to think that whether they mime the food, or do indeed by a kind of conjuring routine produce seemingly endless things to eat from packs and pockets, there is pointed attention to the plenty before them. There is a strong sense of celebration here, and such a tone is appropriate to the Mass.

The parody in *Second Shepherds* centres around a visual pun, a move which enhances the symbolism of the Nativity. The use of folk material here burlesques the sacred conclusion as Weimann pointed out.[10] The sheep in Mak's cradle inevitably points to the baby in Bethlehem and perhaps also to Mak and Gill who with their marital tension are a figure for the holy pair who are shown in this cycle and elsewhere as not entirely harmonious – at least as far as Joseph is concerned. The tension itself is not scriptural but more related to fabliau material, especially in the abuse of Mary as a loose woman. Moreover Gill's asseveration based upon eating the child/lamb again points to the Eucharist (13/774–6).[11]

The ambivalences in the Mak story, itself having folk origins, give rise to questions about how to read the role of Mak.[12] It is presumably inappropriate to seek a psychologically consistent interpretation: his role functions differently in a play of this kind from a modernist realist text. Most likely the practice of the Wakefield Master elsewhere gives us a clue to how to appreciate the villainy here. His persistent interest in evil characters suggests that this invention should be seen in parallel. The other Shepherds do not think much of him and little of what he does invites sympathy because he is a trickster. The hostility to him may well be due to his status as a 'maintained' man.[13] Perhaps his use of magic is also a means of alienation.

In addition to the link between the Mak story and a group of folk tales collected by Cosbey, we note that the Shepherds plays are rich in proverbs, notoriously ambivalent, and that they in themselves draw upon other folk motifs. The tales of Mol, who came home from the well with a broken pitcher, and of the Fools of Gotham (12/220–30, 247–60) suggest a deliberate use of stories which might be commonly known and bring into the narrative the enigmatic nature of folk tales. The remark by Slawpase, eager to demonstrate the folly of the other Shepherds, that they 'fysh before the nett' (12/201), is itself proverbial and also an image of folly. The action requires that Slawpase goes on to demonstrate that the lost grain can never be recovered, graphically imaging the folly of the other Shepherds but forgetting his own.[14] It apparently needs Jak Garcio, yet another impudent servant, to illuminate the folly of his bosses.[15] These aspects of *First Shepherds* are consistent in placing the Shepherds in a poor light and especially in underlining the folly of their behaviour. They are made more potent by the detailed dramatization of the dispute which breaks out over the non-existent sheep, an incident which is part of the tale of the Fools of Gotham. It is worth noting that the Shepherds in the Chester version are also discomforted by their servant Trowle wrestling before the Angel's summons transforms them.[16]

The material so far discussed appears in plays for which the Wakefield Master was wholly responsible. We now need to discuss those plays where he apparently had no influence and yet the writer reflects some of the earlier cultic material. The point of this is that it clarifies these features in the cycle and points up the nature of the Wakefield Master's development of them. There are two significant threads. The first relates to the anti-feminist material noticed earlier. In *Annunciation* when Joseph learns of Mary's pregnancy he laments in a folk motif the folly of the old husband who marries a young wife (10/170). Also in *Annunciation* the story of Joseph's wand, which no doubt came into currency through early Christian legend in the apocryphal infancy gospels and was a medieval commonplace, seems to suggest a folk process for finding a husband worthy of a fairy tale. Later, in *Thomas* Peter and Paul pour scorn on Mary Magdalene bringing news of the Resurrection. Here the misogyny of Paul may have some scriptural authority but there is no doubting his bitter condemnation of how women behave. Once again the presence of a folk motif is suggested by a proverb which warns against the rottenness within an apple (28/41–3). This passage demonstrates the strong effect which could be obtained by combining scriptural material with elements from popular culture, and there is little doubt that it was a valuable resource for the Towneley dramatists.

The treatment of Christ by the cruel prelates in *Conspiracy* also suggests a subversiveness towards the established hierarchy. These characters, Annas and Caiaphas, behave with cruel persistence and they misuse the authority of their office. Thus by implication they suggest a criticism of contemporary ecclesiastics. The exposure of their arrogance may indeed be linked with the attack upon heresy. However, in Towneley this is not quite so explicit as it is in N Town, where Caiaphas makes a specific claim that his role is to suppress heretics (26/170). The key point is that to suggest ecclesiastical suppression of Lollardry by such cruel and arrogant prelates would seem to be a questioning of orthodoxy.

The mockery of Christ himself is a widespread convention in the cycle plays. It derives from the scriptural account but there is little doubt that its dramatic potential was widely appreciated. In some respects this led to the deeper perception of the Man of Sorrows we have noticed. Yet the manipulation of language ridiculing him is a general feature.[17] It may well be that the Wakefield Master exploited it extensively, but the importance of it for our purposes is that it is found in parts of the cycle not influenced by him. This is especially the case in *Crucifixion* (23) where the mockery of Christ is intense. It includes belittling Christ as a king figure:

> In fayth, syr, sen ye callyd you a kyng,
> You must prufe a worthy thyng
> That falles vnto the were:
> Ye must iust in tournamente;
> Bot ye sytt fast, els be ye shentt,
> Els downe I shall you bere.   (23/89–94)

We now turn to an important feature of Towneley which is connected in part with the cultic material we have been discussing. The ways in which tyrants are embodied in the text are relevant to the process by which attempts were made to give the cycle an overall design. They relate to carnival and folk analogues by their mockery of true human leadership and, at times, by their parody of divine power and justice. They repeatedly present an abuse of power in several plays in the cycle.[18] There is no doubt that some of these are the work of the Wakefield Master but it is apparent that the compiler did not rely solely upon his contributions for these passages. There do seem to be some deliberate decisions in the way these characters are distributed. Two appear in the Old Testament section in the form of *Pharaoh* (8) and *Caesar* (9). The first is a direct borrowing from York, which means that it is most probable that the concept of the tyrant was not initiated by the Towneley dramatists and that others had appreciated the theatrical advantages of this dramatic device. Indeed there are some analogues in the subversive behaviour of the angry Herod of the liturgical drama. Karl Young writes, '[Herod] invaded part of the liturgy where his violence was an unseemly intrusion only to be tolerated under the general spirit of misrule prevailing during the Christmas season'; he goes on to quote a thirteenth-century liturgical play at Padua in which Herod, entering in an untidy tunic and with a wooden sword, reads a lesson while his attendants belabour the bishop, the canons and the choristers with a bladder.[19] The *Caesar* episode, in which the Emperor imposes a tax through the empire, is unique to Towneley, which means that in all likelihood it was deliberately composed so as to make use of this narrative, based as it is upon a brief reference in scripture, and perhaps to anticipate the prominence of tyrants in the New Testament sequence.

In fact it is the last play before the initiation of the Nativity sequence in *Annunciation* (10) and it may have been placed here to carry out an introductory function.[20] There are two appearances of the tyrannical Herod in the Nativity section, in *Magi* (14) and *Herod* (16). These occur in places where his rage may be regarded as conventional and based upon scriptural authority: the response to the departure of the Magi, and the decision to order the killing of the Innocents. While the latter play is written in the Wakefield Master's stanza throughout, the former is not, and the play is uniformly different in style and versification. There is a strong possibility that the author was relying on the York model even though this is not a verbatim copy.[21] The remaining four appearances of tyrants occur in the Passion sequence, where Pilate is developed as cruel and unrelenting, a characterization which contrasts with the rather divided figure presented elsewhere.[22]

The intervention by the Wakefield Master in *Crucifixion* is somewhat questionable since the stanza form does not quite match the usual pattern, though lines 9–21 are very similar, and the style matches. It is a unique feature of Towneley that a Herod does not appear in the Passion, though there are some brief references to him, as we shall see.[23]

No doubt the Wakefield Master's decision to write new material for the cycle was dependent upon a number of factors. For example, we shall be discussing violence and the presentation of evil later (see Chapter 3.4), but the nature of his interventions in the role of the tyrants shows that he was interested in the form of the boast which initially draws attention to the need for silence and places the audience, rather comically, in the position of the unfortunate subjects of a tyrant who attempts to bully them. In *Herod* the King's boast is preceded by one spoken by the Nuncius on his behalf (16/1–115). Gardner notes the change wrought in the audience's view of Herod before and after the massacre. When he returns to his boasting near the end of the play the comic tone has darkened.[24] The ridiculous claims and assertions in these speeches must have ensured that they were not taken seriously, even though the actions which followed, such as the slaughter of the Innocents or the scourging of Christ were indeed horrific. But yet even these portentous episodes were themselves presented with a kind of subversive irony by means of cultic material as well, as we see in the outspoken and indecorous angry mothers of *Herod* (16/551–5)[25] and the game of hot cockles in *Buffeting* (21/560–98). So perhaps the boasts had a function in anticipating the tone of the later horrors and this may account for the interest in setting the tone of these individual plays at their outset.

However, the tactics controlling the interventions of the Wakefield Master into the Passion sequence are not easy to define and they vary from play to play. *Conspiracy* is a composite play: the Wakefield Master's contribution being six stanzas at the beginning (1–77) and four near to the end concerned with Pilate's blessing upon the soldiers who are setting out to make the arrest (624–75). The opening boast, heavy with alliteration, is full of menace as Pilate threatens to break the bones of those who do not listen to him, even the aged – presumably this applied to the audience as a mock threat. He mentions his relationship with Mahowne, a hallmark of these boasts even though in all probability it was suggested by similar passages originating in York. He asserts a regal status: 'Was neuer kyng with crowne, / More worthy' (21–2). Besides brandishing his sword he adds that he will play on 'both parties' (33), and then turns to consider what he knows about Christ. In describing what has happened he draws attention to the Trinity, the Virgin Birth and the coming Crucifixion. As usual his account has the effect of revealing his own malice as well as drawing attention to the strength and depth of the divine mysteries. The tone of these stanzas is conventional for a boast but they do link neatly with the following passage in which Caiaphas and Annas seek to bring Christ to answer for his so-called violations of the law. Their cruelty and cunning follow naturally upon Pilate's evil inception of events.

*Buffeting* (21), the next play in the cycle, is entirely by the Wakefield Master but it has no preliminary boast. The action plunges straight into the bullying by the Torturers. In *Scourging* (22) we have another example of the Wakefield Master's intervention at the start of a play. There are several passages later in the play which are close to York but he works in an initial boast, followed by an interchange with the Torturers prompting further cruelty. In this instance the poet modifies his characteristic verse form.[26] For the boast itself (22/1–52) each stanza has longer lines than usual for the first eight lines but when Pilate comes to speak to the Torturers the normal form of verse comes back into use. His boast again draws attention to his capacity to play 'on both sydes' and, invoking Mahowne once more, again he bitterly mentions what others would perceive as the virtues of Christ as though they were crimes. His boastful summary of his own villainy is climactic:

> I am full of sotelty,
> Falshed, gyll and trechery;
> Therfor am I namyd by clergy
> As *malis actoris*. (22/10–13)

A short boast is used to introduce *Crucifixion* (23) and it offers some interesting evidence. As Stevens and Cawley point out, Pilate's twenty-eight lines are unnecessary dramatically since he does and says nothing until line 608. They are written in a verse form which is not that of the Wakefield Master but some of the lines (9–21) form a thirteen-line stanza which is rather similar. Once again he brandishes a sword and, as he swears by Mahowne's blood, he threatens terrible pains and a devil to drag the miscreants to hell. One line, however, puts his threats in a different light and makes it appear that the audience might well not take much notice, for he splutters: 'Will ye not peasse when I bid you?' (23/13).

*Dicing* (24) is anomalous in a number of ways. It is the only surviving play devoted solely to this episode, which in itself has some scriptural authority, and it is a different presentation of it from that which occurs very briefly as part of the previous play, *Crucifixion* (23/554–74). This makes it likely that the insertion of *Dicing* was not fully thought out and that a revision might have been contemplated at some point, though it was apparently not carried out. It has been suggested that the original may have been the lost York play which was discarded in 1422.[27] The central episode, the dialogue accompanying the actual gambling between Pilate and the soldiers – which is not scriptural in as much as Pilate here participates actively – may well have been borrowed from there. The Wakefield Master has added Pilate's boast in a remarkable passage largely in Latin (24/1–65) and the play ends with three of his stanzas spoken by the Torturers and one irregular stanza by Pilate (24/377–438). Towards the end of Pilate's opening boast the verse form changes somewhat but the style is much the same (24/66–91). The rhetoric is exaggerated and grotesque and it implies that Pilate here is both a mock king and an inverted god. It is a manifestation of the popular culture vein with which we are concerned. He claims to be *dominus dominarum* (lord of lords), a title given to God in Revelation 17:14 and one also attributed to Herod in an earlier episode (16/55). Besides this attribution Herod also describes himself as 'all-weldand', generally used for God.[28] The Latin is parodic of the liturgy and is used to point up his blasphemous claims as well as to suggest regal honour as King David:

Myghty lord of all,
*Me Cesar magnificauit.*
Downe on knees ye fall!
*Grett god me sanctificauit,*
Me to obey ouer all
*Regi reliquo quasi Dauid.* (24/40–5)

The subsequent macaronic passage with alternate Latin and English lines may indeed invite chanting.

As *Resurrection* is one of the plays largely taken over from York it must owe its design to the York dramatists, but the openings of the two versions are different. The York text begins with Pilate in conversation with Annas and Caiaphas, but there is no boast. The Towneley play begins with one which has been written in the same six-line stanza (aaabab) as the rest of the play's York predecessor: clearly it is intended as a close match. It contains a demand for attention and is abusive and threatening towards onlookers. There is also pride and self-conceit. However, it is by no means as sensational as the boasts in other plays, though it may have been influenced by them. It is problematic whether this interpolation was written by the Wakefield Master but even if it was not, its author was plainly interested in the boasts which are so prominent a part of the Towneley cycle and he sought to approximate this to the practice.

It appears, then, that these elements of popular culture, whether we regard them as folkloric or carnivalesque, are widely distributed in the cycle and they come to attention in a variety of situations and characterizations. It looks as though the Wakefield Master had a predilection for them and to some extent they perhaps reveal something essential in his outlook. Some of these boasts may have been prompted by elements in the York Cycle where items of popular culture are unmistakable. But as well as incorporating pre-existing material he also initiated new plays whose content includes a substantial presence of them and he also inserted some elements into the work of other Towneley dramatists. But in all likelihood his interpolations, whilst they enriched the dramatic and spiritual texture of the episodes he worked on, did not inhibit the overall movement towards redemption even though he might have been interested in the manifestation of subversion.[29] However, his contribution has to be weighed against those of the other contributing dramatists. It seems likely that the presence of cultic material discussed here may well point to tensions within the structure of belief and reflect fifteenth-century anxieties.

# 3.3

# Social Contexts

In addition to the consideration of gender in Chapter 3.1, we need to address social and economic aspects reflected in Towneley. Such contexts may in some ways be difficult to determine primarily because of the uncertainties about date and the circumstances which might have obtained for performance. Nevertheless, if the cycle was compiled in the fifteenth century there is no doubt that there were many features of national life which gave cause for disquiet, anxiety and tribulation. Some of the cycle might indeed have been written somewhat earlier as our previous discussion has made clear. After the Black Death in the mid-fourteenth century the Peasants' Revolt had followed in 1381: the argument that this upheaval was accompanied by the end of serfdom is compelling and symptomatic of a good deal of social disturbance. There was then a period of dynastic struggle leading to the murder of Richard II in 1399, followed by the internal strife in the reign of Henry IV. In the middle of the fifteenth century the dynastic trouble broke out again and it is very likely that the Towneley Cycle was put together during or shortly after the Wars of the Roses, and some or all of it may have been written against such a background. There are indeed some distinctive features which suggest interests in social matters and reflect the possible circumstances surrounding the text. One of the most important, and one related perhaps to the violence associated with royal authority, is the nature of political power and we have discussed several aspects of this in the previous chapter dealing with tyrants. The same might also be said regarding the problem of the Lollards and the responses to them, including Arundel's *Constitutions* (1407) which set about regulating heresies.[1] It is not necessary to repeat the material here but we can reaffirm that authority, both secular and clerical, is the object of satirical attention in a number of the plays. The grotesque cruelty of royal and ecclesiastical leaders is a significant and emphatic feature of this cycle and in this it follows and elaborates some aspects already present at York. Moreover the severity of justice and punishment were clearly matters of concern. The other side of this is the position of ordinary working people and it is to this we must first turn. This will be followed by some aspects of the law. Here the confrontation of abuses in ecclesiastical as well as secular courts is to be found. This corruption is no doubt a result of the difficulties presented by problems in the maintenance of public authority.

As James Simpson has pointed out, the perception of the world of work for the poor is often brutal and damaging in the cycle plays in general, no doubt reflecting the stress created by an uncertain economy.[2] In Towneley this has been made very plain in some episodes and it is apparent that some of the passages attributed to the Wakefield Master depend upon sharp perception of the sufferings of the poor and the labouring classes. Indeed it appears that this is something he added to the cycle without there being anything really comparable elsewhere in it. His satiric tone and his characteristically pungent language make these stand out. The most prominent of his contributions in this respect comes in the two Shepherds plays. One of the chief effects from a religious point of view is that the events of the Nativity are seen in a late medieval setting, and thus the original sacred events are given a contemporary significance and are dependent upon recognizable topical items. It is also interesting that there are two such plays and in each he concerns himself with the difficulties of the poor, but he varies the focus quite considerably.

In *First Shepherds* the First Shepherd (Gyb) begins with a traditional theme, the mutability of fortune: 'When ryches is he ['high'], / Then comys pouerté' (12/23–4). In his case the sheep plague has killed all his animals. To make things worse he is subject to taxes ('fermes', 44) which he cannot pay. Nevertheless, he intends to try to buy some more sheep at the fair and so to take a gamble on future prosperity:

> To the fare will I me,
> To by shepe, perdé,
> And yit may I multiplé,
> For all this hard case.   (12/62–5)

With the arrival of the Second Shepherd (John Horne) the focus shifts to the misery encountered from thieves and others who threaten violence. His animus is directed chiefly against a proud exploiter who has grand ways and yet makes demands upon the speaker which he cannot refuse:

If he hask me oght
That he wold to his pay,
Full dere bese it boght
If I say nay.   (12/105–8)

This character may well be another version of a similar oppressor in *Second Shepherds* (13/53). Like his companion – to whom he has not yet spoken directly – John Horne begs for God's help. But when the two do talk together they combine in hopelessness:

Is none in this ryke
A shepard, farys wars.
. . .
Poore men ar in the dyke
And oft-tyme mars.
The warld is slyke;
Also helpars
Is none here.   (12/133–9)

It is from this base that the rest of the play is developed, and indeed the main direction is away from it towards a transformation in their fortunes and outlook. But first they must go through the demonstration of their folly we have noted, and then in Bethlehem they are 'restorde' (12/716) and they end the play singing.

The most striking thing about the structure of this play for our purpose is the concentration upon misery at the beginning, and it is remarkable that in *Second Shepherds* the play begins in similar fashion. Whatever the reason for writing two plays on the same topic, the fact that the Wakefield Master again begins with a portrayal of social oppression and economic hardship is remarkable. His preoccupation is all the more so in comparison with the York Shepherds (15). The latter are not presented with the same emphasis upon poverty and it may well be that this is an expression of criticism by the Wakefield Master of the York version. Unfortunately the latter has a lacuna in the early part but, as it stands, it offers no evidence that the social and economic circumstances of the impoverished Shepherds were of concern to the York dramatist. For the Towneley First Shepherd (Gyb) the burden is the stormy weather and the taxes imposed by 'gentlery-men' (13/16): his word 'ramyd' (24) suggests 'plundered'.[3] These liveried servants of greater men oppress the poor and themselves live in plenty under the protection of their remote and powerful masters. Even if one of them comes and demands a plough, the farmer is constrained to give it. There is also the question of the predicament of the Shepherds who are really farmers (cf. 'husbandys') but are now forced to keep sheep because their land has been enclosed and they cannot make a living from their former fields:

> Bot we sely husbandys
> That walkys on the moore,
> In fayth we ar nerehandys
> Outt of the doore.
> No wonder, as it standys,
> If we be poore,
> For the tylthe of oure landys
> Lyys falowe as the floore,
> As ye ken.   (13/14–22)[4]

Coll uses two words of French origin which hint at class division and at the legal language of oppression: 'purveance' (49) was requisitioning food for the king and for other powerful leaders with inadequate or non-existent recompense; 'mantenance' (51) was the practice of keeping large numbers of retainers by magnates.[5] The complaints of the Second Shepherd (Gyb) are less concerned with social oppression: he laments the weather and then goes on to the many burdens of marriage. Though this makes use of conventional anti-feminist attitudes and formulations, we should not overlook the link between the circumstances of poverty created by social oppression and the difficulty of maintaining the well-being of families. But the arrival of the Third Shepherd (Daw), who is also cast down by the weather, brings back directly the theme of social oppression. Those who oppress the shepherds live richly and pay wages meanly and too late:

> Both oure dame and oure syre,
> When we haue ryn in the myre,
> Thay can nyp at oure hyre,
> And pay vs full lately.   (13/231–4)

However, they cheer up and sing a song, and the mood does not turn dark again until the arrival of Mak. In some ways he shares the burdens of the Shepherds as he too has difficulty in feeding his rapidly growing family but his approach to them is crafty, and he comes with a shady reputation. He claims to be a yeoman of the king and their superior, affecting a few scraps of southern speech, and threatens to report them. The conversation between Mak and the Shepherds is tetchy and suspicious.

Possibly they think of him as one of the unpopular 'gentlery-men', though there is some ambiguity in his status. They do not talk about particular ills though the matter of sheep stealing does come up, and it is apparent that they suspect Mak already. As Gyll, his wife, says later, that would be a hanging matter. But there are many small details in the complaints of these characters which emphasize the tension between them and which also point to discomfort and discontent. In all probability this part of the play was intended as a representation of the state of fallen man labouring under the difficulties and the sense of the ordinary hardship of life is palpable, with a distinct consciousness of underlying grievance. The sharpness of the language is intensified by the curtness characteristic of the Yorkshire dialect and by occasional proverbs. For example, when Mak complains that he is sick in his stomach, Daw replies: 'Seldom lyys the dewyll / Dede by the gate' (13/332–3: *gate*, road). This grimly perceptive language does much to increase the sense of the grinding severity of the lives of these characters and their response to it. When Coll asks Mak about his wife the problem of maintaining a family reappears. Even though this is conveyed in misogynistic language and even though the speaker is Mak, who is treated with suspicion, the reiteration of this difficulty is remarkable and part of the impression of social stress. The inclusion of these details of hardship, penury and misfortune is clearly a deliberate step, and it is much pointed by the linguistic style which links it with two other episodes where social issues are notable, *Abel* (2) and *Judgement* (30). It may well be that the poverty revealed here by the Wakefield Master is purposefully directed towards the idea that though poor they share a kind of truth, and that the poverty is a basis for insight. In the last section of the play their threadbare gifts unite them in poverty with the infant Christ.[6]

The circumstances of Cain and his response to them appear to be rather similar to those of the Shepherds: he lives in agricultural poverty and in his case suffers difficulties as he ploughs the land. Like the Shepherds he has much to say about his misfortunes and burdens. However, he does not complain about the weather or oppression by the servants of magnates: his mood is more generally malevolent. Instead he criticizes his plough team which won't pull hard enough for him and quarrels with his boy (Pikeharnes), who returns his hostility with such vigour that they come to blows. His main complaint is about having to pay tithes and a good deal of the action shows him trying to do the best for himself regardless of his spiritual and social obligations.[7] The religious aspects here, his refusal of grace and opposition to God's will, are no doubt the main reasons for the inclusion of this sequence, and the passage also expresses the widespread resentment felt against it. But details about the team and how to drive it and the unforgiving relationship with Pikeharnes exemplify the wretched state of things and Cain's meanness over the tithes is symptomatic of the struggle for existence.[8] It is also true that this is the first episode after the fall, a time when the severity of labour in order to live was thought to be a punishment for Adam's transgression. As with the Shepherds plays, a matter of religious importance is mediated through the circumstances of hard working conditions and the presence of these elements suggests the circumstances of humble working people in a community like a manor farm. There is little here to suggest the problems of urban life or indeed of the culture of craft guilds. Indeed the Wakefield Master seems interested in shifting the social context away from York's urban culture towards a more difficult rural predicament.

After the murder of Abel, Cain's guilt leads into a passage with legal implications.[9] God curses him and consequently Cain attempts to shrug off blame and punishment. In order to do this he has Pikeharnes help him to proclaim his own pardon. This is a kind of trickery with legal overtones since God has already said that no one may harm Cain (2/372–5) and Cain tries to use the form of a royal proclamation to protect himself. It has been suggested by Brockman that this passage has a satirical intent and is based upon two kinds of legal documents, the royal letter of protection given to itinerant ambassadors and, perhaps more critically, the royal letter of pardon which was seen as an abuse since it interfered with the normal process of the law.[10] The mockery of the passage is intensified in a distinctly theatrical way because Pikeharnes, standing aloft in order to ensure a broadcast of Cain's text and using the technique of stichomythia, interposes his own complaints about his poor diet and other diversions instead of proclaiming his master's pardon (2/421–41).

Further legal satire is inserted by the Wakefield Master into the conflicts between Annas and Caiaphas during the preparations for the punishment of Christ in *Buffeting*, as we have noticed (21/261–493). Besides the scriptural importance attached to the concept that Christ's coming brought the replacement of the Old Law by the New, the main point at issue here is how far the letter of the law should be adhered to in the context of the legal power of ecclesiastical authorities. Annas insists upon the distinction between ecclesiastical and temporal law: 'Men of temperall lawes, / They may deme sich cause; / And so may not we' (21/401, and similarly at 417–25). The disagreement between the prelates about how to treat Christ bearing in mind the application of the law is prefaced by the Torturers who see Christ as a threat to the laws (21/31–2) and they claim to bring him to the prelates in order to prevent this happening: 'For ye two, as I traw, / May defende all oure lawe' (21/166–7). The dramatist is able to rely upon contemporary sensitivity about these matters to create dramatic conflict, particularly in the dissension between Annas and Caiaphas, the latter being eager to proceed to violence while the former is more particular about the constraints of the law. In doing so he was in part following the York precedent but he puts his own emphasis upon it. It is also clear that this secular law is corrupt, though interestingly Caiaphas expresses this by means of a proverbial expression: 'Whoso kepis the law, I gess, / He gettys more by purches / Then bi his fre rent' (21/232–4).[11]

We should recollect too that these aspects of legal satire are only a part of the dramatic impact of this play: its extraordinary vigour depends upon a complex of effects of which the social satire is only one.

The Wakefield Master has another contribution to make on legal matters in his interpolation into *Judgement* (30). This play in the section taken from York is concerned with justice and not surprisingly legal matters are involved. For example the Third Bad Soul, in a passage from York, laments not having kept the Commandments and the appearance of Christ is 'To dele my dome' (30/127). The beginning of this play has been revised away from the York version and it contains satire upon the law. The Second Bad Soul fears that no lawyer can help him, and in doing so he reflects on how lawyers could indeed get their clients off:

Alas, I stande great aghe
To loke on that iustyce!
Ther may no man of lagh
Help with no quantyce.

Vokettys ten or twelfe          [*Advocates*]
May none help at this need,
Bot ilk man for hisself
Shall answere for his dede.   (30/13–20)

The speeches of the Demons have a number of references to the legal process (30/181–2, 196, 210, 279, 328). They take pleasure in the amassing of evidence and their purpose at the trial is to present lists of those who have offended: to this end they are equipped with 'rolles' (30/238, 269) and 'rentals' (30/196). Their function is focused by Tutivillus, who describes himself as a 'courte-rollar' (30/310). The Second Demon praises his court knowledge (30/335), his traditional role as witness against idle and careless users of language at Judgement Day being well established.[12] Some of the things he lists hit at ecclesiastical practice, including 'lufars of symonee' (30/433; also at 528). The 'fals swerars' may be misusers of the legal system as witnesses who were paid for false evidence.[13] The overall dramatic effect in *Judgement* with its specific interest in social matters is very different from that of the York original and it is primarily the Wakefield Master's contributions which ensure that this is so. After the first episode by the Demons and Tutivillus containing the legal satire as well as other issues particularly aimed at women, Christ speaks the substantial borrowing from York concerning his sacrifice (30/560–705). There follows another passage by the Demons and Tutivillus and here there is an increasing tempo as more and more Bad Souls are crammed into hell. Kolve noted that this induced mirth among the audience at a performance at the Mermaid Theatre, but it is equally possible to see that passage as a crescendo of horror and frenzy and one which contributes a grim note to the end of history.[14]

    The attention given by the Wakefield Master to the social matters discussed here is both pointed and persistent and it is clear that he was much concerned with them.[15] This may have affected the choices he made about which episodes to write or re-write. He may of course have been writing at a different time from the authors of other passages and he may have been prompted by particular local circumstances, and even possibly by his own professional considerations, though such a speculation is subject to our uncertainty about his own social status and the nature of his education. It is striking that the episodes in which he extended himself do show some interconnections both in terms of the impoverished rural society and the definition and corruption of the law we have noticed. These matters are not so clear in other parts of the cycle, and the disparity is enhanced by the fact that other plays were taken from York where different values might have been obtained. Indeed it may well be that the revelation of divine power could only be achieved through his sense of the toughness of the here and now. Such a stance may imply a critique of more emollient approaches elsewhere in Towneley and in York.

# 3.4

# Interrelations in the Psychology of Evil

The Towneley plays have attracted much attention because of their emphatic presentation of evil characters. These run through much of the cycle from Cain and on to Pharaoh, Caesar (who is at least ambivalent), Mak, Herod, Pilate, Annas and Caiaphas. Often these are spectacular and highly compelling figures of tyranny and at times they are supported by torturers and soldiers, who also exhibit various wicked characteristics and operate in threatening groups. There is also a recurrent and persistent interest in the elaboration of some of the demonic characters. It may well be that the particular handling of these figures does present us with some consistency and that they have both structural and ideological functions. It does appear that the traits attributed to them do at times bear some relationship to one another. Their impact is partly the cumulative result of the selection process by which the cycle was compiled, however diverse their origins. The most useful analyses of them are to be found in the work of Arnold Williams, John Gardner and Jeffrey Helterman.[1]

Gardner attempts to link the manifestations of evil in the cycle as part of his conception of unity, and his overall perception, now difficult to sustain, that the cycle is the work of one writer and construct which may be assessed on the basis of one creative, unified intention. In doing so he stresses ways in which evil characters act in a manner which parodies the holy and the sanctified. His analysis seeks to link together Cain, Herod and Pilate, and at times to associate these with the demonic, though in fact as characterization the role of Cain seems rather different from that of the two tyrants. The structure he perceives is closely linked with the fact that most of the work on these characters is in plays attributable to the Wake-field Master. However, it is important at this point to notice that although this dramatist made a substantial contribution here, there are distinct signs that he was developing the work of others in his presentation of some of these characters. Using the criterion of his characteristic stanza, let us recall what he seems to have contributed in the Passion sequence. In *Conspiracy* he wrote six stanzas for Pilate's opening boast as well as four stanzas covering Pilate's sending of Malchus and two soldiers to arrest Christ (20/1–77; 624–75). *Buffeting* (21) is entirely in his stanza. The first part of *Scourging* (22/1–351) shows initially Pilate's cruelty and pride, and this is followed by the beating of Christ by the Torturers, who force him to carry the cross: twenty-seven stanzas in all. Only one stanza can be tentatively attributed to him in *Crucifixion* in which John seeks to comfort Mary (23/383–95). Pilate begins *Dicing* with a boast, some of it in Latin (24/1–65, five stanzas). Later in the same play the Torturers talk about the evils of dicing and one shows some signs of repentance (24/378–428, especially 422–8). In other words, the main purpose of his intervention in the Passion is to elaborate the presentation of evil characters, mostly in respect of boasting and physical cruelty

We can develop the treatment of Herod in a number of ways. Like Pilate the intensity of his evil characteristics makes him absurd, and invites ridicule.[2] Helterman has shown that there may well be a link between his speeches in *Herod* and the idea of the Antichrist. This is based upon a reference to him as the king of kings, and also his compulsion to present himself as though he were an imitation of Christ and a ruler of many kingdoms.[3] Gardner finds that Herod shares a parody of heaven with the Shepherds and with Cain and attributes an 'allegorical' intention. Noting that *Pharaoh* derives largely from the York precedent, he points out that there are some verbal changes in the use of broken lines and the addition of scriptural detail.[4] He also links these items with the extensive elaboration of the appearances of Pilate. Starting from the observations in the work of Arnold Williams of a shift from the vacillating York Pilate, who shows indications in some episodes, as in the York *Mortificacio Christi* (36/33–9), of wanting to distance himself from the cruelty of what is being done, Gardner develops a view of an unremittingly evil tyrant in Towneley.[5]

This does seem to be a substantial point and it can be supported by many details. It is striking that Pilate is used to introduce several plays in Towneley and that this emphasis does present him as the opponent of Christ, as Williams has noted.[6] Gardner also notices that the character and the speeches of Pilate in *Scourging* echo those in *Conspiracy* (114). However, as Williams demonstrated, the behaviour of Caesar (9) and Herod (20/14) seems to be independent of the work of the Wakefield Master and this raises the possibility that his handling of Pilate may in part be an extension of an interest in tyrants manifested in earlier treatments, most likely at York. It also seems clear that we ought to see the Wakefield Master's characterization of Pilate in the context of all the other villains and evil characters, and that there is a measure of cross-reference. One of the features making this more plausible is their habit of referring to Mahowne, a convention found outside the work of the Wakefield Master and also apparent in York and elsewhere.[7]

A related process may be found if we compare Pilate's behaviour in the York *Second Accusation before Pilate* (32) with that in the Towneley *Dicing* (24). In both these plays there is a critical presentation of Pilate, one designed to bring out his selfish meanness. In the former Pilate tricks the Knight who owns the potter's field into handing over the deed to it. Once he has possession of the document Pilate refuses to return it and sends the Knight away empty handed. This is not repeated in the Towneley episode but *Dicing* shows a Pilate who is just as mean and selfish.[8] We recall that the scriptural sharing of Christ's clothing had already been treated in the previous Towneley play, *Crucifixion*, making this rehandling of the incident strictly unnecessary. The decision to show or include a second version may of course be seen as a parallel to the appearance of the two Shepherds plays earlier in the codex, something which may be only a codicological convenience rather than a deliberate structural repetition. Here then we find in *Dicing* a play largely devoted to the presentation of a selfish Pilate who insists upon taking Christ's garment for himself even though he loses the game of dice with the soldiers, which had ostensibly been intended as a means of settling the ownership. In the discussion of this play in Chapter 1.4 above it emerged that it is not the work of the Wakefield Master entirely and that there is some grounds in terms of its versification for supposing that it is a reflection of a lost play at York. Even if this is so, the inclusion of it in Towneley suggests that the compiler saw in it material which would intensify the portrait of a cruel and selfish Pilate in accordance with decisions made with respect to this characterization in other Towneley plays, and this decision was made in spite of duplication.

Besides the shift in the character of Pilate, there is an important original passage in *Conspiracy* (20). We have noticed that this is a complex play and that it is probably an accumulation of episodes from several quarters, including at least one passage by the Wakefield Master (20/1–77, and probably 624–75). But the passage containing the conspiracy itself (20/78–337), which does not seem to have been written by him, brings together a remarkable assembly of evil characters. It follows on from Pilate's initial boast. Annas and Caiaphas build up a series of accusations against Christ based upon the good things he has done which they interpret as threatening, a trope to which we shall return. The theatrical device of having these two villains work closely together as they threaten Christ also occurs in York, *Second Accusation before Pilate* (32), but the Towneley dramatist has changed the way they interact. Pilate is an outraged listener and his interventions, several of which call upon Mahowne and the Devil, rise to a climax in which he determines to have Christ arrested but he reluctantly agrees to hold back until after the Sabbath. These conspirators and the Soldiers who echo their fierce intent are then interrupted by Judas. At first they reject him, quarrelling with him and threatening him, but the turning point comes when he offers to sell Christ to them (20/228–9). The scene is written in a tense dialogue as Caiaphas and Annas advise Pilate and urge him on. Judas explains why he wishes to sell Christ in a speech which is derived from John 12:4–6 but much expanded in regard to the woman who washed and anointed Christ's feet (not here designated as Mary Magdalene).[9] The bargain is concluded, not without some suspicion and an assertion of the need for secrecy, and the Soldiers willingly comply with their new instructions to make the arrest. The most striking thing about this passage is that the dramatist has created it in such a way as to show the interaction of all these evil characters.

There is a kind of follow-up to this scene in *Hanging of Judas* (32), which intensifies the impression of evil surrounding Judas. Such an effect is underlined by iconological treatment of him which shows him as one of the principal inhabitants of hell, as in Giotto's portrayal of the Last Judgement in the Arena Chapel in Padua. But the episode's place in the manuscript is not really very convincing or coherent: it is written in a different and later hand and there is much doubt about whether this is a play at all. It reflects the sensational elaboration of the life of Judas, which was generally available and widely disseminated.

In his exploitation of the group dynamics of evil Torturers and Soldiers the Wakefield Master is clearly following an established pattern and one which was almost certainly developed earlier in the York Cycle. These groups appear in many places and their activities often present situations of great stress. Very often their activities also involve a victim, usually Christ, whose silent response emphasizes their wickedness, but there are also more vociferous exchanges. We should note, though, that sometimes these characters are ridiculous and that their evil nature is revealed partly through their limitations. Concentrating narrowly upon the details of the cruel task in hand, they often exhibit no conscience or awareness of what they are really doing. One significant and recurring motif is their calling upon Mahowne, as do the major evil characters. As the cycle develops chronologically such groups of Torturers and Soldiers first appear in *Pharaoh* (8), one of the closest of the borrowings from York. In this episode they seem to set a precedent for the behaviour of the later groups. This is especially noticeable in their function as reporters: here, they give Pharaoh information about Moses in a manner which is prophetic in spite of themselves, and later it is they who detail the horrors of the plagues. This process or function is a useful resource because it enables scriptural details and scriptural language to be incorporated in the action of the play. The recurring phenomenon can have a dual function, as we shall see, and at the end of this play it is combined with their disposition to violence as they threaten the Jews: 'We shall not seasse, bot dyng all downe / To all be dede withouten drede' (8/408–9). But their threat comes to nought as they are overwhelmed in the Red Sea.

In the Old Testament version of this episode there is just a hint of their role, and there is a similar small prompt for the next significant action by a group of soldiers in the three invented by the Wakefield Master for *Herod* (16). Here they are called 'knights', perhaps an echo of the *armati* of the liturgical drama,[10] and there is some play on their chivalric appearance when summoned by Herod, though this is obviously meant to be ironic. They report on the deceptive departure of the three kings ('thay went sodanly / Or any man wyst' 16/261–2). But the main purpose here is to reveal their cruelty as they mockingly abuse the mothers of the Innocents. We may note that the dramatist exploits extensively the flexibility of the thirteen-line stanza in the dialogue between soldiers and mothers which accompanies the vigorous action. Once the killing is over, they return to Herod and boast of their achievements: 'morderd haue we / Many thowsandys', (16/606–7). Their evil deeds are compounded by Herod's extravagant rewards and his call upon Mahowne to watch over them (16/662–3).

But perhaps the most striking thing about these groups of soldiers and torturers is their frequency in the Passion sequence as they appear successively in *Conspiracy* (20), *Buffeting* (21), *Scourging* (22), *Crucifixion* (23), *Dicing* (24) and *Resurrection* (26). When the episodes are played consecutively, a great deal of the action and the dramatic effect is found to be concentrated upon their activities and their language. In casting these episodes one could indeed use the same actors in several of them if one were aiming at a performance on a fixed location. The Wakefield Master's work shows a preoccupation with these features that cannot be overlooked but all the details are not solely his: *Resurrection*, for example, is

substantially a York borrowing. In these episodes these characters follow
the precedents we have noticed, frequently recounting details, as for the
revival of Lazarus (20/150–1 and 21/144–7) and the healing of the halt and
the blind (21/118–21). This device, really amounting to a convention, is
especially powerful here because it draws attention to the good Christ has
done even though it is recounted by evil and accusatory voices: it reflects
both well upon him and badly upon them. The narrative recall is turned
to a different effect in *Dicing* where the Torturers recall the events that
have been displayed in the Crucifixion and their part in it. The tone of the
Second Torturer is established by his grim fooling with the words 'play'
and 'game' which starts with: 'I was at Caluery this same day, / Where
the kyng of Iues lay, / And ther I taght hym a newe play . . .' (24/144–6).[11]

   But their worst manifestation is doubtless their tormenting of Christ
which is enacted with graphic detail in *Buffeting*, *Scourging* and *Crucifixion*. The persistent verbal abuse, including treating him as an animal
(21/621, 22/71) is a marked feature. The first of these plays is in the stanza
of the Wakefield Master, but the composition of the other two is more
difficult to establish. *Crucifixion* has but a few examples of this verse and
the detail of extending the body to fit the holes bored in the cross is strongly
reminiscent of the action in the York counterpart. But this is a general
motif, present for example in iconographic representations such as the
*Holkham Bible Picture Book*, as noted by Cawley and Stevens, and it may
therefore not be derived from York at all.[12] *Scourging* is more complex,
since the Wakefield Master has written the passage where the Torturers
deliver their blows upon the silent Christ (22/166–82) and also the passages
recalling his ministry including the feast, the leper, the blind man and
the alleged misuse of the Sabbath (22/196–247). But the closing episode
of this play, in which they impose their will upon Simon, is a direct borrowing from York. The interrelationship between these passages thus raises
important questions about unity: the fact that there is demonstratively
different authorship does not mean that they do not fit together and
participate in a general design, a feature which one could also attribute
to York where there is palpably a measure of diversity. Here the tone of
the individual episodes and the persistent intention to show Christ as a
victim of repeatedly wicked acts of torture and cruelty give this sequence
in the cycle a grim impact and make the interpretation of Christ's Passion
effective in the context of human wickedness. To this extent it appears
that the dramatists were working to a common purpose and that in these
plays some careful and pointed intermingling of work by different writers
was being interconnected.

To these manifestations of evil in Towneley we should add the part played by the devils. Their overall impact is partly limited by two textual matters which might have involved them: the temptation of Eve and Adam probably took place in the passage lost from *Creation* (1); the absence of plays showing the temptation of Christ and the appearance to Pilate's wife, as occurs in other cycles. Devils are referred to frequently enough by the evil characters, but they make only three appearances: Lucifer in *Creation*, Satan and associates in *Harrowing* (25), and the devils including Tutivillus in *Judgement* (30). The functions of these devils do not seem to be interrelated and they are best seen as created for each of the specific contexts in which they appear. Thus Lucifer in *Creation* is emphatic in his self praise, 'thowsandfold' brighter than the sun, and the dramatist has chosen to point up his assumption of divinity and his interest in taking over the throne of the Trinity; the Evil Angels, soon to become devils, back this up with flattering comparison between Lucifer and the divinity. When he tries to fly, however, he falls at once, and the demons immediately begin quarrelling and blaming him for their new pain.

The context for the enlargement of the devils in *Harrowing* is the conflict between Christ and Satan. This is facilitated by the invention of the junior devil, Rybald – who does not appear in the closely related York version – and by an elaboration of the dialogue of the devils, including Belzabub. When Satan does finally appear in order to take control where the others have failed, he is more arrogant and confident than in York (T25/147–50, 153–4) but Christ does not let him escape when he thinks he has made a favourable bargain (327–8).

We have already considered the social context for the Wakefield Master's innovation of introducing the traditional figure of Tutivillus in *Judgement*, but here we should note that there is probably a theological justification also for it. The York version highlights the importance of the Deeds of Mercy, themselves a means of bringing relief to others suffering in various ways, but the sins of greed and luxury, which Tutivillus and the other devils are made to add in the Towneley version, are themselves an exploitation of others and may have been intended as a direct contrast to the embedded virtues.[13]

Although these appearances of devils independently introduced by the Towneley dramatists or added to York precedents do not show a great deal of integration or cross-reference, their presence does enhance the persistent interest in evil which is characteristic of Towneley. Much the same is true of three human characters invented or developed by the Wakefield

Master, though here we have something of a contrasting blend. The wickedness of Judas we have seen as an established trope inside and outside the drama. In many ways Cain matches him since he too is unable to receive mercy because he is unrepentantly evil. As with Judas, God takes special measures with him, in this case preventing anyone from killing him. God also calls him mad (2/352) and there is an irrationality about much of his behaviour. Most of what he does demonstrates the barrenness of evil. It does seem that the dramatist has sought to remove any possibility of sympathy for him: he has no way to turn. But such an intense presentation of evil is somewhat modified in two other characters, Noah's wife and Mak, the shepherd. The effect of the former's irritability and obstinacy is considerably modified by the fallibility of her violent husband who loses a good deal of sympathy by his aggression towards her. The intervention by their sons pinpoints the fact that in the early part of the play both parents are to blame (3/599–602). This portrait of human fallibility is to be seen against the transforming harmony which arrives when they are installed in the Ark and trust is restored. For Mak, thief though he is, there may also be some sympathy. The elaboration of the ills he suffers from his poverty must place him in a position which is morally ambivalent, and to some extent his misfortunes are shared with the shepherds. Although he is guilty and he does exhibit the dangerous trait of using magic, his moral status may well be recognized, and indeed illuminated, by the rather mild and unexpected punishment which is meted out to him: he apparently avoids the pains of hell. It is particularly intriguing that his main fault is stealing a sheep. This must have been seen as a crime, and it would no doubt have attracted widespread condemnation. It could also be an act of covetousness, or a sin against the seventh commandment as indicated by the young Christ with the Doctors, forbidding theft (18/165). But the presentation of Mak leaves us with some doubt because of the social context.

The many examples of evil we have discussed here give us ground for concluding that Towneley does contain enough to represent the fallen world and its necessity for salvation, a point made firmly by Christ, come to destroy the Devil, at the beginning of *Harrowing*, surely a telling moment:

> The feynde theym wan with trayn,
> Thrugh fraude of erthly fode;
> I have theym boght agan
> With shedyng of my blode. (25/13–16)

It may well be that no single creative mind constructed Towneley in the form we now find it in the manuscript, but whether it were performed or read in the sixteenth century or whether it is encountered in the twenty-first, it does show us a world corrupted by the sins of humans and devils, and one which needs salvation. However, this fallen world embodied in the interrelationships of evil also contains some images of virtuous men and women, and to these we turn next.

# 3.5

# Good Men and Women

The medieval Christian view of men and women was a divided one; we can perceive this most markedly in morality plays in England and France. These plays often show an overall perspective on human life, frequently as in *Castle of Perseverance*, *The World and the Child* and *L'Omme Pecheur*, tracing life from the cradle to the grave and beyond. Sometimes this long view is reflected in a shorter scenario as in *Wisdom* and *Everyman*. In this genre the human situation is seen as containing contrasting images. Men – it is usually put in terms of men, though in *Wisdom* the protagonist Anima is female – are shown to be made of clay, vulnerable, weak and liable to folly and indulgence. They are subject to the seven deadly sins and salvation is by no means ensured. The sense of mortality is ever present: 'Whou Mankynde into this werld born is ful bare / And bare schal beryd be at hys last ende' (*Perseverance*, 16–17). But the often repeated complementary view offers an extreme and draws attention to man's being made in God's image. Anima is described as: 'the ymage of Gode that all began / And not only ymage, but hys lyknes ye are' (*Wisdom*, 103–4). This is an image of beauty and is a direct link with the divinity. One related theme was the beauty attributed to Lucifer before his fall: 'He is so lufly and so bright / It is grete ioy to se that sight' (T1/73–4). Sometimes the contrasting views are placed in sharp proximity: 'Fragille est il, mortel et corruptible / puis quen luy est beaulte imcomparable' (*L'Omme Pecheur*, aiiii).[1]

In the previous chapter we have discussed the pervading attention to evil as it is shown in the cycle, reflecting as it does the choices made by the compiler in making up the text. A similar process is present in the representation of virtue in human beings, and the location of these is significant as a contribution to the overall impact of the Towneley Cycle. In some ways this is rather a simple matter. There is a notable accumulation

of virtuous characters in the Old Testament plays and many of these, as
John Gardner has suggested, may be there as prefigures of Christ.[2]
In creating Adam, Deus tells of the qualities with which he is endowed:

> I gif the witt, I gif the strenght
> Of all thou sees, of brede and lengthe;
> Thou shall be wonder wise,
> Myrth and ioy to haue at will.   (1/173–7)

The emphasis upon mental powers and understanding is in ironic
anticipation of what is to come, but it is essential to establish this divine
and powerful gift. Other virtues become apparent among the protagonists
as the Old Testament episodes unfold. Piety and obedience are shown by
Abel, Noah and Abraham. Noah, as conceived by the Wakefield Master,
has a wide and wise view of sacred history and he makes the point that
in the creation the Lord 'To his liknes maide man' (3/41). In this context
'his' seems to refer to being like the beautiful Lucifer whose downfall
Noah has just described and whose place man was intended to take. Noah
also has a perception of God's promise of salvation in the oil of mercy
and the threat posed by the deadly sins (3/66–78).[3] Deus chooses to save
Noah and his wife from his vengeance upon mankind because 'thay wold
neuer stryfe / With me then me offend' (3/155–6). Noah is distinguished
by his plea for mercy and also by his obedience and he ends with a prayer
for God's grace as a means of overcoming human sin. But we have also
seen that this Noah is aggressive and violent and he is therefore a paradoxical figure embodying the contrasting human characteristics we have
noted in the morality plays.

Abraham may be seen as a more appealing figure in that his obedience
is pure and the conflict in which he is caught up is emotional as well as
moral. He shares the view of the human predicament expressed by Noah
and the need for the oil of mercy. *Abraham* begins with his lament for all
those now in hell (including Adam, Abel and Noah) followed by his request
for God's help. Deus comments, out of Abraham's hearing, that he will
help 'Might I luf and lewté fynd' (4/50). Abraham's sorrow is portrayed
poignantly in the Towneley version: it is a commonplace and an important motif in other mystery cycles and in the separated Brome version, but
the tension between his obedience and his paternal love is particularly
intense here. As the test of Abraham begins, his love for Isaac is shown
in his words and his actions, even though he accepts the commandment
to sacrifice him completely: 'That shal be done in every steede' (4/86).

The intensity of his love and his cruel predicament create great sympathy for him and the dramatic presentation makes much of this. At the climax he goes away from where Isaac lies and, in the seconds before the divine intervention, he desperately prepares himself apart to carry out the deed which is so hard for him. In his anguish he plans to bring the matter to a head precipitately: 'I will ryn on a res [in a rush] / And slo hym here, right as he lyse' (4/255–6). When the release comes the Angel praises his 'mekenes' (4/265).

The plays about *Isaac* (5) and *Jacob* (6) are unique to Towneley, and to an extent they follow the emotional emphasis of *Abraham*. The love of Isaac for Jacob is expressed in both plays in emotional language, as in: 'The smell of my son is lyke / To a feld with flouris or hony-bike' (5/3–4). Both plays end with a kiss and it is likely that, being stylistically similar, they were conceived as sequels working towards the reconciliation of Jacob with his brother Esau. In spite of the envy and separation shown in the narrative and derived accurately but selectively from Genesis 27:18–46, Esau rushes into Jacob's arms at the end (6/122sd, as in Genesis 33:4). Deus plays an active role in support of Jacob in exile and assures him of the blessings to come upon his offspring (6/19–26). The inclusion of these plays may well be intended as a contrast with the outcome of the fraternal hate shown in *Abel*. Unfortunately the lacuna at the beginning of *Isaac* denies us positive clues about such a link but the emphasis upon love, following upon *Abraham*, the reconciliation of two hostile brothers, and the sense of divine intervention are significant and help to suggest a coherent interest.

The next important virtuous figure is Moses who appears in *Prophets* (7) and *Pharaoh* (8). In the former he leads the procession and foretells the coming of Christ, who will redeem Adam and his 'blode' from hell (7/12). He then adds the details of the Ten Commandments and refers to God's choosing him on Mount Sinai. His role is more active in *Pharaoh*. Deus recalls his blessing upon Abraham, Isaac and Jacob (8/121–2), and he sends Moses to the Pharaoh to secure the release of his people. Moses emphasizes God's might and like the other leading virtuous figures of the Old Testament, he obediently does God's bidding. Eventually the plagues persuade Pharaoh of his errors and Moses leads his people to the Red Sea. He urges the Jews to show love to God and the Trinity. Moses is perhaps a more public and even political figure than the other Old Testament figures of virtue. Under God's guidance he acts bravely and faces up to the tyrannical Pharaoh on behalf of his people. He is joined by David in *Prophets* who sings God's praises and also foretells the coming of Christ.

With *Annunciation* the main preoccupation of the narrative changes from prophetic anticipation to a focus on the life of Christ and the use made of virtuous characters changes accordingly. Leaving aside the possible exception of the aged Simeon in *Purification*, who is a prophetic figure, the virtuous characters are now part of the gospel narrative or elaborations of it. In fact these characters are few in number and nearly all of them make a series of appearances. Apart from Christ himself, we may notice Mary the Virgin, Mary Magdalene, Joseph, John the Baptist, John and Peter; and there are lesser characters used more sparingly in Mary Salome and Mary Jacobi, Paul Thomas, and the other Apostles. Their activities are to some extent circumscribed by the requirements of the gospel narrative but the dramatists and the compiler have been able to create emphases and exercise selection.

Of these characters we have discussed the Virgin and Mary Magdalene in terms of gender (Chapter 3.1). Here we need to identify their good qualities. The Virgin is the most frequently used, appearing in ten of the episodes. Her actions and words are largely dictated by the circumstances of each, and they can be very different. Sometimes the conventional requirements, with scripture underlying, seem uppermost, as when she says (or sings) the *Magnificat* in *Salutation* (11/49–78). She is an emotional figure as well as an iconic one. Her suffering is demonstrated repeatedly, and it is also noticed by other characters in *Scourging* and *Crucifixion*. The range of emotions includes fear in *Flight* and maternal anxiety for her missing son in *Doctors*. She endures Joseph's accusations and forgives him graciously in *Annunciation*. The damage to the manuscript, involving a loss of twelve leaves near the end, has probably removed the end of her life and her elevation into heaven: in *Ascension* she is filled with wonder and asks her son to take her there with him (29/396). At this point she shows that her earlier sorrows are eased by the comfort she receives from John. However, these intense emotional experiences may not necessarily require us to see her as a coherently constructed character. In production one might make them come together by using the same actress and by consistency of costume and movement, but the texts themselves do not make these necessities. Many of her responses are conventional and can be paralleled in the liturgical drama, particularly in her lamentations:[4] the use of lyrical structures for some of these passages may increase this impression. Moreover, the iconic aspects Mary reveals tend to reduce the possibility of realistic coherence. She receives the worship of the Shepherds on behalf of her son in the two Shepherds plays, and in *Ascension* she enjoins the eleven to spread the truth about her son: 'He is God and man that stevynd into heuen; [ascended] / Preche thus to the pepyll that most ar in price' (29/444–5). The appearances of Mary Magdalene are less frequent. She participates in four episodes: *Scourging*, *Resurrection*, *Thomas* and *Lazarus*. The original unity of this character in scripture is problematic in itself. She is a conflation by Gregory the Great of several biblical women: the sister of Martha and Lazarus; the woman who washes Christ's feet and anoints them; one of the women who find the tomb empty; the woman who mistakes the resurrected Christ for the gardener.[5] Gregory's construction was widely followed and a great deal was added to the mythology subsequently, as can be seen in the dramatic version of her life in the Digby *Mary Magdalene*.[6] These episodes mentioned are presented in Towneley though one of them, the woman who anointed Christ's feet, is not shown directly and is not identified specifically with Mary Magdalene in the retrospective account by Judas (*Conspiracy* 20/274–305). Her direct contact with Christ is somewhat limited but as Coletti has noted it has a distinctly physical dimension in the recognition in the garden.[7] To these are added the role of comforter to the Virgin in *Scourging* and the episode in *Thomas* where she brings news of the Resurrection, having witnessed it in the garden, to the apostles. Peter and Paul refuse to believe her and there is little doubt that this passage was conceived as a thematic prelude to the rest of this play which shows how Thomas doubted and how his doubts were overcome. The mythological accretions to her story place much emphasis upon her former life of sin and the intensity of her repentance. This may well be reflected in her lamentation over Christ and her relief over the forgiveness she had received (*Resurrection* 26/429–47). However, it is to be noted that her characterization hardly arouses the critical reaction she engendered in other works where her threat to orthodoxy, sometimes with a sexual dimension, makes her piety rather ambivalent, especially in the N Town Cycle.[8] It seems that here her appearances are more closely concerned with emotional experiences rather than a reflection of the ambiguities of holy women.

Whilst John the Apostle always appears blameless in Towneley, succouring the Virgin in the conspiracy in *Crucifixion* and *Ascension*, and Christ in *Lazarus*, most of the other virtuous characters after the Annunciation share fallibility with Mary Magdalene. Thus Thomas has a long way to go in overcoming his doubts, and his final speech in *Thomas* is a sustained plea for mercy (28/569–616). Peter disgraces himself, as in the Gospels, by his denial.[9] He is reproved by Christ over the washing of the feet and for cutting off the ear of Malchus and he shares an acrimonious disbelief of Mary Magdalene in *Thomas* with Paul. Joseph is also flawed because of his suspicion over Mary's pregnancy but in other places he supports her fears and comforts her as in *Flight* and *Doctors*. But, as we noticed with the Virgin, many of these items are required by the Gospel account and they are hardly evidence of sustained characterization. Nevertheless, they do present us with a sense of human fallibility as they are caught up in the turmoil of the Passion and its aftermath. Their emotional responses, particularly those by the Virgin, Mary Magdalene, Peter and John the Apostle, are also a means of increasing the emotional involvement of the audience. Perhaps even more importantly their cumulative effect is something of a complement to the spectacular impact of the concentration of evil characters, especially in the Passion sequences. To an extent the rants of the tyrants are counterbalanced by the lyrical strength of their virtuous emotions, even when they speak passionately in their unhappiness.

In the elements discussed in Part III we can discern that Towneley may share a good deal with other cycles, but it is also distinctive from them. In particular, ambivalence in its treatment of gender, its religious orthodoxy, the presence of elements from popular culture, its address of certain social issues and its persistent attention to evil characters and their virtuous counterparts all contribute to our perception of its meanings and our sense of its specific nature, even if these aspects are found in the other cycles.

# IV

## NEGOTIATING THE TEXT

# 4

# Prologue

In this last part of our study we shall assess the implications of the approaches we have made to the nature of the Towneley Cycle and the possibility of its unity. Reaching conclusions for these plays is somewhat constrained because there are still many areas of uncertainty and some areas for further investigation. Because of the limitations in the documentary evidence, some of these may have to remain forever unfathomed. For this reason the discussion I propose here is more a matter of negotiating between different evaluations of the Towneley Cycle rather than presenting a single view. Nevertheless, we should not disregard the many features which match one another and which add support to discernible structures and internal relationships. Although the sum of our preceding discussions is that we cannot view the cycle as the result of one defining and unifying creative process, we should not therefore assume that there is nothing distinctive about it, nothing which helps to give it its own voice or voices and to make it speak somewhat differently from other analogous works of the period during which it was developed. Such considerations may in part depend upon local contexts in so far as they can be ascertained. Moreover, the work remains an authentic late medieval text having dramatic and linguistic characteristics which cannot be ignored, nor can it be plausibly attributed to any other time than the fifteenth and sixteenth centuries. In this sense it is an authentic document and one whose existence, however anomalous or fragmented, demands our attention as such. Attempts to redefine the cyclicity of these plays are not likely to alter the time of its genesis. Thus the activities of the compiler indicate a deliberate editing process orientated towards the production of a cyclic drama with some distinctive features.

The survival of other English texts from the period, and also those in other European languages, makes the unity, or at least some measure of coherence, in Towneley all the more likely since it is part of a culture of cycle plays. Though there are some hints of the beginning of this genre in the fourteenth century, the main development does seem to have been in the fifteenth century, especially for York and also most likely for Coventry and Chester in England, as well as for the Cornish *Ordinalia*. Besides these there is also in France the influential work of Eustache Mercadé (*c*.1440), Arnoul Gréban (*c*.1450) and Jean Michel (1486). There are significant German cycles at Alsfeld and Künzelsau, and the Dutch *Bliscapen* on the Joys of Mary was developed by 1446 and performed for a century afterwards. To put it bluntly cycle plays, not necessarily solely linked with the development and celebration of the feast of Corpus Christi, became fashionable in the fifteenth century in several parts of Europe. But it is clear that the work of creating and adapting cycles went on well into the sixteenth century, concurrent with and presumably even stimulated by the crisis of faith presented by the challenges to orthodox medieval Catholicism.[1] Such a view of cyclic drama in general, and of the Towneley plays in particular, may have been challenged in recent years by persuasive concerns about provenance and origins, but I suggest that what is perceivable in critical thinking today is more a flexible understanding and description of what has survived rather than that we are simply coming to destruction or disintegration. On the other hand the older assessments by Helterman, Gardner and Williams have to be in part set aside in respect of their attempts to illuminate monolithic or highly coordinated authorship, which is patently not there. These plays do not really answer to a critical regime which seeks to interpret them as though they were the work of one tragedian: a better model indeed might be epic poetry. But many of the elements these earlier critics observed in Towneley may still help us to describe what is actually there, and to reveal the development, the playing and reception of the cycle and, perhaps most important of all, the process of its interpretation, which in itself is rich with conflicting elements. In the fourth part of our study we shall now turn to these three broad aspects. In doing so we shall need to bear in mind the many objections to a monolithic approach, and yet the result should be tangibly connected by our experience of these plays whether in the study or in performance.

We have discussed many aspects of such a performance and here it is necessary to restate that although we have little evidence about specifics, the potential for live realization was high from the time when the Towneley Cycle was assembled. Indeed such a potential may well have existed for some individual plays before anyone thought of putting them into a cyclic format. A parallel with N Town is inviting. There are certain elements concentrating upon the Life of the Virgin and the Passion that have been shown to have had a separate existence before the codex was assembled.[2] Once the various plays came together into the Towneley Cycle, whether specifically in this manuscript or in a predecessor, the performance potential became inherent and in modern times, if not earlier, some of it has been shown to be manifestly effective.

# 4.1

# Development

The development of Towneley requires that we think of a process having two substantial parts. The first lies in the fifteenth century when some parts of the York Cycle were adapted. Though there are changes in terms of dialect, much (but not all) that now appears in certain Towneley plays is remarkably close to York in details of verbal expression and thus it seems that the language is substantially of the fifteenth century. Some details of clothing also fall into line with this.[1] Moreover, the orthodox Catholic emphasis of many parts of the Towneley Cycle suggests that at least part of it comes from a time when this religious culture was being asserted against encroachments from Wycliffite or Lollard subversions.

We should also ask at this point whether there are any distinctive features in the parts taken over from York. Probably no one feature will be present in all of them and the impulses to borrow were diverse, but it does seem that several of the plays may be grouped together as giving a strong presence to the appearance of Christ and his effect upon events. The instances of this are in *Doctors*, *Harrowing*, *Resurrection* and *Judgement*. In each of these Christ plays a distinctive and assertive role in the action and what he does and what he stands for are positive and even triumphant.[2] It is notable that in her analysis of the York plays Sarah Beckwith places emphasis upon the visibility of the body of Christ and upon actualizing it at certain parts of the cycle, especially in *Resurrection* and *Judgement*.[3] It may well be that the decision to incorporate these Christ-centred episodes from York into Towneley depended, among other considerations, upon an awareness that they would contribute this special effect. If we were to take the York borrowings away from Towneley the impact of Christ upon events would be poorer.

But the second process, that of the making of the manuscript, now seems to have taken place as late as the middle of the sixteenth century. If this were indeed in the Marian period it would be very likely that it was convenient and desirable at that time to make a manuscript which re-asserted Catholic values. A reprise of the anti-Lollard sentiment in some of the plays originally written in the previous century might well have seemed opportune.[4] Moreover, the very brief records we have from Wakefield leave little doubt that in 1556 the town had a Corpus Christi play with pageants and speeches set forth by the craft guilds, and that there was a 'regenall' or book associated with the dramatic practices adumbrated in the records. It may be useful to recall the wording of these at this point:

1556

Item a payne is sett that everye crafte and occupacion doo bringe furthe / theire pagyauntes of Corpus Christi daye as hathe bene heretofore used and to / gyve furthe the speches of the same in Easter holydayes in payne of / everye one not so doynge to forfett / xl s.

1559

Item a payn ys layd þat gyles dollefe shall brenge In or Causse to be broght þe regenall of Corpus Christy play befo[re] þis & wytsonday In pane . . . Item a payn ys layde þat þe mest[er]es of þe Corpus Christi playe shall Come & mayke thayre a Countes before þe gentyllmen & burgessus of þe to[wn] / before thys & may day next In payn of evere on not so doynge – xx s.

But though these records call the play 'pagyauntes of Corpus Christi daye' it is not, in the absence of external corroboration, absolutely certain that this event necessarily happened on the feast of Corpus Christi itself. Both the 1556 Wakefield record ('as hathe bene heretofore used') and the later York Diocesan prohibition of 1576 ('a plaie commonlie called Corpus Christi plaie, which hath bene hereto fore used': see p. 6) indicate that the play (or plays) in question had been performed for some time, though we cannot tell how far back that might have extended. Moreover, an exacting scrutiny of this evidence does not specifically link the surviving Towneley text with the plays that were apparently performed in mid-century, though we may go so far as to say that the likelihood is acceptable. The only serious objection is that the variety of dramatic styles in the plays in the manuscript is so great that a uniform method of production on pageant carts might have been difficult. *Second Shepherds*, for example, is very long.[5] However, it is clear that some variety of style was tolerated at York (less so at Chester and in the Cornish *Ordinalia*) and possibly the Towneley text does not cross the boundary of what was practical. As a genre cycle plays were tolerant of diversity.

From the first process we may well assume that extensive work by the Wakefield Master was going on in the fifteenth century, but in considering that we come up against the difficulty that Wakefield was a small place before 1500, and it may not have had enough craft guilds to sustain a York-type performance. The additions of a few craft names in sixteenth-century hands, but not in that of the main scribe, may tend to support this. It looks as though any allocation of individual plays for any sort of performance by guilds was undertaken after the manuscript was evolved, even though the 1556 record notices 'everye crafte and occupacion' as though it were retrospective. These factors may indicate that some of the plays at least were not originally written for an urban society but possibly for a more rural one centred upon a manorial culture. There is a good deal of circumstantial evidence in the satirical and subversive work of the Wakefield Master pointing in this direction, especially from that directed to the rural occupations in *Abel* and the *Shepherds* plays.[6] In short, the dating of some details in his work, his interpolation of stanzas into York plays established in the fifteenth century and the presumption that Wakefield was too small to sustain a cycle at that time seem to fit together. We should, however, insert a note of caution in respect of the details that have emerged about the Corpus Christi play revived at New Romney in the mid-sixteenth century. This was a small place and yet it was apparently able to mount a Corpus Christi play conceived in cyclic form.[7] It would seem that it is the interlocking of these pieces of evidence from Wakefield which may be persuasive, rather than the one individual strand concerning size. But by the mid-sixteenth century it does seem from the 1556 record and from the added names of crafts that craft guilds, as distinct from purely religious societies or confraternities, were in some way to be associated with performances by that time.

A number of issues arise from these two distinct phases of development. If there was an expansion in the sixteenth century to meet some sort of civic requirement, in parallel, but perhaps on a lesser scale with the palpable civic aspirations at York, it does not seem likely that these were present for the plays composed in the fifteenth century. This in turn reminds us that a considerable number of the plays do not seem to have been conceived necessarily for wagon performance, and among these are the plays written by the Wakefield Master. One feature of his work has special interest in that most of the plays which were written entirely by him were conceived for a small group of actors. It is also clear that he did intervene on a smaller scale in the plays which had fifteenth-century currency at York. It doesn't look as though he were writing for a pageant-wagon performance, whatever became of his plays later on. This raises the possibility that such a mode of performance developed later in the history of the cycle, and once again York might have provided a model.

However, the hypothesized generation of the manuscript in the mid-sixteenth century does make it possible that there was at that time a strong urge to create or use such a work. The way the scribe has planned and executed the text, including the decorated capitals, argues for this. We should not forget that the size and quality of the manuscript as we now have it are the result of a large amount of effort and a high and sustained level of commitment. The reference to the 'regenall' noted above suggests some civic concern about the state of a text, which may indeed be the one we now have. If this process can be attributed to a Marian context, then there is also likely to have been a religious impulse interwoven with civic aspiration.[8] But the absence of further documentation prevents us from seeing whether the genesis of the manuscript was a regulatory process similar to the one which obtained at York. For the latter we can detect a need for the text of the register to be an instrument of control over the performance by the city authorities, evidenced further by the monitoring for many years into the sixteenth century by John Clerke, the town clerk.

The compilation or copying of the Towneley text in the 1550s may well be a part of a strengthening of Catholic sentiment, but it is also possible that it was stimulated by the contemporary reputation of cycles performed in urban centres elsewhere. We may note that such a date for the compilation of the manuscript and for the possible consolidation of the Towneley Cycle is later than the dates now proposed for the earliest appearance of the Chester Cycle in a form that can be reconciled with the post-1590 recensions.[9] It is also likely that this was later than the creation of the N Town manuscript, and it is worth recalling that this cycle was added to after its inception.[10] As there was also some development of the Coventry Cycle in the 1530s it would seem that work on Towneley in the mid-sixteenth century had some recent examples to prompt it.[11] Moreover, the process of compilation whereby existing material was incorporated and shaped was still very much part of the medieval practices of authorship described by A. J. Minnis and applied to Towneley by Martin Stevens.[12] Another relevant aspect is the process of circulation and interaction between manuscripts. The presence of the York elements argues for this even though we have not in England as much circumstantial detail as can be found in France where, from the mid-fifteenth century, texts were commonly passed from one place to another and then adapted for local circumstances.[13]

This outline of the development of the Towneley Cycle also needs to take account of some distinctive elements in it not so far discussed. These are the plays not derived from York and those which do not show any evidence of the work of the Wakefield Master. I shall consider these in three groups. The first is the pair of plays *Isaac* (5) and *Jacob* (6). The subjects they are concerned with are unusual for the English cycles and they have a distinctive dramatic style of which their striking realism is a significant feature. They were obviously conceived as a pair and their structures are similar. Quite possibly they are early in date and were meant to be free-standing plays, and were subsequently incorporated by the compiler as part of his desire to develop Old Testament elements for his cyclic design.

Secondly, there are two composite plays, *Annunciation* (10) and *Conspiracy* (20), which show signs of adaptation and reconstruction. We have seen that the former carries a structural significance as the beginning of the Nativity sequence, a feature especially marked by the presence of the introductory speech by Deus himself. There may be a sort of narrative rationale for the juxtaposition of this speech with the next part of this play, the Annunciation itself, but this is followed by the episode of Joseph's doubts. The tone of these episodes in this rather lengthy play varies somewhat but the versification has only two major forms: couplets for the speech by Deus, and six-line tail-rhyme stanzas for the rest. Parts of this play may once have had an independent existence, but its function in its present position in the cycle, as the beginning of the Nativity sequence, is clearly strategic.

*Conspiracy* has a similar role at the beginning of the Passion sequence. The play which precedes it is *Baptist* (19), the only one in the collection dealing with Christ as an adult, apart from the somewhat anomalous *Lazarus* placed near the end of the manuscript. *Conspiracy*, comprising the Conspiracy by Pilate and the High Priests to take Jesus, the Last Supper, the Agony in the Garden and the Arrest, contains some stanzas in the form used by the Wakefield Master but these are in the minority and the rest of the play is written largely in three other verse patterns, as we have noticed. Moreover, the dramatic style of the various components varies considerably. It looks as though the whole play has been assembled to cover a significant swathe of narrative. It begins with a boast by Pilate which follows the conventions of writing for tyrants observed elsewhere in the cycle and perhaps deriving ultimately from precedents at York. If this opening speech by Pilate has a strategic significance as the beginning of the Passion, it is in marked contrast to the speech of Deus which begins

*Annunciation*: foreboding and corrupt rather than divinely beneficent. This section (20/1–77) is written in the thirteen-line stanzas of the Wakefield Master and its presence at this point, if the presumed dating of his work is correct, means that this beginning at least was written long before the present manuscript was copied. The diversity found in the other sections, however, means that parts of the play may have been written later.[14] The play has an 'explicit' in which it is designated *Capcio Jesu* (after 20/779). The inconsistency of this with the title, 'conspiracio [et]c', written at the head of the play, may suggest that the scribe or compiler was working from different manuscripts in organizing the components of this text. The presence of such a play, taking account of its strategic importance in the narrative together with its apparent diversity, is a significant indication of the way in which the process of compiling the cycle was carried out. It is apparent that this composite play matches neither the pattern of the York plays, which are rarely composite even though they may have more than one location, as in *Dream of Pilate's Wife* (30) or the York *Resurrection* (38); nor is it similar to the common two-phase structure characteristic of the Chester plays. It seems likely that this irregular structure is a feature of the compilation process rather than being determined by the practice of performance. Indeed it rather militates against a theory of performance, as we have noted. We might also point out that if *Conspiracy* were performed its flowing structure and multi-located scenario would suit a place and scaffold setting rather than one on a pageant wagon. A further element in *Conspiracy* suggests that it has strategic importance. When Christ is at the Mount of Olives he is advised and comforted by a character called Trinitas. This voice has a long and sweeping view of salvation history not unlike that of Deus in *Annunciation*. Even if it is anachronistic, Trinitas refers to the importance of the Passion:

To tyme that childe to deth were dight,
And rasyd hymself apon the thryd day,
And stevend to heuen thrugh his awne myght.
Who may do that bot God veray?   (20/568–71)[15]

To these aspects we should add two further features of the plays not showing the work of the Wakefield Master: some indications of theatrical technique and the presence of lyrical passages.[16] In a way these features are rather contradictory: some plays in the first aspect show a sophisticated skill in the creation of dramatic dialogue and the development of what might appear in a modern performance as tense theatrical situations in the dynamic of the relationship between the characters, whilst the second aspect means that this very dynamism can be interrupted by or juxtaposed to speeches of a more static nature. For the former we have discussed the dramatic sophistication of the dialogue in *Abraham* and *Thomas* (above, pp. 132–4). The qualities of dramatic expression we have observed argue for a strong grasp of ways of developing a biblical narrative in a vigorous dramatic way, and using the advantages of dramatic form, especially dialogue and movement, to increase the effect of the incidents upon the audience.

Lyrical passages are scattered across several plays in the cycle and their presence undoubtedly diversifies the dramatic experience. They are usually composed in a variety of strict prosodic forms, which in themselves make a striking contrast with other forms of verse embodying the rest of the dialogue. They are often a means of building up what we might describe as religious emotion. That is to say that they have a devotional import-ance expressed through their emotional content and one may suspect that these passages are linked with some devotional practices outside the plays. It is also true that some of them have distinctive non-dramatic analogues or indeed that they are themselves versions of poems which have been found elsewhere and in non-dramatic contexts. The use of such passages is not unique to Towneley and their presence in other cycles suggests that devotion is clearly part of the experience of being present at the plays. Here they include Gabriel's salutation of Mary in *Annunciation* (10/77–106) and the adoration by both groups of Shepherds and the Magi (12/660–98, 13/1024–62, 14/541–58). Mary's lamentation in *Crucifixion* (23/396–423) is another traditional feature and one occurring widely within dramatic contexts and outside them. The same is perhaps true of Christ's address to the Daughters of Jerusalem and his words to the people from the cross (23/233–96). The latter is echoed in his two later speeches on his wounds: the one in *Resurrection* is apparently original to Towneley (26/230–350) and that in *Judgement* is found in a passage based on the York version (30/560–607). Thomas has a magnificent lyric as his plea for mercy after his recognition of Christ (28/569–616). The horrors experi-enced by Lazarus are also expressed in lyric form in a passage derived from a sermon, but here they are given poetic form in two consecutive but distinct verse forms (31/111–93 and 194–217).[17] Among these passages only the speeches by the Shepherds are in the Wakefield Master's stanza. Even though a few of them derive from York, it seems that other writers who contributed to the cycle chose to incorporate lyrical form.

Finally we note that although Towneley conforms broadly with the selection of incidents in other cycles there are some idiosyncrasies. With regard to the manuscript itself to some extent we have to guess. There are no preliminaries such as a set of banns. More importantly the large lacuna which cuts out the end of *Resurrection* and the beginning of *Judgement* comprised twelve manuscript folios. It seems likely that at this point in the cycle a substantial amount of drama dealing with the end of the life of the Virgin was originally present, in parallel to the text at York, and that the loss is due to Protestant antipathy to such material. However, the loss of some leaves in the Creation may well have been accidental. It is more difficult to explain the unexpected absence of a Nativity play as such and the paucity of work dealing with Christ's Temptation and his Ministry, and yet these absences might well have occurred by default, a lack of available texts at the time of the compilation of the manuscript. Had there ever been a performance of this cycle, about which our reservations have been made plain, it is difficult to imagine that it would not have been a necessity.

# 4.2

# Playing and Reception

---

The assumptions we are making about the nature of the text must reflect upon any kind of performance theory for the Towneley plays. The salient stages in its development suggest two important factors influencing performance: the time at which the cycle was assembled remains obscure even if it was thought worthwhile to copy the material in the 1550s, and indeed it is not certain that this combining happened at one particular time as there is always the possibility of accretion over a number of years. If the Wakefield Master was a fifteenth-century author, and we put his work alongside the York borrowings which must be of roughly the same period, we still do not arrive necessarily at a cycle which was performed annually for a long period. Possibly it remained fragmentary with its parts not fully related for some time. L. M. Clopper has suggested that perhaps a passion play was created initially and this is plausible even if two of the York borrowings, *Pharaoh* and *Doctors*, do not fit the proposition.[1] It is also possible that there was an independent and coherent Advent series.[2] Palpably the texts of individual plays remain obstinately different and carry with them the possibility of quite different performance intentions or outcomes.

On a broader scale these textual considerations lead us to doubt whether there could have been a performance culture for plays at Wakefield in the fifteenth century. Whereas in York, and possibly in Chester and Coventry, the presentation of the local cycle was a community activity and one for which the necessary complex logistical and financial processes were put in place, it is more difficult to deduce such a one for Wakefield. There is a possibility that this might have developed to some extent in the mid-sixteenth century, if the evidence of customary performances before 1556 is reliable, but there seems little likelihood of this occurring in the previous century, as it did at York. In the more established centres performance problems and traditions would be regularly addressed, and since there may well have been rivalry between guilds, each would have developed its own way of doing things. Such a process implies an audience with a particular mindset, or at least implies some common expectations, comparisons (with last year and with other guild performances this year) and the reciprocal feeling that might be established when you know that a neighbour who is a bookbinder in real life is playing the part of Abraham. Such localized responses would have gone along with the devotional aspects which we have found to be of such importance in the experience of witnessing a performance. To this we should add the presence of liturgical music at certain places in the cycle, as noted in Chapter 2.3. Even though this is not as plentiful as it is in the other English cycles it was obviously thought valuable at certain places in Towneley. Presumably such elements would require the presence of musicians and must have been allowed for the arrangements for performance.

We have already indicated the there is some uncertainty about whether the Towneley text implies a wagon-based performance or the use of place and scaffold mode. The issue remains controversial but there does seem to be a distinction between playing within a localized place, such as in a cottage, in a stable or in Pilate's hall, and carrying out the action in a more general unlocalized place which could, by its very nature as not being defined, be more accessible to the audience. This differentiation could occur in playing on a pageant wagon, assuming that it was accepted that it was normal to play down on the street as well as on the wagon.[3] If, as Cami D. Agan suggests, this were the case for the place where the Ark is constructed in the Towneley *Noah* and the place of torment in *Scourging*, it might mean that the unlocalized area was closer to the audience, the dramatic threshold being different. Such a disposition might alter the extent to which the audience felt close to the action, indeed to be implicated in it. If Christ suffered in such a general place, the audience might be given a deeper sense of being part of the action.[4] Witnessing violence accompanied by bloodshed is attractive as well as repulsive and the lowering of liminality might well enhance this by giving greater accessibility.

Bearing the manipulation of playing places in mind, we now turn to the related matter of the length of the plays. It is true that even in the York text, whose relationship to pageant-wagon performance is not now seriously doubted, the plays are not of uniform length, and as Alan H. Nelson pointed out this does give rise to some difficulty about how to timetable the procession as the units are dissimilar in playing time.[5] There is quite a contrast at York between the length of *Creation* (2), with 86 lines, and *The Dream of Pilate's Wife* (30), with 546 lines. But in the Towneley text the contrasts seem to be even greater, especially in regard to *Second Shepherds* (1088) and *Conspiracy* (779) as compared with *Jacob* (142). It would seem that this factor, together with the uncertainty over the use of multi-centred scenarios is the result of the process of compilation rather than one naturally arising out of the dynamics of processional performance. As we have found elsewhere the circumstances of the compilation of the text may well define the problems of performance.

We should also note here some features of the subject matter and the dramatic style. The Wakefield Master's plays are often influenced or motivated by farce and also by satirical impulses closely related to the social abuses he wished to attack. It may be that in this he was in part extending some of the practices already embodied in the York Cycle. The physical distance between York and Wakefield is not great, and York had established a reputation of some importance. But his style of dramatization may not have been developed for processional performance, and his intended audience may have been different from that found in the streets of fifteenth-century York, Coventry or Chester. Though it is difficult to quantify, it also seems likely that the Wakefield Master, in his complete plays, expected a different reaction from his audience from that implied in many of the rest of the Towneley plays. The higher incidence of irony in his plays, for instance, is remarkable. Nevertheless, in other places his minor interventions suggest that he was prepared to go along with the impact expected by the other dramatists and not controvert them.

If these ideas are credible, then we cannot suppose that there was ever one audience for the plays. Even though it is a feature of cycle plays in general that they should embrace varieties of style and performance – a feature which has been evident in many revivals in modern times especially where the directors of individual plays have been allowed free rein – it would seem that the Towneley collection is as exceptionally diverse in respect of the varied expectations of audience response as it is diverse in dramatic styles. The iconic moments such as the adoration of the Shepherds, Christ's words from the cross and his repeated exposure of his wounds in *Thomas* and *Judgement* come from a variety of provenances and their inclusion is a marked feature in the cycle and one which contrasts boldly with the satirical intensity in most of the Wakefield Master's work. It is worth recalling here that in our discussion in Chapter 1.4 of the varieties of language in the cycle, there are some distinctive features in the language employed by the Wakefield Master, particularly in respect of demotic vocabulary and the use of proverbs. In short, his work sounds different from the rest of the cycle.

If we take an overall view of the aspects of playing discussed here, it is plain that there are many aspects of individual plays in the text which imply a strong sense of theatrical effects. Many of the effects achieved can be seen as paralleled in other cycles. The incorporation of elements from the York Cycle means that to some extent at least they were considered appropriate and fitting to place alongside parts of the cycle not borrowed in this way. However, even though diversity in playing style is characteristic of the other cycles, it does seem that Towneley presents a unique challenge in testing the bounds of what can be sustained in a single work. The diversity we have observed does seem to be greater here than elsewhere. Moreover, there is nothing in the other cycles which matches the work of the Wakefield Master: he seems to inject so much that is different, even eccentric, into Towneley, and this requires us to be aware of his assumptions about the nature of the dramatic experience.

# 4.3

# Interpretations and Structure

We have to approach the conclusion of our discussion with the idea that one single comprehensive interpretation of a work as complex as Towneley is hardly possible. To an extent this undermines the evaluation of the notion of unity which has been the chief preoccupation of this study, and this is made the more emphatic because of the divided authorship which is so apparent. This is not to forget that in any case divided authorship does seem to have been a feature at York and most probably at N Town.[1] Here we shall review a number of different interpretations which can be seen to apply to Towneley and through them we may perceive aspects which are characteristic of it. Some of them will also arise in the interpretation of the other extant cycles, but we must always be sensitive to difference as well as to similarity and there is no doubt that in many ways Towneley does differ markedly from its analogues in this genre.

The selection of incidents and their presentation reflects a variety of devotional motifs. The presence of Christ in different capacities offers the paradox of his suffering and his triumph. In the Passion sequence in particular the presentation of his suffering in visual terms is persistent and disturbing over a number of plays. In this sequence there is no clear way of identifying individual authors even though the Wakefield Master does seem to have participated in many of the plays, to the extent that one feels that he had a particular interest in the portrayal of the sufferings of Christ, presumably with pious motives. The visual effect is made the sharper by the mocking words added to the blows. As at York, Christ is largely silent through these spectacles but that does not detract from the dramatic effect of his presence.[2] This silent presence has continued to have a powerful effect in modern productions of the cycle.

One further aspect to the actions of Christ makes some impact in the later stages of the Towneley Cycle. There is a good deal of emphasis upon mystery involved in his appearances after the Crucifixion in the

*Resurrection* (26), *Pilgrims* (27) and *Thomas* (28). The fact that this is a sequence, deliberately arranged, increases the impact of the mystery of his presence after the Resurrection. As Beckwith has pointed out in her study of the York Cycle, these appearances and their accompanying disappearances require that Christ be both recognizable and not recognizable.[3] The dramatic handling of these episodes in Towneley makes much of the surprise and mystery here, and we should recall that most of this material is original to Towneley and bears little sign of the work of the Wakefield Master. In both the Passion sequence, where Christ suffers and triumphs, and the episodes after the Passion the presence and the impact of Christ have been much developed by the contributing writers.

But Christ also appears triumphant and powerful especially in some of the episodes borrowed from York. This is apparent in *Harrowing* and *Judgement* where a Towneley dramatist has built upon the York original as well as in *Pilgrims* and *Thomas*, which are both plays written separately from the York version and indeed not showing the influence of the Wakefield Master. Further potent elements occur when Christ is shown in contact with his mother (*Scourging* 22/375–442; *Crucifixion* 23/411–502). This has a notable effect upon the way in which Christ is perceived. At the same time these interchanges bring out the devotional importance of the Virgin. Indeed her presence is much in evidence and she acts as a silent witness to most of the important events, including in *Ascension* (29/334–451). We have seen that she is given a number of potent speeches composed in lyric form which were no doubt meant to stimulate an emotional response from the audience. The impact she makes in this respect is remarkable and we should notice that such effects, which are a reflection and an embodiment of devotional practices, are not unique to Towneley. They are brought about in a variety of different ways from cycle to cycle. In *Passion d'Auvergne*, for example, the cycle is constructed to be performed over several days and it appears from the surviving fragments from three individual days that each day's performance was so constructed that it ended with a meeting between her and Christ.[4]

The selection of incidents in Towneley presents us with two other notable features: the shape of the Old Testament narrative and the presence of the devils. The Old Testament episodes carry out the function of showing human fallibility and also the complementary obedience shown by Noah, Abraham and Moses. But we also find that these iconic characters are given individuality and a palpable reality, a feature we have noticed in the characterization of Isaac and Jacob. As Michael O'Connell has suggested, the sacred history is humanized in this cycle.[5] This may well apply even to Cain and Mak, although they are obviously not in the group of the specially chosen characters destined for salvation. In this process the Wakefield Master no doubt made a significant contribution but it is clear that his was not the only voice, and it may well be that by his selection of material the compiler has brought out this feature emphatically. The establishment of the principal characters in the Old Testament history is also part of the linking with later elements in the life of Christ: Adam as pre-figuring Christ, Isaac as sacrificial victim anticipating the Crucifixion, and the passage of the Israelites through the Red Sea as Baptism. The compiler was no doubt impelled to reflect such links in his selection of material and thus to follow and promote what may well be regarded as conventional links. I would suggest that this is likely to happen even if there are not specific pointers to such parallels. The links were made too often in iconography and indeed in other dramas for them not to be available and within the experience of the audience. J. W. Earl points to the Old Testament sequence up to Moses as being concerned with the time of deviation and indicates that the readings it comprised were part of the Septuagesima liturgy.[6]

Towneley has been much noticed for its presentation of evil characters. The devils play a major role in *Harrowing* and *Judgement*, and they are one of the features which especially interested the Wakefield Master who expanded them. I think, however, that we should avoid over-emphasizing the coherence of the demonology. It is notable that C. W. Marx did not include Towneley into his theory about the plotting of the devil and the counteraction of divine deception which he had noticed in other cycle plays, particularly N Town.[7] There is no play about the dream of Pilate's wife in Towneley, an episode showing the devil's intervention in human affairs at a late stage in the life of Christ.[8] It was there apparently in York to be borrowed but apparently the choice was not made. Instead Towneley offers spectacular devil incidents, some of them innovative, as in *Harrowing* and *Judgement*, but it also gives much scope for human wickedness in individuals in the Old Testament stories and those of the New Testament. Indeed the main narrative of the Passion, from *Conspiracy* to *Dicing* (20–4) presents us emphatically with human cruelty and wickedness. These too may be described as spectacular in as much as the dialogues of the Torturers and Soldiers and the threats and machinations of the tyrants form a distinctive element in the cycle.

We have discussed a variety of social matters in the Towneley plays. The absence of a developed urban culture turns our attention to different issues from those embodying the guild politics of York. In its place we find reflections of tyranny and oppression as well as a good deal of attention to the predicaments of the poor: 'Poore men ar in the dyke,' says John Horne, the shepherd (12/135). The difficulty of labour and the need to come to terms with the working world are also themes, presented mostly by the Wakefield Master.[9] The underlying purpose in dealing with these themes may well be to enhance the devotional urge but there is always a feeling that subversion is not far away. The secular authorities are almost always portrayed as tyrannical.[10] Such tyranny separates men from divine law and perverts the process of uniting all, which is the special role of Christ. There is a polarity between corrupt earthly power and divine kingship.[11] Much of this is centred on the role of Pilate who emerges as a dominating villain in a number of plays, particularly in *Dicing*.[12] Here and elsewhere tyrants are used by the dramatists – not only the Wakefield Master – with the social purpose of making a comment on the misuse of authority. At the same time the interaction with their chief victim – even though he is a silent participant in the exchange – makes for a reflection upon him too. The necessity of his suffering and his submission is set off by the extravagancies of corrupt authority. His own exercise of authority is *ipso facto* beyond criticism in *Harrowing* and *Judgement*.

A great deal depends upon whether one sees the Wakefield Master, with all his carnival impulses, as subversive or conformist. The departure from orthodoxy implied in the celebration of vigorous dissent may well point away from the latter. But in the end he does bring the Shepherds to the Christ-child and they are changed, as Slawpase says: 'We mon all be restorde – / God graunt it be so!' (12/716–17) Conversely Cain cannot be redeemed and he is hardly a lovable rogue. His subversiveness is ingeniously presented, but it is hardly approved. Nevertheless, a Marxist perspective might suggest that the explicit presentation of the social and economic forces of repression do not reveal a society capable of improvement. It seems likely that this tension between subversion and orthodoxy is one of the features of the plays that makes them interesting, at least as far as those by the Wakefield Master are concerned. But perhaps we should also link thematically his articulation of the suffering of the poor with the suffering of Christ which is presented in the Passion sequence.

One outstanding feature here is the effect of *Lazarus*, anomalously placed after *Judgement*. Perhaps this placing makes the play all the more emphatic. If one takes a figurative view, Lazarus is commonly an anticipation of the Resurrection, but that is effectively negated by the play's present position. However, it does contain one of the most positive statements by Christ of his mission and that may go some way towards justifying the placing here:

I warne you, both man and wyfe,
That I am rysyng and I am life;
And whoso truly trowys in me,
That I was euer and ay shall be,
Oone thyng I shall hym gif:
Though he be dede, yit shall he lif.    (31/51–6)

The particular phraseology of this may well recall the words of Deus in *Annunciation* linking Adam and Eve to Mary and Christ (10/32–4), and the Trinitas in *Conspiracy* (especially 20/568–71, quoted above, p. 217). Two terminal features may well be operating in *Lazarus*, and one may see in them indications of the overall significance of this episode based upon its location. 'That I was euer and ay shall be' is a recall of the 'alpha and omega' motif which stands as the first idea in the cycle (1/1–2), as it does conventionally with other cycles. The second is that Christ's declaration is a warning (51) and what follows in the eloquent speech of Lazarus brings home the warning in no uncertain terms by its threat about what is to come to those who ignore the warning (103–231). In the rhetoric of this speech the structure switches from the repeated 'Ye . . . Youre . . .' to the imperative 'Take hede . . . Amende . . . Amende'.[13]

There is a further articulation of the oppressed when it comes to the role of women in the cycle. For several of them the possibility of dissent and the assertion of the difficulties of ordinary life are a vigorous issue in a number of plays. And just as we have a turning for the Shepherds towards a better life, so for Noah's Wife there arises trust and cooperation in place of suspicion and violence. Mak's Wife is apparently not touched by the rather limited retribution visited upon her husband. She remains a vigorous and independent voice and one who expresses the predicament and the burdens of marriage and childbearing. The vigour of this presentation is in marked contrast, a dialectic opposition, to the crude caricatures of women's lives by Gyb, the Second Shepherd, and Mak, and it is interesting that the Wakefield Master makes these so questionable by means of their crudeness.

Several of the women's roles outside those envisaged by the Wakefield Master fulfil a more conventional pattern, especially with regard to family contexts, as with Rebecca (*Isaac*), Rachel (*Jacob*) and Elizabeth

(*Salutation*).[14] Mary the Virgin follows this in *Flight* and in *Doctors*, though in this respect Towneley reduces her function from that in the York version. But in the Passion sequence her major role, as we have suggested, is to be the witness of Christ's suffering and to share in it emotionally. In this she is complemented by Mary Magdalene (*Scourging* 22/450–61; *Resurrection* 26/351–441). Thus the Virgin's role shifts away from the social aspects of gender towards devotion. Indeed her body, notwithstanding her emotions, is an iconic feature of these plays, though the loss from the text before *Judgement* makes this difficult to assess fully. It would seem that through the power of such icons her physical presence is meant to match that of her son, but to enhance it and not to be a rival.

The salient features we have considered suggest that there are a number of features in the cycle which are distinctive and which make for coherence. However, it is not possible to attribute to Towneley the same kind of consistencies which might appear in the cycles from York and Chester. This may be the result of the distinctive features of the context of Wakefield in contrast with the other two. But if we consider the York and Chester cycles more closely we find that they too are held together by differing bonds. Cycle plays were widespread in Europe in general and even though there are relatively few in England they do seem to have constituted a successful genre, and one which lasted in active performance for up to two hundred years. The members of this class, however, do not conform to strict patterns and the means by which they are held together are individual and diverse. The genesis of the Towneley Cycle lies within this broad tradition and though some elements may be relatively early, it seems likely that it was put together when the genre was well established and in some measure of conformity with it. It is distinguished by a varied authorship and by a considerable range of dramatic styles. Cycle drama evidently tolerated variety and no doubt thrived upon it, but perhaps Towneley was more diverse than many others. The extensive borrowing from York and the presence of large interventions by the Wakefield Master are not closely matched by other elements in the cycle many of which have distinctive dramatic qualities of their own. Indeed, the peculiar abilities of the Wakefield Master, which amount to eccentricity in some respects, are in general not well integrated into the cycle, though it must be admitted that many of his minor interventions are hardly at odds with the plays in which they are found. This means that a critical approach to the cycle must always take account of centrifugal aspects, and that generalization about its qualities should be qualified by the limitations to its unity we have been discussing. It is true to say that much criticism in the past has been negligent or even ignorant of the complexity of this text.

But if the Wakefield Master's work is in some ways divisive, it is also rich, suggestive and successful, and it takes a place among a variety of other striking effects. The compilation of the cycle reveals strength in a number of other ways which we should finally recall here. The accumulation of the heroes of the Old Testament who represent the time of deviation is powerful and impressive. There is an engaging cluster of plays following the intervention of Deus at the Annunciation and surrounding the Advent sequence. Though the Ministry is slightly represented, the Passion sequence is theatrically powerful. During this, the presence of Christ in the various constituent events is both potent and disturbing. The cruel features of his suffering, much emphasized by the affective piety prevalent in the fifteenth century, are exploited by the Wakefield Master and by other contributing authors.[15] The sequence showing this is followed by a group of plays which continue to present him but with a different emphasis, pointing instead to mystery and power.

The Towneley Cycle may not have been generated by one dramatist or several deliberately setting out to achieve these effects but they are palpably there, even if the most creative aspect of them is what we have referred to repeatedly as a process of compilation. But then compilation was seen in medieval times as creative in essence. As we now find these plays we can also appreciate that many of the episodes have a practical strength in performance. The individual components are the material from which performance may be generated today, even if the cycle was never performed in the way the manuscript implies. Further practical exploration of the theatrical qualities which are inherent in these texts may well generate a greater awareness of the cycle's distinctive qualities. As regards the bibliographical aspects of the cycle discussed in this study, through them we may gain a more accurate awareness of how the cycle was generated and the diversity of the materials which went into its compilation. However disparate these may be, there is no doubt that some person or persons unknown meant to fit them together within the conventions of late medieval cyclic drama. Even if we sense that the Wakefield Master with his individualistic holiness was pulling away from the other dramatists in the cycle, one of Towneley's most abiding characteristics is its presentation of the mystery of the Christological narrative, and this mystery invites many voices.

## Retrospect

Looking back over this study I should like to sum up what I think it has revealed, and also to point to some persisting areas of uncertainty. The Towneley text is undoubtedly a cycle, put together to conform with contemporary models, and in an intimate, if intermittent, relationship with the cycle at York and possibly with cycles at Beverley, Doncaster and Pontefract, its near neighbours and contemporaries.[16] It contains the work of a number of authors of whom the Wakefield Master is the most powerful contributor. His identifiable work extends over much but not of all of the cycle, but it appears that other dramatists, much neglected in critical accounts, also made distinctive contributions, especially in *Abraham, Isaac, Jacob, Annunciation, Salutation, Conspiracy* and *Thomas*. The Wakefield Master's work is sometimes carefully integrated with the achievement of other writers but sometimes it is so distinctive as to be at odds with it.

There is still much to be done in the study of the language of the cycle and its variations in the aftermath of the publication of the *Linguistic Atlas of Late Medieval English*,[17] but I think that the indications are that the language of the scribe and probably that of the authors (with the exception of those working for the York Cycle) was closely associated with Wakefield or its near environs. Some aspects of the language, some social aspects and some circumstantial details suggest that much, if not all of the cycle, was generated in the fifteenth century even though the manuscript may have been assembled or copied much later. The span between the dates of composition of individual items and the date of the manuscript has widened considerably of late and somewhere in between comes the act of compilation. But we should notice that there is little doubt that this must have happened before the middle of the sixteenth century and probably rather earlier: this is a late medieval work in its entirety.

However, we should not insist that such a compilation happened as one single event. A priori it must be possible – and in fact it does seem more than likely – that a number of sections came into being separately, such as the *Isaac* and *Jacob* pair, the two Shepherds plays, the putative Advent sequence and *Conspiracy*, which seems in itself to be a combination of elements with differing origins. The individuality of such elements argues strongly against a comprehensive unity and we are thus left with a process of 'compilation', of putting differing items together so that they may reflect upon one another in what may now seem an open-ended way. Under the aegis of medieval Catholicism, itself not exactly monolithic, the cycle operates as a work of faith and it reflects many of the mysteries, miracles and paradoxes of religious belief at the time of its creation as well as being for most of the time affirmative of such belief and a reflection of intense emotional experience. It also embodies a number of pressing social issues. These aspects are ascertainable even if the purpose of copying the manuscript is not. Some of its features, especially the rubrication and the elaborate initial capitals, suggest that the objective was for it to be read and contemplated as a book in much the same way as were *Books of Hours*. Its relationship to performance remains problematic.

Nevertheless, the dramatic qualities of the cycle are exceptionally varied, reflecting the different origins of its components. We cannot be certain that this text was ever performed as a whole before the modern attempts, but it does seem highly likely that in the Marian period at least, and perhaps for some time before it, a play associated with Corpus Christi was presented by the guilds at Wakefield. However, we are still left with much uncertainty about exactly what was performed and the circumstances of its enactment. This is especially tantalizing in view of the brilliant theatrical writing in many parts of the cycle which has excited many directors, actors and audiences in modern times and will no doubt continue to do so.

# Notes

## Introduction: The Problem of Unity

[1] John Gardner, *The Construction of the Wakefield Cycle* (Carbondale and Edwardsville: Southern Illinois University Press, 1974), p. 135. See also Jeffrey Helterman, *Symbolic Action in the Plays of the Wakefield Master* (Athens, GA: University of Georgia Press, 1981); Martin Stevens, *Four Middle English Mystery Cycles* (Princeton: Princeton University Press, 1987); J. W. Robinson, *Studies in Fifteenth-Century Stagecraft* (Kalamazoo: Medieval Institute, 1991). Cecilia Pietropoli identifies a precise moral function for the plays and asserts that poetic justice (*giustizia poetica*) is done, *Il teatro dei Miracoli e delle Moralità* (Naples: Liguori, 1996), pp. 82–4. Further material regarding the unity of cycle plays in general is to be found in Jerome Taylor, 'The dramatic structure of the Middle English Corpus Christi, or Cycle, Plays' in Jerome Taylor and Alan H. Nelson (eds), *Medieval English Drama: Essays Critical and Contextual* (Chicago and London: University of Chicago Press, 1972), pp. 148–56, with reference to the importance of Corpus Christi as a focus; and Kevin J. Harty, 'The unity and structure of the Chester Mystery Cycle' in Kevin J. Harty (ed.) *The Chester Mystery Cycle: A Casebook* (New York and London: Garland, 1993), pp. 69–88, in which he identifies 'Monastically inspired concern for prophecy, Christian perfection and the end-times' (p. 85) as unifying forces.

[2] *The Wakefield Pageants in the Towneley Cycle* (Manchester: Manchester University Press, 1958). Unless otherwise specified all references to the Towneley Cycle are to *The Towneley Plays*, ed. Martin Stevens and A. C. Cawley, 2 vols, EETS s.s. 13 (Oxford: Oxford University Press, 1994): Stevens and Cawley, *Plays* henceforward.

[3] Garrett P. J. Epp, 'The Towneley plays and the hazards of cycling', *RORD*, 32 (1993), 121–50 (138). See also James Gordon and Joseph Hunter, (eds), *The Towneley Mysteries* (London: Surtees Society, 1836), p. x; R. Woolf, *The English Mystery Plays* (London: Routledge, 1972), p. 310; David Mills, '"The Towneley Plays" or "The Towneley Cycle"?', *LSE* 17 (1986), 95–104 (95); B. D. Palmer, '"Towneley Plays" or "Wakefield Cycle" Revisited', *CD* 21 (1987–8), 318–48, 'Corpus Christi Cycles in Yorkshire: The Surviving Records', *CD* 27 (1993), 218–31, 'Recycling "The Wakefield Cycle": The Records', *RORD* 41 (2002), 88–130.

4   For the possible Marian dating see Barbara D. Palmer, 'Recycling "The Wakefield Cycle", especially 88, n. 6, and 96.

5   Alexandra F. Johnston, 'The city as patron: York', in Paul Whitfield White and Suzanne R. Westfall (eds), *Shakespeare and Theatrical Patronage in Early Modern England* (Cambridge: Cambridge University Press, 2002), pp. 150–75 (p. 150).

6   S. Spector (ed.), *The N-Town Play: Cotton MS Vespasian D.8*, EETS s.s. 11, vol. 2, (Oxford: Oxford University Press, 1991) 543, noted by Epp, pp. 138–9. Peter Meredith's analysis of the N Town text suggests that it is 'in the process of being put together . . . and not the finished product', 'Manuscript, scribe and performance: further looks at the N Town manuscript', in Felicity Riddy, (ed.), *Regionalism in Late Medieval Manuscripts and Texts* (Cambridge: D. S. Brewer, 1991), pp. 109–28 (p. 109).

7   'English drama: From ungodly *Ludi* to sacred play', in David Wallace (ed.), *The Cambridge History of Medieval English Literature* (Cambridge: Cambridge University Press, 1999), pp. 739–66 (pp. 752–3).

8   For changes in scribal procedure see *The Towneley Cycle: A Facsimile of Huntington MS HMI*, ed. A. C. Cawley and M. Stevens (Leeds: University of Leeds, 1976), pp. xiii–xiv. We shall deal more specifically with the lesser discontinuities in the arrangement of the manuscript in Chapter 1.1 below.

9   The naming of the Wakefield Master may be attributed to C. M. Gayley, who mentioned the 'Wakefield master' [*sic*] as the author of *Dicing* in his collection entitled *Representative English Comedies* (New York: Macmillan, 1903), p. xxviii. A few years later he has a chapter entitled 'The Wakefield Master' in his *Plays of our Forefathers* (London: Chatto and Windus, 1908), pp. 161–90. Anticipating this to some extent, A. W. Pollard identified six plays by a poet he called 'the Wakefield editor', in his Introduction to G. England (ed.), *The Towneley Plays,* EETS e.s. 71 (Oxford: Oxford University Press), p. xxii. The identity was much developed by A. C. Cawley in *The Wakefield Pageants in the Towneley Cycle*.

10  For a consideration of parts of the cycle not attributable to the Wakefield Master see my 'The Towneley Cycle without the Wakefield Master', *RORD,* 45 (2006), 23–38.

11  The full records are transcribed in A. C. Cawley, J. Forrester, and J. Goodchild, 'References to the Corpus Christi Play in the Wakefield Burgess Court rolls: the originals rediscovered', *LSE,* 19 (1988), 85–104, where the evidence about the fabrication is presented. The uncertified elaborations were made in J. W. Walker, 'The Burgess Court, Wakefield: 1533, 1554, 1556, and 1579', *Yorkshire Archaeological Society Records Series*, lxxiv (1929), pp. 16–32. See also B. D. Palmer, ' "Towneley Plays" or "Wakefield Cycle" revisited', 325–8.

12  Barbara Palmer has pointed out that the 1559 record falls into the reign of Elizabeth I, and this may mean that the record refers to the possible suppression of the cycle, 'Recycling "The Wakefield Cycle": the records', 94.

13  The full text of the letter is transcribed in Cawley, *Wakefield Pageants*, p. 125.

14  One inconsistency between this brief description and the plays is that the establishment of the eucharist is not shown in the text as we now have it.

[15]  See my *Cyclic Form and the English Mystery Plays* (Amsterdam and New York: Rodopi, 2004), pp. 34–40.

[16]  The plays in 1415 are listed in A. F. Johnston and M. Rogerson (eds), *REED: York* (Toronto: University of Toronto Press, 1979), pp. 16–26. For the date of the York manuscript, see Richard Beadle, (ed.) *The York Plays* (London: Edward Arnold, 1982), pp. 10–11. For a discussion of the varying relationship between the York guilds and their plays see Alexandra F. Johnston, 'The city as patron: York', pp. 150–75. Meg Twycross has recently questioned the accepted time for beginning the York performance and in consequence there is now a little more uncertainty about the relationship between the 1415 list and the Register compiled at some point in the years 1463 to 1477: 'Forget the 4.30a.m. start: recovering a palimpsest in the York *Ordo paginarum*', *METh*, 25 (2003), 98–152.

[17]  P. Meredith, 'John Clerke's hand in the York Register', *LSE*, 12 (1981), 245–71.

[18]  'Verbal texture and wordplay in the York Cycle', *ET*, 3 (2000), 167–84.

[19]  E. K. Chambers tabulates the selection of incidents in the five complete English cycles, *The Medieval Stage*, vol. 2 (Oxford: Clarendon Press, 1933), pp. 321–3. This shows a remarkable degree of similarity between the four English cycles.

[20]  For a summary of the evidence about the cycle at Beverley, see Alan H. Nelson, *The Medieval English Stage: Corpus Christi Pageants and Plays* (Chicago and London: University of Chicago Press, 1974), pp. 91–4 and n. 20.

[21]  L. M. Clopper, *Drama, Play and Game: English Festive Culture in the Medieval and Early Modern Period*, (Chicago and London: University of Chicago Press, 2002), p. 181. For details of the Chester manuscripts see *The Chester Mystery Cycle*, ed. R. M. Lumiansky and David Mills, 2 vols, EETS s.s. 3, 9 (Oxford: Oxford University Press, 1974 and 1986), vol. 1, pp. ix–xxvii.

[22]  G. J. Betcher, 'A reassessment of the date and provenance of the Cornish *Ordinalia*', *CD*, 29 (1995–6), 35–63.

[23]  The Coventry Plays were no doubt as well known as the York Cycle in the fifteenth century, attracting royal attendance in a comparable manner, but the difficulty inherent in them is that we have no positive evidence that the episodes in this cycle extended back before the Annunciation: See P. M. King and C. Davidson (eds) *The Coventry Corpus Christi Plays* (Kalamazoo: The Medieval Institute, 2000), p. 9.

[24]  A. J. Minnis, *Medieval Theory of Authorship: Scholastic Literary Attitudes in the Later Middle Ages*, second edition (Aldershot: Wildwood House, 1988), pp. 191–205. For the earlier aspects of the 'compilator' see M. B. Parkes, 'The influence of the concepts of ordinatio and compilatio on the development of the book', in his *Scribes, Scripts and Readers: Studies in the Communication, Presentation and Dissemination of Medieval Texts* (London: Hambledon Press, 1991), pp. 25–69 (pp. 58–9).

[25]  The compiler could have an emphatic, even ironic, voice of his own. Minnis, *Medieval Theory of Authorship*, p. 199, discusses Chaucer's exploitation of his own pretended role as a sort of compiler in *The Canterbury Tales, General Prologue*, ll. 725–46.

26  M. Stevens, 'The *Towneley Plays* manuscript: *Compilatio* and *Ordinatio*', *Text*,
    5 (1991), 157–73. The absence of banns is an intriguing question to which we
    shall return.
27  For details see P. Meredith, 'John Clerke's hand in the York Register'.

# 1  Prologue: Place and Date

1   See B. D. Palmer, '"Towneley Plays" or "Wakefield Cycle" Revisited'; 'Corpus
    Christi Cycles in Yorkshire: the surviving records'; 'Early English northern
    entertainment: patterns and peculiarities', *RORD*, 34 (1995); and 'Recycling "The
    Wakefield Cycle": the Records'. In the last Palmer raises the possibility that the
    cycle may have been compiled at Whalley Abbey under the aegis of the Towneley
    family who lived nearby.
2   Cawley, *Wakefield Pageants*, pp. xiv–xv.
3   M. G. Frampton, 'The date of the flourishing of the Wakefield Master', *PMLA*,
    50 (1935), 631–60.
4   Cawley, *Wakefield Pageants*, 130.

## 1.1  The Manuscript

1   Stevens and Cawley, accepting a considerable debt to Louis Wann's exhaustive
    bibliographical study, 'A new examination of the manuscript of the Towneley
    Plays', *PMLA*, 43 (1928), 137–52, place it after 1475 (*Plays*, 1.xv). My discussion
    of the text owes much to both these and to the Introduction to A. C. Cawley and
    M. Stevens (eds), *The Towneley Cycle: A Facsimile of Huntington MS HM1*
    (Leeds: University of Leeds, 1976). For the theory that the manuscript was Marian,
    see B. D. Palmer, 'Recycling "The Wakefield Cycle": the Records'.
2   The possible date of the composition of the cycle is reviewed in Chapter 4.3 below.
3   The key phrases are 'thurt the craue' and 'as a sympull knaue' (Towneley 25/262,
    264), as compared with 'þus þe I telle' and 'symple braide' (York 37/242, 244),
    where the rhyme has been lost. Full details are given in Stevens's *Four Middle
    English Mystery Cycles*, (Princeton: Princeton University Press, 1987), pp. 120–1.
    Richard Beadle printed the Towneley readings as evidenced by Clerke, in the text
    of his edition, and he records the main York scribe's version in notes, *The York
    Plays* (London: Edward Arnold, 1982), 37/242 and 244. Because the Towneley
    version rhymes correctly, the York must be a corruption.
4   See above p. 6. The pages of the manuscript showing hard use as listed are fols
    26v (9/64–108), 38v (13/18–84), 39r (13/85–149), 40v (13/278–342), 62v
    (18/57–104), 70r (20/376–425), 77r (21/447–512); see Louis Wann, 'A new exam-
    ination of the manuscript of the Towneley Plays', *PMLA*, 43 (1928), 137–52.
5   Stevens and Cawley, *Plays*, p. xvi. The appearance of this pressmark on the
    extant first page suggests that the loss of the first quire had already happened
    and there may have been an ideological cause for this.

6   The practices of placing speech headings to the right and of using horizontal
    separating lines are clear in the *York* manuscript (see *Facsimile*, p. xxvi), and they
    were followed by John Clerke when he copied two belated play texts into it *c.*1558–9
    (*The York Plays: A Facsimile of British Library MS Additional 35290*, ed. Richard
    Beadle and Peter Meredith (Leeds: University of Leeds, 1983), p. xxi). Similar
    procedure is followed in the N Town manuscript (late fifteenth century), though
    there the normal practice is to underline the name with a hooked red line (*The
    N-Town Plays: A Facsimile of British Library MS Cotton Vespasian D.VIII*, ed.
    Peter Meredith and S. J. Kahrl (Leeds: University of Leeds, 1977), p. xix.

7   Cawley and Stevens, *Facsimile*, xi m.1, xiii u, 7.

8   The practice of using brackets for rhymes is similar in the York manuscript,
    though there are some errors: see Beadle and Meredith, *The York Play: A
    Facsimile*, p. xxvi.

9   Stevens and Cawley present some evidence that they are the same hand: see
    *Plays*, p. xvii, n. 3.

10  The *First Shepherds* play has a similar procedure, and it may well be that it arose
    because he wanted to avoid confusion arising from the unusual step of having
    two plays on Shepherds: see Cawley and Stevens, *Facsimile*, pp. xiii–xiv. Having
    hit upon the method, it could have been re-used for the later sequence.

11  L. M. Clopper raises the possibility that the roles might refer to an ad hoc selection
    of individual plays for a performance rather than a presentation of the whole
    cycle: see *Drama, Play and Game: English Festive Culture in the Medieval and
    Early Modern Period* (Chicago and London: University of Chicago Press, 2002),
    p. 180. Barbara Palmer notes the possibility that John Payne Collier may have
    'meddled' with the manuscript when it was in his possession 1831–3, 'Recycling
    "The Wakefield Cycle": the Records', 91 and n. 20.

12  Stevens and Cawley, *Plays*, vol. 2, p. 651.

13  We should note however that Wann comments upon an irregularity in the sewing
    of the last quire which puts into question the contents of fols 129–32 containing
    the last two plays (139). When the scribe did make an error of transcription of
    fols 5v and 6, in *Mactatio Abel*, he was careful to show the correct order in which
    the sheets should be read: see Wann 142–3, and Stevens and Cawley, *Plays*,
    vol. 2, p. 444, n. 273–4.

14  Noted by G. R. Owst, *Literature and Pulpit in Medieval England* (Cambridge:
    Cambridge University Press, 1933), p. 487.

15  Black only 1, 3, 4, 5, 6, 13, 17, 19, 22, 25, 28, 29, 30, 31; red 20, 26; red and
    black 8, 18, 27. Wann notes 'that every one of the plays which deviates from
    the uniform use of black stage directions in Latin (8, 14, 18, 20, 26 and 27)
    belongs to the "York-borrowing" stage', (147). A fuller discussion of the theatrical
    function of the stage directions appears in Chapter 2.1 below.

16  This last removal also took away the opening lines of *Judgement*. For a broader
    account of Protestant changes to the mystery cycles see my ' "Erazed in the Booke":
    the mystery cycles and reform', in Lloyd Kermode, Jason Scott-Warren and
    Martine van Elk (eds), *Tudor Drama before Shakespeare, 1485–1590: New
    Directions for Research, Criticism, and Pedagogy* (New York and Basingstoke:

Palgrave, 2004), pp. 15–33; Cawley and Stevens, *Facsimile*, p. xii, n. 2. The role of Mary in the cycle will be considered in Chapter 3.1.

## 1.2 York and Towneley

1. M. C. Lyle, *The Original Identity of the York and Towneley Plays* (Minneapolis: University of Minnesota Press, 1919), p. 108.
2. On some aspects of linguistic homogeneity in York see R. Beadle, 'Verbal texture and wordplay in the York Cycle', *ET*, 3 (2000), 167–84. This apparent evenness of texture may in part be the result of 'ironing out' linguistic forms and normalizing by the dominant York scribe.
3. M. G. Frampton, 'The date of the flourishing of the Wakefield Master', *PMLA*, 50 (1935), 631–60. See also P. J. P. Goldberg, 'Craft guilds, the Corpus Christi play, and civic government', in his *Society, Politics and Culture* (Cambridge: Cambridge University Press, 1986), pp. 16–47.
4. The York connections, as in 'Let my people pas' (T8/136; T25/210) and 'maistries' (T8/34; T25/116, 222, 237), are discussed in R. Beadle, 'The York hosiers' play of *Moses and Pharaoh*: a middle English dramatist at work', *Poetica* (Tokyo), 19 (1984), 3–26 (20–1).
5. Septenars, rhyming ababab ab$_4$cdcd$_3$, are found in *Pharaoh* (8) and *Harrowing* (25), also deriving from York: see Stevens and Cawley, *Plays*, vol. 2, p. 591. Beadle, *York Plays*, p. 422, points out that this metre appears in twelve York plays, and also in the *Middle English Metrical Paraphrase of the Old Testament*, a source for the York *Abraham and Isaac* (10).
6. In general, as Stevens and Cawley point out, York and Towneley are closer together than any other Doctors play in the surviving mystery plays, which are themselves all derived from York (*Plays*, vol. 2, p. 534).
7. Stevens and Cawley, *Plays*, vol. 2, p. 291.
8. Stevens and Cawley offer this estimate of one-fifth, but it should be noted that it is based on their new line numbering which amounts to far more than in earlier editions because of their decision to print the Wakefield Master's stanzas as thirteen-liners, and there is consequently an increase in the line total over previous editions. If these stanzas were counted as nine-liners the proportion of York lines retained in Towneley would seem higher.
9. See Lyle, *Original Identity*, pp. 54–87.
10. Stevens and Cawley, *Plays*, vol. 1, p. xxvii.
11. Stevens and Cawley, *Plays*, p. 480, n. 51, 54. They point out that the structural similarities noted by Lyle may be due to following the same scriptural narrative rather than imitation.
12. P. Meredith, 'The Towneley Cycle', in R. Beadle (ed.), *The Cambridge Companion to Medieval English Theatre* (Cambridge: Cambridge University Press, 1994), pp. 134–62 (p. 147).
13. One York stanza, Y34/250–9, is omitted from this passage.
14. P. Meredith, 'The York millers' pageant and the Towneley *Processus Talentorum*', *METh*, 4 (1982), 104–14 (111); *REED: York*, 1.48.

[15] A. C. Cawley and M. Stevens, 'The Towneley *Processus Talentorum*: text and commentary', *LSE*, 17 (1986), 105–30.

[16] Stevens and Cawley, *Plays* (vol. 1, p. xxviii) and P. Meredith, 'The Towneley Cycle', p. 148, raise this possibility.

[17] P. Meredith, 'The Towneley Cycle', p. 148; for the common clerk, see his 'John Clerke's hand in the York Register', *LSE*, 12 (1981), 245–71.

[18] The most useful studies of the Towneley language and the changes from York are M. Trusler, 'The language of the Wakefield playwright', *SP*, 33 (1936), 15–39; A. C. Cawley (ed.), *The Wakefield Pageants in the Towneley Cycle* (Manchester: Manchester University Press, 1958), pp. xxxi–iii, and p. 130; M. Stevens, 'The accuracy of the Towneley scribe', *HLQ*, 22 (1958), 1–9; and, with particular reference to York, R. Beadle, 'Verbal texture and wordplay in the York Cycle'.

[19] M. L. Holford, 'Language and regional identity in the York Corpus Christi Cycle', *LSE*, 33 (2002), 171–96.

[20] T2/5–7, 148–9, Trusler, 'The language of the Wakefield playwright', 21, n. 21. The consistency of the Towneley scribe is also noted by Holford, 'Language and regional identity in the York Corpus Christi Cycle', 185.

[21] Trusler, 'The language of the Wakefield playwright', 38–9,: for example, he frequently uses 'wrang' as at 12/73, 446.

[22] For this shift from a northern to a Midland form see Cawley, *The Wakefield Pageants*, p. xxxii.

[23] See the note on 'sall' in relation to *The Dicing* (T24) in P. Meredith, 'The York millers' pageant and the Towneley *Processus Talentorum*', 107. Holford tabulates the frequency of northern 'sal' forms in some York pageants and shows that more southern forms were introduced by the scribe in some pageants: see table 1, 'Language and regional identity in the York Corpus Christi Cycle', 188.

[24] J. W. Robinson, *Studies in Fifteenth-Century Stagecraft* (Kalamazoo: Medieval Institute, 1991), pp. 86, 144, 176 and 183.

## 1.3 Provenances and Authorship

[1] *Representative English Comedies*, see above p. 234, n. 9.

[2] '. . . a major redactor of the full cycle, if not the compiler himself', Stevens and Cawley, *Plays*, 1.xxxi. Stevens's account of the dominating role of the Wakefield Master is even more assertive in his *Four Middle English Mystery Cycles* (Princeton: Princeton University Press, 1987): 'a strong case can be made for the Wakefield Master to have been the principal compiler and the guiding intelligence of the cycle' (pp. 88–9). These claims have been somewhat undermined by the proposed new date for the copying of the manuscript in the 1550s, Palmer 'Recycling "The Wakefield Cycle": the Records', 88, 96.

[3] E. Schell comments upon the way in which the play is paced, suggesting that Abraham's emotional tension means that everything must happen in a rush, banishing everything but the act itself, 'The distinctions of the Towneley *Abraham*', *MLQ*, 41 (1980), 315–27 (320).

4   Stevens and Cawley, *Plays*, vol. 2, p. 459. They also note a twelfth-century version
    in K. Young, *The Drama of the Medieval Church*, vol. 2 (Oxford: Clarendon
    Press, 1933), pp. 126–38. However, as Young points out (p. 131), because the
    *lectio* was substantially abbreviated in some churches, the extension to nine other
    speakers cannot be taken for granted.
5   M. Paull, 'The figure of Mahomet in the Towneley Cycle', *CD*, 6 (1972–3),
    187–204.
6   Unfortunately, the lacuna at the end of *Creation* means that we cannot check
    whether the promise of the oil of mercy featured near the beginning of the
    Towneley text is in its conventional place; it is however mentioned in *Noah*
    (3/66) and *Abraham* (4/6).
7   This is linked with the concept of Antichrist: see pp. 67, 192, 252, n. 24.
8   Stevens and Cawley note that the essential events in this play, including the
    Nuncius, follow conventions established in the liturgical drama, *Plays*, vol. 2,
    p. 512.
9   See R. Woolf, *The English Religious Lyric in the Middle Ages* (Oxford: Clarendon
    Press, 1968), pp. 103–6.
10  J. Dutka, *Music in the English Mystery Plays* (Kalamazoo: The Medieval Institute,
    1980), p. 37.
11  See A. C. Cawley, 'Middle English versions of the decalogue with reference to
    the English Corpus Christi Cycle', *LSE*, 8 (1975), 129–45.
12  See W. F. Munson, 'Self, action, and sign in the Towneley and York plays on
    the baptism of Christ and in Ockhamist salvation theology', in H. Keiper,
    C. Bode and R. I. Utz (eds), *Nominalism and Literary Discourse* (Amsterdam:
    Rodopi, 1997), pp. 191–216.
13  The stage direction translates 'Then Jesus comes and sings "Peace be with you,
    and it shall not be long; this is the day that the Lord hath made".' The song
    was probably sung in a liturgical style, though it has not been identified (Dutka,
    p. 73). Stevens and Cawley suggest it is a conflation of three scriptural elements
    (*Plays*, vol. 2, p. 620). That Christ should sing is a rarity in English cycles (Rastall,
    p. 177) but his role is often very musical in German cycles such as the *Alsfelder
    Passionsspiel*.
14  For the Judas story see Jacob de Voragine, *The Golden Legend: Readings on the
    Saints*, trans. W. G. Ryan, vol. 1 (Princeton: Princeton University Press, 1993),
    pp. 67–8.
15  J. W. Earl links the displacement of Judas with that of Pharaoh, 'The shape of
    Old Testament history in the Towneley Plays', *SP*, 69 (1972), 434–52.

## 1.4 The Wakefield Master

1   For parallels with liturgical drama see E. C. Dunn, 'The literary style of the
    Towneley plays', *American Benedictine Review*, 20 (1969), 481–504 (498–502).
2   M. Stevens, *Four Middle English Mystery Cycles* (Princeton: Princeton University
    Press, 1987), p. 148.

³ Words asterisked (*) are listed as unique to the Wakefield Master group in G. B. Kinneavy, *A Concordance to the Towneley Plays* (New York and London: Garland, 1990). Stevens has a similar list to this, but interestingly it is drawn from passages attributed to the Wakefield Master occurring largely outside the six plays under consideration here: *Four Middle English Mystery Cycles*, p. 163.

⁴ This is proverbial: cf. John Heywood, *Johan Johan*, in Richard Axton and Peter Happé (eds), *The Plays of John Heywood* (Cambridge: D. S. Brewer, 1991), pp. 75–109.

⁵ The plays he identified as having none or few proverbs are *Creation, Abraham, Jacob, Pharaoh, Caesar, Salutation, Magi, Baptist, Harrowing, Pilgrims, Ascension*. B. J. Whiting, *Proverbs in the Earlier English Drama* (Cambridge, Mass.: Harvard University Press, 1938, repr. New York: Octagon, 1969), p. 12, and n. 6 and 7. Of these, *Caesar* and *Harrowing* are dependent upon York. He also notes that some Towneley plays dealing with Mary have fewer proverbs than the dramatization of similar episodes in *Coventry* and in *N Town*, p. 13.

⁶ *Studies in Fifteenth-Century Stagecraft* (Kalamazoo: Medieval Institute, 1991), p. 127; cf. B. J. Whiting, *Proverbs, Sentences and Proverbial Writings* (Cambridge, Mass.: Harvard University Press, 1968), p. 383.

⁷ Robinson has suggested that this Towneley version shows some dependence upon the York *Trial before Annas and Caiphas* (29), *Studies in Fifteenth-Century Stagecraft*, pp. 176–95. It is notable that the York Christ here is also silent.

⁸ M. Paull, 'The figure of Mahomet in the Towneley Cycle', *CD*, 6 (1972–3), 187–204.

⁹ In iconographical representations Herod is shown with crossed legs to express this, as in the roof boss in the north transept of Norwich cathedral: cf. M. Rose and J. Hedgecoe, *Stories in Stone* (London: Herbert Press, 1997), pp. 119, 134.

¹⁰ E. T. Schell, 'The limits of typology in the Wakefield Master's *Processus Noe*', *CD*, 25 (1991), 168–87 (177).

¹¹ Cawley, *The Wakefield Pageants*, p. 106, n. 109: cf. 13/158.

¹² Margaret Rogerson, 'The medieval plough team on stage: judicial process as satiric theme in the Wakefield *Mactatio Abel*', *CD*, 28 (1994), 182–200.

¹³ See the comparative chart in R. Rastall, *The Heaven Singing: Music in Early English Religious Drama: vol. 1* (Cambridge: D. S. Brewer, 1996), p. 348.

¹⁴ Luke 2:13. The Vulgate has *laudantium* and the *New English Bible* 'singing the praises of God'.

¹⁵ J. Dutka, *Music in the English Mystery Plays*, p. 111.

¹⁶ This passage is an interpolation: see Beadle, *York*, p. 76 and note on ll. 73–99.

¹⁷ See A. C. Cawley, 'Iak Garcio of the *Prima Pastorum*', *MLN*, 68 (1953), 169–72.

¹⁸ *Le Mystère de la Passion d'Arnoul Gréban* O. Jodogne, ed. (Brussels: Académie Royale de Belgique, 1965), ll. 22781–816.

¹⁹ The origins of this piece of demonology are obscure, but the name is traceable to an unknown Franciscan early in the fourteenth century, who gives a version of the Latin verses at 30/365–6: see M. Jennings, 'Tutivillus: the literary career of the recording demon', Texts and Studies, *SP*, 74 (1977), 15.

20  See M. G. Frampton, 'The *Processus Talentorum*: (Towneley XXIV)', *PMLA*,
    59 (1944), 646–54; P. Meredith, 'The York millers' pageant and the Towneley
    *Processus Talentorum*', *METh*, 4 (1982), 104–14.
21  See L. Toulmin Smith, *York Plays*, p. xxv.
22  The theory is linked with the possible misplacing of the Pharaoh in the Old
    Testament sequence: see J. W. Earl, 'The shape of Old Testament history in the
    Towneley Plays', *SP*, 69 (1972), 434–52 (450–1).
23  For liturgical survivals see K. Young, *The Drama of the Medieval Church*, 2
    vols (vol. 1) (Oxford: Clarendon Press, 1933), pp. 451–83, especially the com-
    prehensive twelfth-century version from Sicily, pp. 476–81.
24  See specific comments on *Abel, Abraham, Shepherds* and *Pilgrims* by Lauren
    Lepow, *Enacting the Sacrament: Counter-Lollardry in the Towneley Cycle*
    (London and Toronto: Associated University Presses, 1990), pp. 58–9, Cain as
    a caricature of a Lollard; pp. 72–3, Abraham as priest; pp. 84–8, Shepherds and
    the Mass and sacraments; pp. 124–6, Real Presence.

## 2.1 Dramaturgy

1   For details see Cawley and Stevens *MS*, p. x and n. 25. As *Pharaoh* is the first
    play in the manuscript to come from York, it is just possible that the scribe began
    to follow the York practice at this point, but the matter is not easy to decide in
    that it is more than likely that he had a different exemplar.
2   T. H. Howard-Hill makes a strong case that initially it was normal to put stage
    directions in Latin throughout the corpus of early plays in manuscript, whether
    there was a close link with performance or not, 'The evolution of the form of
    plays during the Renaissance', *Renaissance Quarterly*, 43 (1990), 112–45
    (117–26).
3   The York stage direction at 38/186 may have prompted the song cue at T26/229.
    Towneley also takes no account of the York stage directions at Y37/37 and
    Y47/218 in passages just before the borrowing begins at T25/25 and T30/560.
4   In the following discussion I am indebted to the valuable list by Alan H. Nelson
    in *RORD*, 13–14 (1970–1), 215–19, but my own examination of the text has
    revealed rather more such details than those he recorded.
5   See Abel's speeches at 2/76, 108, 133, 146 and 170.
6   Hills are also involved later in the cycle in *Conspiracy* (20/515), *Crucifixion*
    (23/83) and *Ascension* (29/420).
7   The action is very compressed here, and the stage direction at l.369 'Then let
    John and Peter prepare the table' (trans. Stevens and Cawley) says nothing of
    the movement to the chamber by Jesus and the other Apostles.
8   For an analysis of the dramatization in this episode, see Edgar Schell, 'The
    distinctions of the Towneley *Abraham*', *MLQ*, 41 (1980), 315–27.
9   There appears to be a numbering error in Stevens and Cawley, *Plays*, at this
    point.
10  *Catholic Encyclopaedia*.

[11] In the Towneley *Noah* there is no detail in the text about the animals going into the Ark, in marked contrast with the Chester treatment where there is a delightful list (Ch3/160–92).

[12] Stevens and Cawley gloss 'pall' as 'scarlet' implying the blood-stained body of Christ.

## 2.2 *Modern Revivals*

[1] John R. Elliott, Jr., *Playing God: Medieval Mysteries on the Modern Stage* (Toronto: University of Toronto Press, 1989), provides a comprehensive account up to 1980; there is a great deal of information in the form of reviews and articles in *Medieval English Theatre*, *Research Opportunities in Renaissance Drama* and *Early Theatre*.

[2] Elliott, *Playing God*, pp. 114–16.

[3] For the Towneley productions see *The Wakefield Mystery Plays*, ed. Martial Rose (London: Evans Bros, 1961); the reviews in *The Times*, 4 April 1961 (Mermaid), and in *RORD*, 23 (1980), 81–2 (at Wakefield); M. Stevens, '*Processus Torontoniensis*: A performance of the Wakefield Cycle', *RORD*, 28 (1985), 189–200; D. Mills, 'The Towneley Cycle of Toronto: the audience as actor', *METh*, 7 (1985), 51–4. The York performances were reported in *RORD*, 20 (1977), 102–21; D. Parry, 'The York Mystery Cycle at Toronto', *METh*, 1 (1979), 19–31; S. Lindenbaum, 'The York Cycle at Toronto: staging, performance, style', *Theatre Research International*, 4 (1978), 31–41; A. F. Johnston, 'Four York pageants performed in the streets of York', *RORD*, 31 (1992), 101–4; B. Palmer, D. Bevington, Garrett P. J. Epp, R. Blasting, D. Mills and P. Meredith, 'The York Cycle in Performance: Toronto and York', *ET*, 1 (1998), 139–69; and, with special reference to the Toronto performance in 1998, in Helen Ostovich (ed.), *The York Cycle Then and Now: Special Volume*, *ET*, 3 (Hamilton: McMaster University Press, 2000).

[4] See Megan Lloyd, 'Reflections of a York survivor: the York Cycle and its audience', *RORD*, 39 (2000), 223–35.

[5] A. F. Johnston, 'York Cycle 1998: what we learned', *ET*, 3 (2000), 199–203 (199). This has been recently challenged by Margaret Rogerson who suggests that no pageant was played more than twice on the day of performance (forthcoming).

[6] Eileen White, 'Places to hear the play in York', *ET*, 3 (2000), 49–78.

[7] David Parry, 'The York Mystery Cycle at Toronto', 20.

[8] 'Raging in the streets of medieval York', *ET*, 3 (2000), 105–25. The argument turns upon whether the famous Coventry stage direction about Herod raging 'in the street also' is a rare exception or normal practice: see Pamela M. King and Clifford Davidson (eds), *The Coventry Corpus Christi Plays*, (Kalamazoo: Medieval Institute, 2000): *The Pageant of the Shearmen and Taylors*, 728sd.

[9] L. W. Soule, 'Performing the mysteries: demystification, story-telling and over-acting like the devil', *EMD*, 1 (1997), 219–31 (222).

244         NOTES

[10] John McKinnell, 'The medieval pageant wagons at York: their orientation and height', *ET*, 3 (2000), 79–99 (93–8).

[11] The diagrams are reproduced in E. Norris, *The Ancient Cornish Drama*, vol. 1 (Oxford: Oxford University Press, 1859), pp. 219, 479. This was the practice followed in the reconstructed performance in the Piran Round in 1969 by the company from Bristol University: see N. Denny 'Arena staging a dramatic quality in the Cornish passion play', in *Medieval Drama*, ed. N. Denny, Stratford-upon-Avon Studies, 16 (London: Edward Arnold, 1973), pp. 124–53 and K. Roddy, 'Revival of the Cornish mystery plays in St Piran 'round' and of the York Cycle 1969', *New Theatre Magazine*, 9 (1969), 16–19. See also my 'Performing passion plays in France and England', *EMD*, 4 (2000), 57–75 (73–4).

[12] Margaret Rogerson, ' "Everybody got their brown dress": mystery plays for the millennium', *New Theatre Quarterly*, 17 (2001), 123–40 (129).

[13] Elliott, *Playing God*, p. 75.

[14] Elliott, *Playing God*, p. 66.

[15] S. J. Kahrl writes of a production at Ely: 'Those members of chorus who had drowned in the Flood (i.e. sinners) were suddenly resurrected by Noah's family after the Ark touched down and proceeded to circle the stage singing 'Land of Hope and Glory', 'Medieval drama in England, 1973: Chester and Ely', *RORD*, 15–16 (1972–3), 117–23 (123).

[16] See Elliott, *Playing God*, p. 115.

[17] See *RORD*, 22 (1979), 137–9.

[18] See the commentary on the northern mystery by D. Atkinson, 'Northern mystery plays, Crucible, Sheffield 23.6 – 15.7.89', *Cahiers Elisabéthaines*, 39 (1989). This production contained *Abel* (2) and *Second Shepherds* (13). Besides the liveliness of speech there was also an attempt to bring out local folk elements and popular culture.

[19] 'The National Theatre's production of *The Mysteries*: some observations', *RORD*, 40 (1986), 70–3.

[20] P. Butterworth, 'Discipline, dignity and beauty: the Wakefield mystery plays, Bretton Hall, 1958', *LSE*, 32 (2001), 49–80 (52). This essay includes eleven photographs from the 1958 performance.

[21] The performance was divided into two sections, one with episodes appropriate for Christmas 1957 and one similarly for Easter 1958, Butterworth, 'Discipline, dignity, beauty: the Wakefield mystery plays, Bretton Hall, 1958', 56.

[22] Elliott, *Playing God*, pp. 111–13.

[23] 'When the processions moved from stage to stage the crowd parted like the Red Sea and babies were removed from their path': see my review in *RORD*, 23 (1979), vol. 1, p. 109 (1476), 11, 6–17.

[24] I remember hearing one busy mother say to her husband something like 'You stay here with him [baby in pram] and watch the play while I pop into the chemist's for the aspirins.' One of a group of youths with motorbikes, meanwhile, declared his admiration for the actor who was playing Christ virtually naked.

[25] A. F. Johnston and Margaret Rogerson, *REED: York*, vol. 1 (Toronto: University of Toronto Press, 1979, 109 (1976), pp. 6–17.

26  'Processus Torontoniensis: A performance of the Wakefield Cycle', 190.

27  'The Towneley Cycle at Toronto', METh, 8 (1986), 51–60.

28  'The Towneley Cycle of Toronto: the audience as actor', METh, 7 (1985), 51–4.

29  The English expectation would have been different from the corresponding one in France where the Passions tended to run from the Baptism to the Ascension: see my Cyclic Form and the English Mystery Plays (Amsterdam and New York: Rodopi, 2004), pp. 138–47.

30  'Original-staging productions of English medieval plays: ideals, evidence and practice', in Popular Drama in Northern Europe in the Later Middle Ages, ed. Flemming G. Andersen et al., (Odense: Odense University Press, 1988), pp. 65–100 (p. 73).

31  Meg Twycross, 'The Toronto passion play', METh, 3 (1981), 122–31 (126).

32  See the 'Informal minutes of seminar 17', RORD, 13–14 (1970–1), 203–20.

33  'The Wakefield Corpus Christi play', RORD, 13–14 (1970–1), 221–33 (228–9).

34  See my 'Procession and the cycle drama in England and Europe: some dramatic possibilities', EMD, 6 (2002), 31–47.

35  'Processus Torontoniensis: a performance of the Wakefield Cycle', 193.

36  See D. Atkinson, 'Northern mystery plays', 99, and Katie Normington, 'Reviving the Royal National Theatre's The Mysteries', RORD, 40 (2001), 133–47 (134). See also Paula Neuss's comments on the effectiveness of the rhyming in the Towneley Judgement (30) at Wakefield in 1980, 'God and embarrassment', Themes in Drama 5: Drama and Religion, ed. James Redmond (Cambridge: Cambridge University Press, 1983), pp. 241–53 (p. 251), and M. Billington on the Mysteries in The Guardian, 21.12.99.

37  RORD, 20 (1977), 100.

38  Peter Meredith, 'Original-staging productions of English medieval plays: ideals, evidence and practice', p. 94.

39  For a discussion of aspects of Brecht and the limitations of his ideas in relation to the mystery plays see Garrett P. J. Epp, 'Visible words: the York plays, Brecht and Gestic writing', CD, 24 (1990–1), 289–305.

40  'Mediaeval acting' in M. G. Briscoe and J. E. Coldewey (eds), Contexts for Early English Drama from L. Petit de Julleville, Les Mystères, 2 vols (Paris: Hachette, 1880), 1.370 (recorded 1485) and 2.133 (recorded 1536).

41  See RORD, 24, (1981), 195–6.

42  I have found the discussion by L. W. Soule particularly helpful, though I have not followed exactly the categories she has proposed: see 'Performing the mysteries: demystification, story-telling and over-acting like the devil', 221–30.

43  Katie Normington, 'The actor/audience contract in modern restagings of the mystery plays', RORD, 43 (2004), 29–37 (31).

44  Margaret Rogerson, ' "Everybody got their brown dress": mystery plays for the millennium', 124.

45  See RORD, 35 (1996), 141–2.

46  See RORD, 29 (1986–7), 111–12.

47  See RORD, 41 (2002), 206–8.

48  T. Corbett, in his review in *RORD*, 41 (2002), 208–11, makes it clear that the *Second Shepherds* play performed by the same actors was deliberately treated more conventionally.

49  Untitled review by Carol Symes, *RORD*, 36 (1997), 196–9.

50  See my review in *RORD*, 22 (1979), 139–41.

51  'Seeing is believing: the Chester play of nativity at Chester Cathedral, summer 1987', *Cahiers Elisabéthaines*, 34 (1988), 1–9 (4).

## 2.3 Special Features

1  Richard Rastall, 'Music in the cycle plays', in Marianne G. Briscoe and John C. Coldewey, (eds), *Contexts for Early English Drama* (Bloomington, IA: Indiana University Press, 1989), pp. 192–218 (p. 199).

2  The singing of the souls in hell is described as 'this ugly noyse' by the devil Rybald (T25/101).

3  Stevens and Cawley assume that the canticle was indeed sung on the basis of the parallel with the other cycles, *Plays*, vol. 2, p. 480. There is a comparative chart for liturgical music in the cycles in JoAnna Dutka, *Music in the English Mystery Plays* (Kalamazoo: The Medieval Institute, 1980), pp. 124–7.

4  Dutka points out that the form in which this item appears in the manuscript, *pax vobis et non tardabit* cannot be found in the liturgy or a liturgical play, and proposes that *et non tardabit* is really a stage direction for Christ to make a rapid disappearance, *Music in the English Mystery Plays*, p. 73. Stevens and Cawley, *Plays*, vol. 2, p. 620, accept that this may be true, but think it does not account for the next line *hec est dies quam fecit Dominus* (Psalm 117:24, gradual of Easter Sunday Mass). But the normal ruled line in the manuscript separating speeches and linking to the speech head right for *Tercius Apostolus* precedes this line of Latin. This may mean either that it is an on-page copy of the first line of the next speech, not to be spoken, or that the Apostle does indeed say it and then translates it as 'This is the day that God maide' in 28/105. The first line of this stage direction is repeated at 28/120 without the following Latin phrase, making Dutka's reading rather more plausible but we still have to assume that the scribe or his copy text made the same mistake twice.

5  Stevens and Cawley, *Plays*, vol. 2, p. 462; cf. Young, *Drama of the Medieval Church*, vol. 2, pp. 125–38 where there are examples of the *lectio*.

6  The phrase is sung in *Das Künzelsauer Fronleichnamspiel*, ed. P. K. Liebenow (Berlin: De Gruyter, 1969), 3731sd, but that cycle, in common with other German-language versions, has far more music than any of the English examples. The antiphon itself, which is based on these words in the form *Tollite portas*, is discussed by K. Young, *Drama of the Medieval Church*, vol. 1, pp. 161–76.

7  As in *The Alsfeld Passion Play*, ed. and trans. Larry E. West (Lampeter: Mellen, 1997), pp. 5756–9 and stage directions. The passage is spoken in Chester 1/152sd.

8  The Towneley *Pharaoh* does not take over the *Cantemus domino* which is sung at the end of the York version (Y/11/406). Some of the praise to God is followed

(428–9) but the Towneley dramatist provides a more warning tone in the last speech by Moses. Rastall points out that loud minstrelsy is provided for Herod in N Town and Chester, 'Music in the cycle plays', p. 210; it is not noted in Towneley.

9   Richard Rastall, 'Music in the cycle plays', p. 194.

10  It is possible that the Third Shepherd's blessing or spell, expressed in incompetent and muddled Latin before the three go to sleep is sung, perhaps in a liturgical mode, but the text gives no indication: *Jesus onazorus / Crucyfixus, / Marcus, Andreus / God be oure spede!* (12/422–5).

11  Twenty-four semiminims to a long is much more elaborate than the Shepherds' style of singing; See Nan C. Carpenter, 'Music in the *Secunda Pastorum*', *Speculum*, 26 (1951), 696–700.

12  An alternative reading, that the Shepherds are going to sing in unison and that the Third Shepherd is timid about beginning alone, is suggested by Richard Rastall, *The Heaven Singing: Music in Early English Religious Drama: I* (Cambridge: D. S. Brewer, 1996), p. 355.

13  It is tempting to think that the Shepherds, as corrupt human beings, might be comically ignorant and that their musical performance might be a travesty of what they and the audience have just heard, but the balance of the evidence here and also in *Second Shepherds* suggests that this is not so. There is no doubting, however, that in the first part of both plays, where there are attempts to portray the hardship and evil of the world into which Christ is born, their foibles are exposed.

14  See the table in Richard Rastall, *The Heaven Singing*, p. 348.

15  *The Heaven Singing*, p. 41.

16  Rastall notes that the textual evidence regarding the performance by the Shepherds in the surviving Coventry plays required a high level of musical competence, perhaps equivalent to professional skills, *The Heaven Singing*, p. 360.

17  See P. J. P. Goldberg, 'Women' in R. Horrox (ed.), *Fifteenth-Century Attitudes: Perceptions of Society in Late Medieval England* (Cambridge: Cambridge University Press, 1994), pp. 112–31 (p. 118).

18  The origin is in the *Summa predicantium*, Stevens and Cawley, *Plays*, vol. 2, p.649.

19  For comments on the linguistic consistency of York see Richard Beadle, 'Verbal texture and wordplay in the York Cycle', *ET*, 3, (2000), 167–84.

## 3.1 Gender

1   Theresa Coletti, 'A feminist approach to the Corpus Christi cycles', in R. K. Emmerson (ed.), *Approaches to Teaching Medieval English Drama* (New York: Modern Language Association of America, 1990), pp. 79–89 (p. 81). On gender issues in general see P. J. P. Goldberg, 'Women', in R. Horrox (ed.), *Fifteenth-Century Attitudes: Perceptions of Society in Late Medieval England* (Cambridge:

248 NOTES

Cambridge University Press, 1994), 112–31, and Katie Normington, *Gender and Medieval Drama* (Cambridge: D. S. Brewer, 2004).

2   *Plays*, vol. 2, p. 437.

3   For ambiguities in the significance of Eve see Maureen Fries, 'The evolution of Eve in Medieval French and English drama', *SP*, 99 (2002), 1–16. However, the differences between York and Towneley are greater than she allows (13).

4   *The English Mystery Plays* (London: Routledge, 1972), p. 139. The figural link is traditional.

5   Ruth Evans, 'Feminist re-enactments: gender and the Towneley *Uxor Noe*', in J. Dor (ed.), *A Wyf ther was: Essays in Honour of Paule Mertens-Fonck* (Liège: University of Liège Press, 1992), pp. 141–54 (p. 150). See also Monica Bzezinsky Potkay and Regula Meyer Evitt, *Minding the Body: Women and Literature in the Middle Ages* (New York: Twayne, 1997), p. 108. The exposure of the stereotypic weaknesses of men is noted by James Simpson, *Reform and Cultural Revolution*, Oxford English Literary History, vol. 2, 1350–547 (Oxford: Oxford University Press, 2002), p. 520. The female caricature reappears with Mak's wife, where the treatment is different: see below p. 144.

6   Jane Tolmie, 'Mrs Noah and didactic abuses', *ET*, 5 (2002), 11–35 (16).

7   Joseph M. Ricke notes Noah's limitations and his less admirable qualities and links the episode of his 'defeat' to festive practices, 'Parody, performance, and the "Ultimate" meaning of Noah's shrew', *Medievalia*, 18 (1995), 263–81 (272). Katie Normington suggests there might be a social protest in her allegiance to spinning and her being forced to give this up. This may be related to contemporary pressure at Wakefield on women's work in the wool trades coming under pressure in the mid-fifteenth century, *Gender and Medieval Drama*, pp. 131–2.

8   Jane Tolmie, 'Mrs Noah and didactic abuses', 24.

9   A. Gash, 'Carnival against Lent: the ambivalence of medieval drama', in David Aers (ed.), *Medieval Literature: Criticism, Ideology and History* (New York: St Martin's Press, 1986), pp. 74–98 (p. 79).

10  We might also suggest that this articulation from a character of inferior status might well tone with the oppressed Shepherds: see Chapter 3.3.

11  Stevens and Cawley, *Plays*, vol. 2, p. 463.

12  Theresa Coletti, 'A feminist approach to the Corpus Christi cycles', p. 87.

13  Compare the analysis of Mary's more pointed disruption of the gender system in W. Fitzhenry, 'The *N-Town Plays* and the politics of metatheater', *SP*, 100 (2003), 22–43.

14  Theresa Coletti, 'Purity and danger: the paradox of Mary's body and the engendering of the infancy narrative in the English mystery cycles', in Linda Lomperis and Sarah Stanbury (eds), *Feminist Approaches to the Body in Medieval Literature* (Philadelphia: University of Pennsylvania Press, 1993), pp. 65–95 (pp. 67, 76, 87). Moreover Mary's dominance and the ambiguity generated by her 'dangerous' body may have challenged medieval stereotypes.

15  See Potkay and Evitt, *Minding the Body*, pp. 120–3, but they assume the play was written by the Wakefield Master without giving grounds for the attribution (p. 120). Stylistically and thematically it has very little in common with the plays confidently attributed to him.

16  Cecilia Pietropoli notes a tension between the traditional stereotype as a shrew and the role of the good wife in this character, *Il teatro dei Miracoli e delle Moralità* (Naples: Liguori, 1996), p. 302.

17  Rosemary Woolf notes the extent of this convention of elaborating his claim to god-like or even devilish powers, *The English Mystery Plays*, p. 203.

18  ' "Ther Be But Women": gender conflict and gender identity in the Middle English innocents plays', *Medievalia*, 18 (1995), 245–61 (254). The intensity of the sense of loss felt by these mothers seems to override the characteristics which suggest the stereotype of 'unruly women': see Katie Normington, 'Giving voice to women: teaching feminist approaches to the mystery plays', *College Literature*, 28 (2001), 130–54; see also her *Gender and Medieval Drama* (Cambridge: D. S. Brewer, 2004).

19  See for example her many appearances in Memling's two cyclic paintings known as 'Scenes from the Passion' and 'The Seven Joys of Mary', in Dirk De Vos, *Hans Memling: The Complete Works* (London: Thames and Hudson, 1994), nos 11 and 38.

20  Characteristic of her continual presence is the device in the *Passion d'Auvergne* where there is apparently a provision for Christ to meet his mother at the end of each day of the performance. See *La Passion d'Auvergne*, ed. Graham A. Runnals (Geneva: Droz, 1982), ll. 1894–911 and note, and 4525–88.

21  The following lines are closely similar though there are some small variations suggesting either that Towneley was copied from a different exemplum or that memory was not quite perfect: Y34/106–15, 126–35 and T22/351–72. The re-writing may well have been accidental rather than a deliberate revision.

22  Compare Luke 23:29 with Matthew 24:19. The identification of the women addressed at this point in scripture ('many women', Luke 23:28) with Mary and her companions is rare in meditations and iconography, Rosemary Woolf, *The English Mystery Plays*, p. 403, n. 58.

23  See my 'The Towneley Cycle without the Wakefield Master', *RORD*, 45 (2006), 23–38.

24  Rosemary Woolf notes parallels in vernacular lyrics, including the reproach to Gabriel for raising her hopes (23/481–910), *The English Mystery Plays*, p. 403, n. 62.

25  The actions and events attributed to Mary Magdalene that are not strictly scriptural were put together in exegetical writings, especially by Gregory the Great, from apparently unrelated incidents in the Bible; see Theresa Coletti, *Mary Magdalene and the Drama of Saints: Theater, Gender and Religion in Late Medieval England* (Philadelphia: University of Pennsylvania Press, 2004), pp. 22 and 170. For the threat posed by Holy Women to the ecclesiastical authorities see Janette Dillon, 'Holy women and their confessors or confessors and their holy women? Margery Kemp and continental tradition', in Rosalynn Voaden (ed.), *Prophets Abroad: The Reception of Continental Holy Women in Late Medieval England* (Cambridge: D. S. Brewer, 1996), pp. 115–40.

26  Stevens and Cawley also refer to the occurrence of this in sermons: see *Plays*, vol. 2, p. 618, and G. R. Owst, *Literature and Pulpit in Medieval England* (Cambridge: Cambridge University Press, 1933), p. 385.

[27] The relationship is further discussed in an account which also discriminates between the two by Chester N. Scoville, *Saints and the Audience in Middle English Biblical Drama* (Toronto: University of Toronto Press, 2004).

[28] The incident of the anointing of Christ at the house of Simon is described by Judas when he makes the bargain with the High Priests, but it is not enacted and it is not specifically attributed to Mary Magdalene (*Conspiracy*, 20/272–305).

[29] Noted by Coletti, *Mary Magdalene and the Drama of Saints*, p. 206.

[30] See Sarah Beckwith, *Christ's Body: Identity, Culture and Society in Late Medieval Writings* (London and New York: Routledge, 1993), and Caroline Walker Bynum, 'The body of Christ in the later Middle Ages: a reply to Leo Steinberg', *Renaissance Quarterly*, 39 (1986), 399–439. Garrett P. J. Epp, discussing the sexuality of the naked Christ, notes that the Wycliffite *Tretise of Miraclis Pleyinge* criticizes the fleshly pleasures of theatrical representation, but he shows that Nicholas Love sought to make 'the bodyes or bodily þinges' stimulate devotion, 'Ecce Homo', in Glenn Burger and Steven F. Kruger (eds), *Queering the Middle Ages* (Minneapolis: University of Minnesota Press, 2001), pp. 236–51 (pp. 237–9).

[31] See, for example, J. H. Marrow, *Passion Iconography in Northern European Art of the Late Middle Ages and Early Renaissance* (Courtrai: Van Ghemmert, 1979).

[32] For the function of Corpus Christi as expressing a social bond, see Mervyn James, 'Ritual body and social drama in the late medieval English town', *Past and Present*, 98 (1983), 3–29 (4). Paradigms for Christ's body are discussed by Peter W. Travis, 'The social body of the dramatic Christ in medieval England', in Albert H. Tricomi (ed.), *Early Drama to 1600, Acta XIII* (Binghamton: State University of New York, 1987), pp. 17–36, and 'The semiotics of Christ's body in the English cycles', in R. K. Emmerson (ed.), *Approaches to Teaching Medieval English Drama* (New York: Modern Language Association of America, 1990), pp. 67–78.

[33] Travis, 'The social body of the dramatic Christ in medieval England', pp. 26–8. See also Katie Normington, *Gender and Medieval Drama*, p. 85.

[34] See Ruth Evans, 'Body politics: engendering medieval cycle drama', in Ruth Evans and Lesley Johnson (eds), *Feminist Readings in Middle English Literature* (London and New York: Routledge, 1994), pp. 112–39 (p. 119). For further ideas about Christ as a maternal figure and iconographic representations of him as nourishing his followers, see Travis, 'The social body of the dramatic Christ in medieval England', 1976, and Leo Steinberg, *The Sexuality of Christ in Renaissance Art and in Modern Oblivion* (New York: Random, 1983).

## 3.2.1 Religion

[1] E. C. Dunn, 'The literary style of the Towneley plays', *American Benedictine Review*, 20 (1969), 481–504.

[2] See E. M. Ross, *The Grief of God: Images of the Suffering of Jesus in Late Medieval England* (Oxford: Oxford University Press, 1997). R. N. Swanson suggests that Anselm's question *Cur Deus Homo* (Why God [as] Man?) was one

of the key influences in the shift towards the image of Christ as Man of Sorrows, 'Passion and practice: the social and ecclesiastical implications of passion devotion in the late Middle Ages', in A. A. MacDonald, H. N. B. Ridderbos and R. M. Schlusemann (eds), *The Broken Body: Passion Devotion in Late Medieval Culture* (Groningen: Forsten, 1998), pp. 1–30. On the relationship between religion and cyclic form see my *Cyclic Form and the English Mystery Plays* (Amsterdam and New York: Redopi, 2004), pp. 23–30.

3  W. A. Pantin, *The English Church in the Fourteenth Century* (Cambridge: Cambridge University Press, 1955), p. 190; on specifically didactic tendencies, see J. O. Fichte, *Expository Voices in Medieval Drama: Essays on the Mode and Function of Dramatic Exposition* (Nürnberg: Carl, 1975), pp. 67–8. On the symbolism of the Passion see John Bossy, *Christianity in the West 1400–1700* (Oxford: Oxford University Press, 1985), pp. 6–7.

4  See Chapter 3.3, n. 4.

5  W. A. Pantin, *The English Church in the Fourteenth Century*, pp. 191–3.

6  'Middle English versions of the Decalogue with reference to the English Corpus Christi cycles', *LSE*, 8 (1975), 129–45 (130–2), specifying the Ten Commandments, *Prophets* (7), *Doctors* (18); the sacrament of baptism, *Baptist* (19); the Eucharist, *Resurrection* (26), *Pilgrims* (27), *Thomas* (28); Penance, *Annunciation* (10), *Thomas* (28); and Good Works, *Judgement* (30).

7  Margaret Aston, *Faith and Fire: Popular and Unpopular Religion 1350–1600* (London: Hambledon Press, 1993), p. 84.

8  See A. Henry (ed.), *The Mirour of Mans Saluacioun* (Aldershot: Scolar Press, 1986), p. 10.

9  For some further aspects of the religious culture at York see A. F. Johnston, 'The Word made Flesh: Augustinian Elements in the York Cycle', in R. A. Taylor et al. (eds), *The Centre and its Compass: Studies in Medieval Literature in Honor of Professor John Layerle*, Studies in Medieval Culture, 33 (Kalamazoo: Medieval Institute Publications, 1993), 225–46.

10  *The Mirror of the Blessed Life of Jesu Christ*, trans. Nicholas Love (London: Burns, Oates and Washburne, 1926). Gail McMurray Gibson draws attention to the powerful, even exceptional, influence of this book on lay piety, *The Theater of Devotion: East Anglian Drama and Society in the Late Middle Ages* (Chicago and London: University of Chicago Press, 1994), p. 21. Archbishop Arundel approved the book in 1410: Margaret Aston, *Faith and Fire*, p. 82. See also *The Mirror of the Blessed Life of Jesus Christ: A Reading Text*, ed. Michael G. Sargeant (Exeter: Exeter University Press, 2004), pp. xvii–xx, for the anti-Lollard stance.

11  Ruth Nissé, 'Staged interpretations: civic rhetoric and Lollard politics in the York plays', *JMEMS*, 28 (1998), 427–52; Lauren Lepow, *Enacting the Sacrament: Counter-Lollardry in the Towneley Cycle* (London and Toronto: Associated University Presses, 1990), pp. 47–8; W. Fitzhenry, 'The *N-Town Plays* and the politics of metatheater', 22–43.

12  For later phases in the political and religious disputes at Chester see David Mills, *Recycling the Cycle: The City of Chester and its Whitsun Plays* (Toronto: University of Toronto Press, 1998).

[13]  See L. Remly, '*Deus Caritas*: the Christian message of the *Secunda Pastorum*', *Neuphilologische Mitteilungen*, 72 (1971), 742–8 (747).

[14]  Martial Rose and Julia Hedgecoe, *Stories in Stone* (London: Herbert Press, 1997), p. 82; Clifford Davidson and David E. O'Connor, *York Art* (Kalamazoo: Medieval Institute, 1978), pp. 85–6.

[15]  There are other references to the Trinity at 1/61, 3/121, 3/245, 3/367.

[16]  The legend originates in the *Gospel of Nicodemus* and was frequently repeated. It is dramatized in the Cornish *Ordinalia*, a text which appears to precede Towneley, *Origo Mundi*, pp. 733–80.

[17]  The Second King also uses the title as the Kings pray for guidance to Bethlehem (14/513).

[18]  This play also shows one of the Sorrows of Mary in her lament for her lost son, and it may well be an example of how the incorporating of material from York was indeed occasioned by an interest in asserting what might be termed orthodox traditions. Another of the Sorrows appears in *Flight into Egypt* when Mary fears for her son and in doing so anticipates the Crucifixion (15/79–89).

[19]  For 'boytt' see *bote* n. (1) in *MED*, where the phrase 'bote of bale' is described as proverbial: cf. Tilley, *A Dictionary of the proverbs in England in the Sixteenth and Seventeenth Centuries* (Ann Arbor: University of Michigan Press, 1950), B59. See also *beten* v. (2) 1a mend, and *bale* n. (1).

[20]  Lauren Lepow, *Enacting the Sacrament*, pp. 56–7. There is a misericord in Ripon Cathedral portraying this proverb: cf. Tilley, F656.

[21]  'leche' can mean either 'physician' or 'remedy', see *MED*, *leche* n. (3), 1 and 2.

[22]  *Le Mystère de la Passion d'Arnoul Gréban*, ed. O. Jodogne (Brussels: Académie Royale de Belgique, 1965). These ideas are less direct in York and are handled quite differently in the speech by the Doctor beginning *Annunciation* (Y12/1–143).

[23]  Later in this discussion we shall take note of other lyrical passages; E. C. Dunn has proposed that a lyrical mode is one of the stylistic characteristics of Towneley: see 'The literary style of the Towneley plays', 484–5. Her article wisely avoids the assumption that there is only one style.

[24]  There is no hint that Towneley concerned itself with the Antichrist sequence, which takes up two plays at the end of the Chester Cycle, but possibly the evil characters in the cycle make up a composite figure: see David Mills, 'Religious drama and civic ceremonial', in A. C. Cawley et al., *The Revels History of Drama in English: Volume I, Medieval Drama* (London and New York: Methuen, 1983), p. 186.

[25]  This is a devotional commonplace: see Stevens and Cawley, *Plays*, vol. 2, p. 606, n. 294. Clifford Davidson notes that the body here presented becomes linked with the Eucharist: see *History, Religion, and Violence: Cultural Contexts for Medieval and Renaissance English Drama* (Aldershot: Ashgate, 2002), pp. 193–4.

[26]  Ritchie D. Kendall, *The Drama of Dissent: The Radical Poetics of Nonconformity, 1380–1590* (Chapel Hill: University of North Carolina Press, 1986), p. 20. See also Lepow, *Enacting the Sacrament*, p. 121. Michael O'Connell regards 'the

Lollard opposition to religious representation as the most serious challenge to images in Europe prior to the Reformation', *The Idolatrous Eye: Iconoclasm and Theatre in Early Modern England* (Oxford: Oxford University Press, 2000), p. 42.

27  Sixteen seven-line stanzas, rhyming aaabccb, the fourth line a dimeter reminiscent of the short ninth line in the Wakefield Master's stanza.

28  The origin and status of this song, *Pax vobis et non tardabit; hec est dies quam fecit Dominus*, is disputed: see Stevens and Cawley, *Plays*, vol. 2, p. 620, n. 104 + sd. Richard Rastall, however, mentions a similarity with the song of angels, as it appears for the Shepherds and in other places, though he does point out that the emphasis here is upon Christ's corporeality rather than his divinity: see *The Heaven Singing*, p. 177.

29  *Plays*, vol. 2, p. 626.

30  David Mills points out that one of the chief Lollard objections to the biblical plays in *A Tretise of Miraclis Pleyinge* was their dangerous resemblance to worship and instruction: 'Medieval and modern views of drama', in A. C. Cawley et al. (eds), *The Revels History of Drama in English: Volume I, Medieval Drama* (London and New York: Methuen, 1983), p. 91.

31  It can be found in *Flight* 15/79–82, 157–60 and *Doctors* 18/197–204.

32  Clifford Davidson, 'An interpretation of the Wakefield *Judicium*', *Annuale Medievale*, 10 (1969), 117.

33  Lepow suggests that the verbal excess of Tutivillus is related to the alleged abuse of language by Lollards, *Enacting the Sacrament*, p. 140.

34  'The shape of Old Testament history in the Towneley plays', *SP*, 69 (1972), 434–52.

## 3.2.2 Popular Culture

1  John Bossy suggests that the main purpose of carnival was to reveal what was normally concealed so that it could be expiated through the penitence of Lent which began as soon as the six days of carnival ended on Shrove Tuesday, *Christianity in the West 1400–1700*, pp. 42–5.

2  Peter Burke, *Popular Culture in Early Modern Europe* (Aldershot: Scolar Press, 1978); for a critique see Tim Harris, 'Problematising popular culture', in Tim Harris (ed.), *Popular Culture in England c.1500–1850* (Basingstoke: Macmillan, 1995), pp. 1–27. It is also noteworthy that a high proportion of the activities recorded by the REED project based at the University of Toronto falls readily into line with these subjects, and this is true of urban as well as rural communities.

3  Following E. K. Chambers's exhaustive account of mainly continental examples in *The Medieval Stage*, 2 vols (Oxford: Clarendon Press, 1903), useful details are to be found in Richard Axton, *European Drama of the Early Middle Ages* (London: Hutchinson, 1974), pp. 33–60; David Mills, 'Religious drama and civic ceremonial', in A. C. Cawley et al. (eds), *The Revels History of Drama in English:*

*Volume I, Medieval Drama*, pp. 152–206; and in L. M. Clopper, *Drama, Play and Game: English Festive Culture in the Medieval and Early Modern Period* (Chicago and London: University of Chicago Press, 2002), pp. 177–9. For the pattern of the ritual year, Christmas to midsummer, see Richard Hutton, *The Rise and Fall of Merry England: The Ritual Year, 1400–1700* (Oxford: Oxford University Press, 1994), pp. 5–48 and François Laroque, *Shakespeare's Festive World* (Cambridge: Cambridge University Press, 1991).

4  *A History of the English Church and English People*, trans. L. Sherley-Price, and revised by L. E. Latham (Harmondsworth: Penguin, 1990), 1.30, p. 92. The tension between subversion and conformity in medieval drama is discussed by Darryll Grantley, *Wit's Pilgrimage: Drama and the Social Impact of Education in Early Modern England* (Aldershot: Ashgate, 2000), pp. 11–13.

5  We must note, however, that the Brewbarret passage in the York manuscript occurs in a relatively late interpolation by John Clerke: see Beadle, *York*, p. 76.

6  Michael D. Bristol, 'Theater and popular culture', in John D. Cox and David Scott Kastan (eds), *A New History of Early English Drama* (New York: Columbia University Press, 1997), pp. 23–48 (p. 234).

7  A. Gash, 'Carnival against Lent: the ambivalence of medieval drama', in David Aers (ed.), *Medieval Literature: Criticism, Ideology and History* (New York: St Martin's Press, 1986), pp. 74–98 (pp. 76–7).

8  Monica Bzezinsky Potkay and Regula Meyer Evitt, *Minding the Body: Women and Literature in the Middle Ages* (New York: Twayne, 1997), p. 107.

9  Stevens and Cawley, *Plays*, vol. 2, p. 450, n. 276.

10  Robert Weimann, *Shakespeare and the Popular Tradition in the Theater*, ed. Robert Schwartz (Baltimore and London: Johns Hopkins University Press, 1978), p. 91.

11  At another level the repetition of the phrase 'lytyll day-starne' links Mak's 'baby' with the Christ-child (13/834, 1049).

12  For details see R. C. Cosbey, 'The Mak story and its folklore analogues', *Speculum*, 20 (1945), 310–17. He concludes that the folk tale preceded the Towneley version and was adapted for dramatic needs by the playwright.

13  Lynn Forest-Hill, 'Sins of the mouth: signs of subversion in medieval English cycle plays', in Dermot Cavanagh and Tim Kirk (eds), *Subversion and Scurrility: Popular Discourse in Europe from 1500 to the Present* (Aldershot: Ashgate, 2000), pp. 21–3: see below, Chapter 3.3.

14  Malcolm Jones ' "Slawpase fro the Myln-Wheele": seeing between the lines', in Meg Twycross (ed.), *Festive Drama* (Cambridge: D. S. Brewer, 1996), pp. 242–58.

15  Here we need to bear in mind that there is some uncertainty in the text about the identity of Jak Garcio: see Stevens and Cawley, *Plays*, vol. 2, p. 487, n. 257.

16  On the implications of rebellion by Trowle in Chester (7/202–87) see Sandra Billington, *Mock Kings in Medieval Society and Renaissance Drama*, (Oxford: Clarendon Press, 1991), pp. 63–4.

17  Cf. Lynn Forest-Hill, *Transgressive Language in Medieval English Drama* (Aldershot: Ashgate, 2000), pp. 82–3.

¹⁸ For the widespread customs concerning the establishment of mock kings, see Sandra Billington, *Mock Kings in Medieval Society and Renaissance Drama*, passim.

¹⁹ *The Drama of the Medieval Church* (Oxford: Clarendon Press, 1933), vol. 2, pp. 99–100. R. Weimann notes Herod as King of Fools in France and Italy, *Shakespeare and the Popular Tradition*, pp. 65–6.

²⁰ Garrett P. J. Epp suggests that this play is part of an Advent sequence which may have had a separate existence. He suggests that it runs *Prophets* (7), *Caesar* (9), *Annunciation* (part) (10), *Salutation* (11), *Annunciation* (part, Joseph). The argument depends upon the view that *Pharaoh* (8) and *Prophets* (7) should be reversed: see '"And every mys amend": editing the Towneley advent sequence', (forthcoming). I am grateful to Professor Epp for allowing me to see his conference paper.

²¹ Stevens and Cawley, *Plays*, vol. 2, p. 513.

²² See Arnold Williams, *The Characterization of Pilate in the Towneley Plays* (East Lansing: Michigan State College Press, 1950), pp. 10–11.

²³ The Herod of the Nativity is Herod the Great (Ascalonita): the Herod of the Passion, who appears in York, is Herod Antipas.

²⁴ John Gardner, *The Construction of the Wakefield Cycle* (1974), p. 98.

²⁵ L. M. Clopper notes the possibility of a regenerative effect by the comic reversal in the women's beating of the soldiers, *Drama, Play and Game*, p. 178.

²⁶ Stevens and Cawley sustain the attribution to the Wakefield Master, *Plays*, vol. 2, pp. 565–6, n. 1–52.

²⁷ A. C. Cawley, 'The Towneley *Processus Talentorum*: a survey and interpretation', *LSE*, 17 (1986), 131–7; Peter Meredith, 'The York millers' pageant and the Towneley *Processus Talentorum*', *METh*, 4 (1982), 104–14. The linguistic evidence adduced by Martin Stevens separates the linguistic characteristics from those of York, indicating composition other than at York: 'The composition of the Towneley *Talents* play: a linguistic examination', *JEGP*, 58 (1959), 423–33 (431). This, however, is challenged by Meredith (105–8).

²⁸ Stevens and Cawley, *Plays*, vol. 2, p. 57, n. 421; see also John Robinson, *Studies in Fifteenth-Century Stagecraft* (Kalamazoo: Medieval Institute Publications, 1991), p. 153.

²⁹ Lynn Forest-Hill has suggested that subversion is here licensed but also stretched, 'Sins of the mouth: signs of subversion in medieval English cycle plays', p. 24.

## 3.3 Social Contexts

¹ The response of the *Constitutions* against the spread of Lollardry may not have been entirely enforceable, and it is thought that there was regional variation in the way they were applied.

² *Reform and Cultural Revolution*, Oxford English Literary History, volume 2: 1350–1547 (Oxford: Oxford University Press, 2002), 523.

³ Cf. *MED reimen* v.2(a).

⁴ Stevens and Cawley, *Plays*, vol. 2, p. 495, note this problem and they link it with the tension between Cain (ploughman) and Abel (shepherd) in *Abel* (2). See also Warren Edminster, 'Punning and political power in *The Second Shepherds' Play*', *English Language Notes*, 40.4 (2003), 1–10, who develops, by means of the puns on 'wether' and 'child', a parallel between this social predicament and that of other 'husbandys' trapped in marriage.

⁵ This practice is criticized in the fifteenth-century morality *Wisdom* (*c.*1460) where the six 'jurors' wear hats of maintenance: see l. 724sd, and l. 761.

⁶ See Ruth Nissé, *Defining Acts: Drama and the Politics of Interpretation in Late Medieval England* (Notre Dame: University of Notre Dame Press, 2005), pp. 86–92. This account also shows a link between the poverty of the Shepherds and that of the Franciscans, p. 93.

⁷ The word 'tithe' is not used in the play, but 'teynd/tend' appears at 2/75, 104, 175, 216, 224. Though the York *Cain and Abel* (7) has a lacuna, the words 'tente/teynde' are used there similarly. It thus seems likely that the Wakefield Master was following a lead from York but he develops it extensively in theatrical as well as social terms.

⁸ For the possibility that Cain is incompetent as a ploughman see Liam O. Purdon, *The Wakefield Master's Dramatic Art: A Drama of Spiritual Understanding* (Gainesville, FL: University of Florida Press, 2003), pp. 24–5.

⁹ For historical aspects of the English legal system and the establishment of the common law in the period after the Conquest, see Theodore K. Lerud, *Social and Political Dimensions of the English Corpus Christi Drama* (New York and London: Garland, 1988), pp. 43–8.

¹⁰ B. A. Brockman, 'The law of man and the peace of God: judicial process as satiric theme in the Wakefield *Mactatio Abel*', *Speculum*, 49 (1974), 699–707 (700–1); see also Theodore K. Lerud, *Social and Political Dimensions of the English Corpus Christi Drama*, pp. 60–1, 157–8.

¹¹ Cf. Chaucer, *Prologue to the Canterbury Tales*, l. 256; noted by Stevens and Cawley, *Plays*, vol. 2, p. 558.

¹² Margaret Jennings, 'Tutivillus: the literary career of the recording demon', Texts and Studies, *SP*, 74 (1977), 58–64.

¹³ The evidence here is not entirely convincing since the context might suggest any kind of swearing, but there is a pointer in the 'fals indytars, / Quest mangers and iurers' welcomed in the Wakefield Master's words given to Pilate in *Conspiracy* (20/36–7): see the note on line 37 in Stevens and Cawley, *Plays*, vol. 2, p. 547.

¹⁴ V. A. Kolve, *The Play Called Corpus Christi* (London: Edward Arnold, 1966), pp. 141–2. It is very difficult to gauge how far perceptions may firmly have changed as between a medieval and a modern audience, but we can be sure that the fear of hell was indeed much greater.

¹⁵ We should note here that Noah's wife's spinning may also be a social issue: see Chapter 3.1, n. 7.

## 3.4 Interrelations in the Psychology of Evil

1   Arnold Williams, *The Characterization of Pilate*; John Gardner, *The Construction of the Wakefield Cycle* (Carbondale and Edwardsville: Southern Illinois University Press, 1974); Jeffrey Helterman, *Symbolic Action in the Plays of the Wakefield Master* (Athens, Ga.: University of Georgia Press, 1981). For this section I have also drawn on some material in my 'Subversion in *The Towneley Cycle*: strategies for evil', in M. Pincombe (ed.), *The Anatomy of Tudor Literature* (Aldershot: Ashgate, 2001), pp. 11–23.

2   Cecilia Pietropoli, 'The characterisation of evil in the Towneley plays', *METh*, 11 (1989), 85–93 (86–7).

3   See Helterman, *Symbolic Action in the Plays of the Wakefield Master*, pp. 117–19.

4   Gardner, *The Construction of the Wakefield Cycle*, pp. 74–5. Cecilia Pietropoli links these two characters in their wilfulness, *Il teatro dei Miracoli e delle Moralità*, p. 82.

5   See Williams, *The Characterization of Pilate*, pp. 4–7. That there were many contradictory ideas in the legends about Pilate is apparent from the discussion by Jean-Pierre Bordier with special reference to the French cycles: see *Le Jeu de la Passion: Le message chrétien et le théâtre français (XIIIe–XVIe s.)* (Paris: Champion, 1998), pp. 447–56. Williams has some useful detail from several German plays, *The Characterization of Pilate*, pp. 4–5.

6   As an illuminating contrast, J. O. Fichte thought that the N Town author tended to enlarge the role of the Devil as an opponent, 'The passion plays in *Ludus Coventriae* and the continental passion plays', in T. Takamiya and R. Beadle (eds), *Chaucer to Shakespeare: Essays in Honour of Shinsuke Ando* (Woodbridge: Boydell and Brewer, 1992), pp. 111–20 (p. 117).

7   M. Paull, 'The figure of Mahomet in the Towneley Cycle', *CD*, 6 (1972–3), 187–204.

8   See Williams, *Characterization of Pilate*, p. 29.

9   This elaboration of Judas's reasons is not original but was developed in a number of popular versions, dramatic and non-dramatic, as Stevens and Cawley make clear, *Plays*, vol. 2, p. 549.

10   Young, *The Drama of the Medieval Church* (Oxford: Clarendon Press, 1933) vol. 2, p. 195, cited by Stevens and Cawley, *Plays*, vol. 2, p. 525.

11   Cf. 'play' (147), 'gam' (151), 'played' (152).

12   W. O. Hassall, *The Holkham Bible Picture Book* (London: Dropmore Press, 1954), Fig. 31v.

13   See John D. Cox, 'The devils and society in the English mystery plays', *CD*, 28 (1994–5), 407–38.

## 3.5 Good Men and Women

1   For a fuller discussion of the contrast see my 'Dramatic images of man in medieval drama and Shakespeare', in P. Dorval (ed.), *Shakespeare et le Moyen Age* (Paris: Société Française Shakespeare, 2002), pp. 71–93 (pp. 71–9). *L'Omme Pecheur*

is in *Moralités françaises*, vol. 1, ed. Werner Helmut (Geneva: Slatkine, 1980), pp. 111–421.

2  *The Construction of the Wakefield Cycle*, p. 133.

3  John Bale's *God's Promises* (*c*.1538) works over much the same ground regarding the moral qualities of virtuous Old Testament figures. He shows them each seeking to sustain the promise of mercy by God and to each particular character a virtue is attributed: Justus Noah, Moses Sanctus, Abraham Fidelis, David Rex Pius.

4  For the *Planctus Mariae* in the liturgical drama see Karl Young, *The Drama of the Medieval Church*, vol. 1, pp. 496–506.

5  Theresa Coletti, *Mary Magdalene and the Drama of Saints: Theater, Gender and Religion in Late Medieval England* (Philadelphia: University of Pennsylvania Press, 2004), pp. 22 and 170.

6  *The Late Medieval Religious Plays of Bodleian MSS Digby 133 and e Museo 160*, ed. Donald C. Baker, John L. Murphy, and Louis B. Hall, Jr., EETS o.s. 283 (Oxford: Oxford University Press, 1982), pp. 24–95.

7  *Mary Magdalene and the Drama of Saints*, p. 206.

8  See Theresa Coletti, *Mary Magdalene and the Drama of Saints*, pp. 90–7. Katie Normington notes that none of the Towneley episodes show Mary as a sinner as she is in Chester and N Town, *Gender and Medieval Drama* (Cambridge: D. S. Brewer, 2004), p. 109.

9  This episode is not enacted, but Christ refers to it twice in *Conspiracy*, 20/404–5 and 452–3, perhaps in an erroneous duplication by the compiler.

# 4 Prologue

1  For further discussion of the development of the genre see my *Cyclic Form and the English Mystery Plays* (Amsterdam and New York: Rodopi, 2004). However, the unity of medieval Catholicism is nevertheless something about which there should be reservations: see Patrick Collinson, *The Reformation* (London: Phoenix, 2005), pp. 1–12; Diarmaid MacCulloch, *Reformation: Europe's House Divided, 1490–1700* (London: Penguin Books, 2004).

2  See P. Meredith (ed.), *The Mary Play* (London: Longman, 1987) and *The Passion Play* (London: Longman, 1990).

## 4.1 Development

1  See M. G. Frampton, 'The date of the Flourishing of the Wakefield Master', *PMLA*, 50 (1935), 631–60, and 'The date of the "Wakefield Master": bibliographical evidence', *PMLA*, 53 (1938), 86–117. The state of the wool trade in mid-fifteenth century Yorkshire may also be a significant factor: cf. Katie Normington, *Gender in Medieval Drama* (Cambridge: D. S. Brewer, 2004), pp. 131–2.

2  In the York *Resurrection* Christ is silent but the visual and iconic impact of rising from the tomb and walking away through the streets of York is magnificent. Meg

Twycross's production with stations in the street of York in 1992 put this point beyond conjecture. The Towneley version adds an extensive lyrical speech for Christ, 26/230–350.

3   *Signifying God: Social Relation and Symbolic Act in the York Corpus Christi Plays* (Chicago: University of Chicago Press, 2001), pp. 114–16.

4   It is possible that the process of accumulating the individual plays took place much earlier and that the Towneley manuscript is only a fair copy of such an earlier collection. However, the piecemeal collecting together of sections of what eventually became the cycle cannot be ruled out.

5   In the new numbering in Stevens and Cawley, *Plays*, there are 1088 lines: in the older edition (*The Towneley Plays*, ed. George England and A. W. Pollard, EETS e.s. 71 (Oxford: Oxford University Press, 1897) the count was 754 lines. Cf. *Conspiracy* with 779 lines discussed below.

6   Martin Stevens has noted that discomfort and poverty and the social stress in *Abel* may well be a reflection of tension in a manorial situation: see *Four Middle English Mystery Cycles* (Princeton: Princeton University Press, 1987), pp. 127–9.

7   See James M. Gibson '*Interludium Passionis Domini*: parish drama in medieval New Romney', in Alexandra F. Johnston and Wim Hüsken (eds), *English Parish Drama* (Amsterdam: Rodopi, 1996), pp. 137–48.

8   The civic aspiration at York is discussed by P. J. P. Goldberg, 'Craft guilds, the Corpus Christi play and civic government', in his *Society, Politics and Culture* (Cambridge: Cambridge University Press, 1986), pp. 16–47. For the possibility of strife between guilds at York see Kathleen M. Ashley, 'Sponsorship, reflexivity and resistance: cultural readings of the York Cycle plays', in J. J. Paxman, L. M. Clopper and S. Tomasch (eds), *The Performance of Middle English Culture: Essays on Chaucer and the Drama in Honor of Martin Stevens* (Cambridge: D. S. Brewer, 1998), pp. 9–24.

9   R. M. Lumiansky and David Mills propose a pre-exemplar which was in existence before the presumed exemplar of the existing Chester Cycle manuscripts: see *The Chester Mystery Cycle: Essays and Documents* (Chapel Hill and London: University of North Carolina Press, 1983), p. 5. For the expansion of Old Testament episodes see L. M. Clopper, *Chester*, REED (Toronto: University of Toronto Press, 1979), p. liv.

10  Stephen Spector, 'The composition and development of an eclectic manuscript: Cotton Vespasian D VIII', *LSE*, 9 (1997), 62–83.

11  For the possible revisions to the Coventry plays see *The Coventry Corpus Christi Plays*, ed. Clifford Davidson and Pamela M. King (Kalamazoo: The Medieval Institute, 2000), pp. 3–5. The Norwich Cycle was also reconfigured in the 1530s, but little of it is now extant: see JoAnna Dutka, 'Mystery plays at Norwich: their formation and development', *LSE*, 10 (1978), 107–20.

12  A. J. Minnis, *Medieval Theory of Authorship: Scholastic Literary Attitudes in the Later Middle Ages*, second edition (Aldershot: Wildwood House, 1988); Martin Stevens, 'The Towneley plays manuscript: *Compilatio* and *Ordinatio*', *Text*, 5 (1991), 157–73. See also M. B. Parkes, 'The influence of the concepts of Ordinatio and Compilatio on the development of the book', in his *Scribes, Scripts and*

*Readers: Studies in the Communication, Presentation and Dissemination of Medieval Texts* (London: Hambledon Press, 1991), pp. 25–69.

[13] See Graham A. Runnalls, *Les Mystères Français Imprimés* (Geneva: Droz, 1999).

[14] Stevens and Cawley, noting that there are some verbal similarities with corresponding episodes, suggest that some parts of the play may originally have been borrowed from York, *Plays*, vol. 2, p. 546.

[15] For further discussion of this and other elements not suggesting the Wakefield Master see my 'The Towneley Cycle without the Wakefield Master', *RORD* 45 (2006).

[16] Reference to Figure 1 on p. 24 indicates that there are fourteen plays not showing the characteristics of the work of the Wakefield Master, in addition to the six substantially borrowed from York: altogether, more than half of the cycle.

[17] The origin of the whole sequence is in the *Summa predicantium*, Stevens and Cawley, *Plays*, vol. 2, p. 649.

## 4.2 Playing and Reception

[1] See quotation on p. 3.

[2] See Garrett P. J. Epp, '"And every mys amend": editing the Towneley advent sequence' (forthcoming).

[3] Playing down on the street from the wagon has been generally assumed for some time and modern directors have not scrupled to do so; for the case against, see Margaret Rogerson, 'Raging in the streets of medieval York', *ET*, 3 (2000), 105–25.

[4] Cami D. Agan, 'The platea in the York and Wakefield Cycles: avenues for liminality and salvation', *SP*, 94 (1997), 344–67.

[5] *The Medieval English Stage: Corpus Christi Pageants and Plays* (Chicago and London: University of Chicago Press, 1974), pp. 15–33. Nelson's case, originally published in *Modern Philology*, 67 (1970), 303–20, was contested by Margaret Dorrell, 'Two studies of the York Corpus Christi play', *LSE*, 6 (1972), 77–111.

## 4.3 Interpretations and Structure

[1] L. M. Clopper notices that the guilds at York apparently did not consult each other, *Drama, Play and Game*, p. 172, but the question of whether there was any coordination at York and who undertook it if there was remains a challenging one. No doubt the traditions by which individual guilds managed their own plays would be an important factor over many years: a feature much less likely with Towneley.

[2] On the silent Christ in York see A. F. Johnston, '"At the still point of the turning world": Augustinian roots of medieval dramaturgy', *EMD*, 2 (1998), 1–19.

[3] Sarah Beckwith, *Signifying God*, pp. 72–5.

⁴ See John R. Elliott, Jr., and Graham A. Runnalls (eds), *The Baptism and Temptation of Christ: The First Day of a Medieval French Passion Play* (New Haven: Yale University Press, 1978), and Graham A. Runnalls, (ed.), *La Passion d'Auvergne* (Geneva: Droz, 1982).

⁵ Michael O'Connell, *The Idolatrous Eye: Iconoclasm and Theatre in Early Modern England* (Oxford: Oxford University Press, 2000), p. 27.

⁶ J. W. Earl, 'The shape of Old Testament history in the Towneley plays', *SP*, 69 (1972), 434–52 (442). He also notes that the escape through the Red Sea anticipates the eventual redemption by Christ (443), as well as the Baptism.

⁷ Cf. C. W. Marx, *The Devil's Right and the Redemption in the Literature of Medieval England* (Cambridge: D. S. Brewer, 1995), pp. 121–4.

⁸ Such a reflection offers a new line of speculation based upon what was available at York and was not chosen by the Towneley compiler: choice can be negative as well as positive.

⁹ For a study of the labouring world as represented by the Wakefield Master in the Towneley Cycle, see Liam O. Purdon, *The Wakefield Master's Dramatic Art: A Drama of Spiritual Understanding* (Gainesville, FL.: University of Florida Press, 2003). This work pays special attention to the 'work' undertaken by the soldiers and torturers.

¹⁰ L. M. Clopper, 'English drama: from ungodly *Ludi* to sacred play', in David Wallace (ed.), *The Cambridge History of Medieval English Literature* (Cambridge: Cambridge University Press, 1999), pp. 739–66 (p. 762).

¹¹ Theresa Coletti, 'Theology and politics in the Towneley *Play of the Talents*', *Medievalia and Humanistica*, 9 (1979), 111–26 (117–18).

¹² The study by Arnold Williams, *The Characterization of Pilate in the Towneley Plays* (East Lansing: Michigan State College Press, 1950), remains an important contribution concerning the emphasis and originality of the Towneley plays, even though Williams tended to see the cycle as the work of one author.

¹³ For the proposition that this play is misplaced see Barbara I. Gusick, 'Death and resurrection in the Towneley *Lazarus*', in B. I. Gusick and E. DuBruck, (eds), *Death and Dying in the Middle Ages* (New York: Peter Lang, 1999), pp. 331–54.

¹⁴ There is a notable contrast, whether deliberate or not, between the harmonious maternity in *Salutation* and what follows in the Shepherds plays. Though the reason for having two of the latter is not very clear, if they were used as alternatives the contrast between harmony and hardship works for both.

¹⁵ Such movement is represented outside the drama by Nicolas Love, *The Mirrour of the blessed lyf of Jesu Christ*, Julian of Norwich, *The Revelation of Divine Love*, and *The Book of Margery Kemp*. See Alexandra F. Johnston, 'The city as Patron: York', in Paul Whitfield White and Suzanne R. Westfall (eds), *York*, REED (Toronto: University of Toronto Press, 1979), pp. 152–3.

¹⁶ Besides Beverley, which we have noted earlier, Barbara Palmer points out the possible existence of Corpus Christi cycles at Pontefract and Doncaster, 'Corpus Christi cycles in Yorkshire: the surviving records', *CD*, 27 (1993), 218–31.

¹⁷ See under Angus McIntosh et al. in the Bibliography.

# Bibliography

## Primary Texts

*The Alsfeld Passion Play*, ed. and trans. Larry E. West (Lampeter: Mellen, 1997).

*The Ancient Cornish Drama*, ed. E. Norris, 2 vols (Oxford: Oxford University Press, 1859).

*The Castle of Perserverance*, in *The Macro Plays*, ed. Mark Eccles, EETS 262 (Oxford: Oxford University Press, 1969), pp. 1–111.

*The Chester Mystery Cycle*, ed. R. M. Lumiansky and David Mills, 2 vols, EETS s.s. 3, 9 (Oxford: Oxford University Press, 1974, 1986).

*The Coventry Corpus Christi Plays*, ed. Clifford Davidson and Pamela M. King (Kalamazoo: The Medieval Institute, 2000).

*Das Künzelsauer Fronleichnamspiel*, ed. P. K. Liebenow (Berlin: De Gruyter, 1969).

*Everyman*, ed. A. C. Cawley (Manchester: University of Manchester Press, 1961).

Heywood, John, *Johan Johan*, in Richard Axton and Peter Happé (eds), *The Plays of John Heywood* (Cambridge: D. S. Brewer, 1991), pp. 75–109.

*The Late Medieval Religious Plays of Bodleian MSS Digby 133 and e. Mus. 160*, ed. Donald C. Baker, John L. Murphy, and Louis B. Hall, Jr., EETS o.s. 283 (Oxford: Oxford University Press, 1982).

*The Macro Plays*, ed. Mark Eccles, EETS 262 (Oxford: Oxford University Press, 1969).

*The Mary Play*, ed. P. Meredith (London: Longman, 1987).

*The Mirour of Mans Saluacioun*, ed. A. Henry (Aldershot: Scolar Press, 1986).

*The Mirror of the Blessed Life of Jesu Christ*, trans. Nicholas Love (London: Burns, Oates and Washburne, 1926).

Love, Nicholas, *The Mirror of the Blessed Life of Jesus Christ: A Reading Test*, ed. Michael G. Sargeant (Exeter: Exeter University Press, 2004).

*Le Mystère de la Passion d'Arnoul Gréban*, ed. O. Jodogne (Brussels: Académie Royale de Belgique, 1965).

*The N Town Play: Cotton MS Vespasian D. 8*, ed. Stephen Spector, 2 vols, EETS s.s. 11 (Oxford: Oxford University Press, 1991).

*The N-Town Plays: A Facsimile of British Library MS Cotton Vespasian D.VIII*, ed. Peter Meredith and S. J. Kahrl (Leeds: University of Leeds, 1977).

*L'Omme Pecheur* in *Moralités françaises*, vol. 1, ed. Werner Helmut (Geneva: Slatkine, 1980), pp. I. 111–421.

*La Passion d'Auvergne*, ed. Graham A. Runnalls (Geneva: Droz, 1982).

*The Passion Play*, ed. P. Meredith (London: Longman, 1990).

*Representative English Comedies*, ed. C. M. Gayley (New York: Macmillan, 1903).

*The Towneley Cycle: A Facsimile of Huntington MS HM1*, ed. A. C. Cawley and M. Stevens (Leeds: University of Leeds, 1976).

*The Towneley Mysteries*, ed. James Gordon and Joseph Hunter (London: The Surtees Society, 1836).

*The Towneley Plays*, ed. George England and A. W. Pollard, EETS e.s. 71 (Oxford: Oxford University Press, 1897).

*The Towneley Plays*, ed. Martin Stevens and A. C. Cawley, 2 vols, EETS s.s. 13 (Oxford: Oxford University Press, 1994).

*The Wakefield Mystery Plays*, ed. Martial Rose (London: Evans Bros, 1961).

*The Wakefield Pageants in the Towneley Cycle*, ed. A. C. Cawley (Manchester: Manchester University Press, 1958).

*Wisdom*, in *The Macro Plays*, ed. Mark Eccles, EETS 262 (Oxford: Oxford University Press, 1969), pp. 113–52.

*The World and the Child*, ed. Clifford Davidson and Peter Happé (Kalamazoo: Medieval Institute, 1999).

*The York Play: A Facsimile of British Library MS Additional 35290*, ed. Richard Beadle and Peter Meredith (Leeds: University of Leeds, 1983).

*York Plays*, ed. Lucy Toulmin Smith (Oxford: Clarendon Press, 1885, repr., New York: Russell and Russell, 1963).

*The York Plays*, ed. Richard Beadle (London: Edward Arnold, 1982).

## Secondary Texts

Adams, Charles Phythian, 'Ceremony and the citizen: the communal year at Coventry 1450–1550', in Peter Clark and Paul Slack (eds), *Crisis and Order in English Towns 1500–1700: Essays in Urban History* (London: Routledge, 1972), pp. 57–85.

Aers, David, and Lynn Staley, *The Powers of the Holy: Religion, Politics, and Gender in Late Medieval English Culture* (University Park: Pennsylvania University Press, 1996).

Agan, Cami D., 'The platea in the York and Wakefield Cycles: avenues for liminality and salvation', *SP*, 94 (1997), pp. 344–67.

Ashley, Kathleen M., ' "Wyt" and "Wysdam" in the N Town Cycle', *PQ*, 58 (1979), 121–35.

——, 'The resurrection of Lazarus in the late medieval English and French cycle drama', *Papers on Language and Literature*, 22 (1986), pp. 227–44.

——, 'Cultural approaches to medieval drama,' in R. K. Emmerson (ed.), *Approaches to Teaching Medieval English Drama* (New York: Modern Language Association of America, 1990), pp. 57–66.

——, (ed.) *Victor Turner and the Construction of Cultural Criticism: Between Literature and Anthropology* (Bloomington: Indiana University Press, 1990).

——, 'Sponsorship, reflexivity and resistance: cultural readings of the York Cycle plays', in J. J. Paxson, L. M. Clopper and S. Tomasch (eds), *The Performance of Middle English Culture* (Cambridge: D. S. Brewer, 1998), pp. 9–24.

Aston, Margaret, *Faith and Fire: Popular and Unpopular Religion 1350–1600* (London: Hambledon Press, 1993).

——, 'Death', in R. Horrox (ed.), *Fifteenth-Century Attitudes: Perceptions of Society in Late Medieval England* (Cambridge: Cambridge University Press, 1994), pp. 202–28.

Axton, Richard, *European Drama of the Early Middle Ages* (London: Hutchinson, 1974).

Bakhtin, Mikhail, *Rabelais and His World*, trans. Hélène Iswolsky (Bloomington: University of Indiana Press, 1984).

Bale, John, *God's Promises*, in Peter Happé (ed.), *The Complete Plays of John Bale*, 2 vols (Cambridge: D. S. Brewer, 1985–6), vol. 2, pp. 1–34.

Banks, William Stott, *A List of Provincial Words in use at Wakefield in Yorkshire* (London: J. R. Smith, 1865).

Baugh, A. C., 'The Mak story', *MP*, 15 (1918), 729–34.

Beadle, Richard, 'The York hosiers' play of *Moses and Pharaoh*: a middle English dramatist at work', *Poetica* (Tokyo), 19 (1984), 3–26.

—— (ed.), *The Cambridge Companion to Medieval English Theatre* (Cambridge: Cambridge University Press, 1994).

——, 'Middle English texts and their transmission, 1350–1500: some geographical criteria', in Margaret Laing and Keith Williamson (eds), *Speaking in our Tongues* (Cambridge: D. S. Brewer, 1994), pp. 69–91.

——, 'Verbal texture and wordplay in the York Cycle', *ET*, 3 (2000), 167–84.

Beckwith, Sarah, 'Ritual, church and theatre: medieval dramas of the sacramental body', in David Aers (ed.), *Culture and History 1350–1600* (Hemel Hempstead: Harvester Wheatsheaf, 1992), pp. 65–90.

——, *Christ's Body: Identity, Culture and Society in Late Medieval Writings* (London and New York: Routledge, 1993).

——, 'Making the world in York and the York Cycle', in S. Kay and Miri Rubin (eds), *Framing Medieval Bodies* (Manchester: Manchester University Press, 1994), pp. 254–76.

——, 'The present of past things: the York Cycle as contemporary theory of memory', *JMEMS*, 26 (1996), 355–79.

——, '*Sacrum Signum*: sacramentality and dissent in York's theatre of Corpus Christi', in R. Copeland (ed.), *Criticism and Dissent in the Middle Ages* (Cambridge: Cambridge University Press, 1996), pp. 264–88.

——, 'Absent presences: the theatre of resurrection in York', in David Aers (ed.), *Medieval Literature and Historical Enquiry* (Cambridge: D. S. Brewer, 2000), pp. 185–205.

——, *Signifying God: Social Relation and Symbolic Act in the York Corpus Christi Plays* (Chicago: University of Chicago Press, 2001).

Bernbrock, J. E., 'Notes on the Towneley Cycle *Slaying of Abel*', *JEGP*, 62 (1963), 317–22.

Betcher, Gloria J., 'A reassessment of the date and provenance of the Cornish *Ordinalia*', *CD*, 29 (1995–6), 35–63.

Billington, Sandra, *Mock Kings in Medieval Society and Renaissance Drama* (Oxford: Clarendon Press, 1991).

Bills, B., 'The "Suppression Theory" and the English Corpus Christi play: a re-examination', *Theatre Journal*, 32 (1980), 157–68.

Bordier, Jean-Pierre, *Le Jeu de la Passion: Le message chrétien et le théâtre français (XIIIe–XVIe s.)* (Paris: Champion, 1998).

Bossy, John, *Christianity in the West 1400–1700* (Oxford: Oxford University Press, 1985).

Brawer, R. A., 'The dramatic function of the ministry group in the Towneley Cycle', *CD*, 4 (1970–1), 166–75.

Brigden, Susan, *London and the Reformation* (Oxford: Clarendon Press, 1989).

Briscoe, Marianne G., and John C. Coldewey (eds), *Contexts for Early English Drama* (Bloomington, IA: Indiana University Press, 1989).

Bristol, Michael D., *Carnival and Theatre* (London: Methuen, 1985).

——, 'Theater and popular culture', in John D. Cox and David Scott Kastan (eds), *A New History of Early English Drama* (New York: Columbia University Press, 1997), pp. 23–48.

Brockman, B. A., 'The law of man and the peace of God: judicial process as satiric theme in the Wakefield *Mactatio Abel*', *Speculum*, 49 (1974), 699–707.

——, 'Comic and tragic counterpoint in the medieval drama: the Wakefield *Mactatio Abel*', *Medieval Studies*, 39 (1977), 331–49.

Brown, C., 'The Towneley *Play of the Doctors* and the *Speculum Christiani*', *MLN*, 31 (1916), 223–6.

Burke, Peter, *Popular Culture in Early Modern Europe* (Aldershot: Scolar Press, 1978).

Burns, E., 'Seeing is believing: the Chester play of nativity at Chester Cathedral, summer 1987', *Cahiers Elisabéthaines*, 34 (1988), 1–9.

Butler, Michelle M., 'The York/Towneley *Harrowing of Hell?*', *FCS*, 25 (2000), 115–26.

Butterworth, Philip, 'Discipline, Dignity and Beauty: the Wakefield mystery plays, Bretton Hall, 1958', *LSE*, 32 (2001), 49–80.

Bynum, Caroline Walker, 'The body of Christ in the later Middle Ages: a reply to Leo Steinberg', *Renaissance Quarterly*, 39 (1986), 399–439.

Cady, F. W., 'The liturgical basis of the Towneley Mysteries', *PMLA*, 24 (1909), 419–69.

——, 'The Couplets and Quatrains in the Towneley mystery plays', *JEGP*, 10 (1911), 572–84.

——, 'The Wakefield group in Towneley', *JEGP*, 11 (1912), 244–62.

——, 'The passion group in Towneley', *MP*, 10 (1913), 587–600.

——, 'Towneley, York, and true-Coventry', *SP*, 26 (1929), 386–400.

Campbell, T. P., 'Why do the shepherds prophesy?', *CD*, 12 (1978), 137–50.

Cantelupe, E. B., and R. Griffith, 'The gifts of the shepherds in the Wakefield "Secunda Pastorum"', *Medieval Studies*, 28 (1966), 328–55.

Carey, Millicent, *The Wakefield Group in the Towneley Cycle* (Baltimore: Johns Hopkins University Press, 1950).

Cargill, Oscar, 'The authorship of the *Secunda Pastorum*', *PMLA*, 41 (1926), 810–31.

Carpenter, Nan C., 'Music in the *Secunda Pastorum*', *Speculum*, 26 (1951), 696–700.

Cawley, A. C., 'Iak Garcio of the *Prima Pastorum*', *MLN*, 68 (1953), 169–72.

——, 'The grotesque feast in the *Prima Pastorum*', *Speculum*, 30 (1955), 213–17.

——, 'Middle English versions of the Decalogue with reference to the English Corpus Christi cycle', *LSE*, 8 (1975), 129–45.

——, 'The Towneley *Processus Talentorum*: a survey and interpretation', *LSE*, 17 (1986), 131–7.

——, Marion Jones, Peter F. McDonald and David Mills, *The Revels History of Drama in English: Volume I, Medieval Drama* (London and New York: Methuen, 1983).

——, and M. Stevens, 'The Towneley *Processus Talentorum*: text and commentary', *LSE*, 17 (1986), 105–30.

——, J. Forrester and J. Goodchild, 'References to the Corpus Christi play in the Wakefield Burgess court rolls: the originals rediscovered', *LSE*, 19 (1988), 85–104.

Chambers, E. K., *The Medieval Stage*, 2 vols (Oxford: Clarendon Press, 1903).

Chidamian, C., 'Mak and the tossing in the blanket', *Speculum*, 22 (1947), 186–90.

Clarke, E. M., 'Liturgical influences in the Towneley plays', *Orate Frates*, 16 (1941), 69–70.

Clopper, Laurence M., *Chester*, REED (Toronto: University of Toronto Press, 1979).

——, 'Tyrants and villains: characterization in the passion sequences of the English cycle plays', *MLQ*, 41 (1980), 3–20.

——, 'English drama: from ungodly *Ludi* to sacred play', in David Wallace (ed.), *The Cambridge History of Medieval English Literature* (Cambridge: Cambridge University Press, 1999), pp. 739–66.

——, *Drama, Play and Game: English Festive Culture in the Medieval and Early Modern Period* (Chicago and London: University of Chicago Press, 2002).

Coletti, Theresa, 'Theology and politics in the Towneley *Play of the Talents*', *Medievalia and Humanistica*, 9 (1979), 111–26.

——, 'A feminist approach to the Corpus Christi cycles', in R. K. Emmerson (ed.), *Approaches to Teaching Medieval English Drama* (New York: Modern Language Association of America, 1990), pp. 79–89.

——, 'Purity and danger: the paradox of Mary's body and the en-gendering of the infancy narrative in the English mystery cycles', in Linda Lomperis and Sarah Stanbury (eds), *Feminist Approaches to the Body in Medieval Literature* (Philadelphia: University of Pennsylvania Press, 1993), pp. 65–95.

——, ' "Ther Be But Women": gender conflict and gender identity in the Middle English innocents plays', *Medievalia*, 18 (1995), 245–61.

——, *Mary Magdalene and the Drama of Saints: Theater, Gender and Religion in Late Medieval England* (Philadelphia: University of Pennsylvania Press, 2004).

Collinson, Patrick, *The Reformation* (London: Phoenix, 2005).

Cook, A. S., 'Another parallel to the Mak story', *MP*, 14 (1916), 11–15.

Coronato, Rocco, *Jonson Versus Bakhtin: Carnival and the Grotesque* (Amsterdam: Rodopi, 2003).

Cosbey, R. C., 'The Mak story and its folklore analogues', *Speculum*, 20 (1945), 310–17.

Cox, John D., 'The devils and society in the English mystery plays', *CD*, 28 (1994–5), 407–38.

——, *The Devil and the Sacred in English Drama, 1350–1642* (Cambridge: Cambridge University Press, 2000).

Craddock, L., 'Franciscan influence on early English drama', *Franciscan Studies*, 10 (1950), 383–417.

Curtis, C. G., 'The York and Towneley plays on *The Harrowing of Hell*', *SP*, 30 (1933), 23–33.

David, A., 'Noah's wife's flood', in Paxson, Clopper and Tomasch (eds), *The Performance of Middle English Culture*, pp. 97–116.

Davidson, Clifford, 'An interpretation of the Wakefield *Judicium*', *Annuale Medievale*, 10 (1969), 104–19.

——, 'Carnival, Lent and early English drama', *RORD*, 36 (1997), 123–42.

——, 'Cain in the mysteries: the iconography of violence', *FCS*, 25 (2000), 204–27.

——, *History, Religion, and Violence: Cultural Contexts for Medieval and Renaissance English Drama* (Aldershot: Ashgate, 2002).

de Voragine, Jacob, *The Golden Legend: Readings on the Saints*, trans. W. G. Ryan, 2 vols (Princeton: Princeton University Press, 1993).

De Vos, Dirk, *Hans Memling: The Complete Works* (London: Thames and Hudson, 1994).

de Welles, T. R., 'The Social and Political Content of the Towneley Cycle', (Unpublished Ph.D. thesis, Toronto: University of Toronto, 1981).

Denny, N., 'Arena staging a dramatic quality in the Cornish Passion play', in N. Denny (ed.), *Medieval Drama*, Stratford-upon-Avon Studies, 16 (London: Edward Arnold, 1973), 124–53.

Diller, Hans-Jurgen, 'The craftsmanship of the Wakefield Master', in Taylor and Nelson (eds), *Medieval English Drama: Essays Critical and Contextual* (Chicago and London: University of Chicago Press, 1972), pp. 245–59.

——, 'The torturers in the English mystery plays', *METh*, 11 (1989), 57–65.

——, and David E. O'Connor, *York Art* (Kalamazoo: Medieval Institute, 1978).

Dillon, Janette, 'Holy women and their confessors or confessors and their holy women? Margery Kemp and continental tradition', in R. Voaden (ed.), *Prophets Abroad: The Reception of Continental Holy Women in Late Medieval England* (Cambridge: D. S. Brewer, 1996), pp. 115–40.

Dobson, R. B., 'Craft guilds and city: the historical origins of the York mystery plays reassessed', in A. E. Knight (ed.), *The Stage as Mirror: Civic Theatre in Late Medieval Europe* (Cambridge: D. S. Brewer, 1997), pp. 91–106.

Dorrell, Margaret, 'Two studies of the York Corpus Christi play', *LSE*, 6 (1972), 77–111.

Duffy, Eamon, *The Stripping of the Altars: Traditional Religion in England c.1400–c.1580* (New Haven: Yale University Press, 1992).

Dunn, E. C., 'The medieval "Cycle" as history play: an approach to the Wakefield plays', *Studies in the Renaissance*, 7 (1961), 79–89.

——, 'Lyrical form and prophetic principle in the Towneley plays', *Medieval Studies*, 23 (1961), 80–90.

——, 'The literary style of the Towneley plays', *American Benedictine Review*, 20 (1969), 481–504.

Dustoor, P. E., 'Some textual notes on the English mystery plays', *MLR*, 21 (1926), 427–31.

——, 'Textual notes on the Towneley Old Testament plays', *Englische Studien*, 43 (1929), 220–8.

Dutka, JoAnna, 'Mystery plays at Norwich: their formation and development', *LSE*, 10 (1978), 107–20.

——, *Music in the English Mystery Plays* (Kalamazoo: The Medieval Institute, 1980).

Earl, J. W., 'The shape of Old Testament history in the Towneley plays', *SP*, 69 (1972), 434–52.

Eaton, H. A., 'A source for the Towneley *Prima Pastorum*', *MLN*, 14 (1899), 265–8.

Edminster, Warren, 'Foolish shepherds and priestly folly: festive influence in the *Prima Pastorum*', *Medieval Perspectives*, 15 (2000), 57–73.

——, 'Punning and political power in *The Second Shepherds' Play*', *English Language Notes*, 40.4 (2003) 1–10.

——, *The Preaching Fox: Festive Subversion in the Plays of the Wakefield Master* (New York: Routledge, 2005).

Elliott Jr., John R., 'Mediaeval acting', in M. G. Briscoe and J. E. Coldewey (eds), *Contexts for Early English Drama* (Bloomington, IN: Indiana University Press, 1989), pp. 238–91.

——, *Playing God: Medieval Mysteries on the Modern Stage* (Toronto: University of Toronto Press, 1989).

——, and Graham A. Runnalls (eds), *The Baptism and Temptation of Christ: The First Day of a Medieval French Passion Play* (New Haven: Yale University Press, 1978).

Emmerson, R. K. (ed.), *Approaches to Teaching Medieval English Drama* (New York: Modern Language Association of America, 1990).

Epp, Garrett P. J., 'Passion, pomp, and parody: alliteration in the York plays', *METh*, 11 (1989), 150–61.

——, 'Visible words: the York plays, Brecht and Gestic writing', *CD*, 24 (1990–1), 289–305.

——, 'The Towneley plays and the hazards of cycling', *RORD*, 32 (1993), 121–50.

——, 'Ecce Homo', in Glenn Burger and Steven F. Kruger (eds), *Queering the Middle Ages* (Minneapolis: University of Minnesota Press, 2001), pp. 236–51.

——, '"Corected and not playd": an unproductive history of the Towneley plays', *RORD*, 43 (2004), 38–53.

——, '"And every mys amend": editing the Towneley advent sequence', (forthcoming).

Evans, Ruth, 'Feminist re-enactments: gender and the Towneley *Uxor Noe*', in J. Dor (ed.), *A Wyf ther was: Essays in Honour of Paule Mertens-Fonck* (Liège: University of Liège Press, 1992), pp. 141–54.

——, 'Body politics: engendering medieval cycle drama', in Ruth Evans and Lesley Johnson (eds), *Feminist Readings in Middle English Literature* (London and New York: Routledge, 1994), pp. 112–39.

Fichte, J. O., *Expository Voices in Medieval Drama: Essays on the Mode and Function of Dramatic Exposition* (Nürnberg: Carl, 1975).

——, 'The passion plays in *Ludus Coventriae* and the continental passion plays', in T. Takamiya and R. Beadle (eds), *Chaucer to Shakespeare: Essays in Honour of Shinsuke Ando* (Woodbridge: Boydell and Brewer, 1992), pp. 111–20.

Fionella, M. G., 'The conversion of the sign in the Towneley passion plays', in M. D. Ledgerwood (ed.), *New Approaches to Medieval Textuality* (New York: Peter Lang, 1998).

Fitzhenry, W., 'The *N-Town Plays* and the politics of metatheater', *SP*, 100 (2003), 22–43.

Flanigan, Clifford C., 'Liminality, carnival, and social structure: the case of late medieval biblical drama', in Ashley (ed.), *Victor Turner and the Construction of Cultural Criticism*, pp. 42–63.

Forest-Hill, Lynn, *Transgressive Language in Medieval English Drama* (Aldershot: Ashgate, 2000).

——, 'Sins of the mouth: signs of subversion in medieval English cycle plays', in Dermot Cavanagh and Tim Kirk (eds), *Subversion and Scurrility: Popular Discourse in Europe from 1500 to the Present* (Aldershot: Ashgate, 2000), pp. 11–25.

Forrester J., and A. C. Cawley, 'The Corpus Christi play at Wakefield: a new look at the Wakefield Burgess Court records', *LSE*, 7 (1974), 108–16.

Frampton, M. G., 'The date of the flourishing of the Wakefield Master', *PMLA*, 50 (1935), 631–60.

——, 'The date of the "Wakefield Master": bibliographical evidence', *PMLA*, 53 (1938), 86–117.

——, 'The Towneley *Harrowing of Hell*', *PMLA*, 56 (1941), 105–19.

——, 'The York play of Christ led up to Calvary (Towneley XXXIV)', *PQ*, 20 (1941), 198–204.

——, 'Towneley XXX: the *Conspiracio* (*et Capcio*)', *PMLA*, 58 (1943), 920–37.

——, 'The *Processus Talentorum*: (Towneley XXIV)', *PMLA*, 59 (1944), 646–54.

Frank, Grace, 'On the relation between the York and Towneley plays', *PMLA*, 44 (1929), 313–19.

Fries, Maureen, 'The evolution of Eve in medieval French and English drama', *SP*, 99 (2002), 1–16.

Furnish, Shearle, 'The play-within-the-play in the dramas of the Wakefield Master', *Medieval Perspective*, 14 (1999), 61–9.

Gardiner, Harold C., *Mysteries' End: An Investigation into the Last Days of the Medieval Religious Stage* (New Haven: Yale University Press, 1946).

Gardner, John, 'Theme and irony in the Wakefield *Mactatio Abel*', *PMLA*, 80 (1965), 515–21.

——, *The Construction of the Wakefield Cycle* (Carbondale and Edwardsville: Southern Illinois University Press, 1974).

Gash, A., 'Carnival against Lent: the ambivalence of medieval drama', in David Aers (ed.), *Medieval Literature: Criticism, Ideology and History* (New York: St Martin's Press, 1986), pp. 74–98.

Gayley, C. M., *Plays of our Forefathers* (London: Chatto and Windus, 1908).

Gerould, G. H., 'Moll of the *Prima Pastorum*', *MLN*, 19 (1904), 225–30.

Gibson, Gail McMurray, *The Theater of Devotion: East Anglian Drama and Society in the Late Middle Ages* (Chicago and London: University of Chicago Press, 1994).

Gibson, James M., '*Interludium Passionis Domini*: parish drama in medieval New Romney', in Alexandra F. Johnston and Wim Hüsken (eds), *English Parish Drama* (Amsterdam: Rodopi, 1996), pp. 137–48.

Goldberg, P. J. P., 'Craft guilds, the Corpus Christi play and civic government', in his *Society, Politics and Culture* (Cambridge: Cambridge University Press, 1986), pp. 16–47.

——, 'Late book ownership in late medieval York: the evidence of wills', *The Library*, 6th series, 16 (1994), 181–9.

——, 'Women', in Horrox (ed.), *Fifteenth-Century Attitudes: Perceptions of Society in Late Medieval England* (Cambridge: Cambridge University Press, 1994), pp. 112–31.

——, 'Performing the word of God: Corpus Christi drama in the northern province', in D. Wood (ed.), *Life and Thought in the Northern Church, c.1100–1700* (Woodbridge: Boydell and Brewer, 1999), pp. 145–70.

Goodland, Katherine, '"Vs for to wepe no man may lett": accommodating female grief in the medieval Lazarus plays', *ET*, 8.1 (2005), 69–94.

Grantley, Darryll, *Wit's Pilgrimage: Drama and the Social Impact of Education in Early Modern England* (Aldershot: Ashgate, 2000).

Green, J. H., 'Yorkshire dialect as spoken in the West Riding during the fifteenth and nineteenth centuries', *Transactions of the Yorkshire Dialect Society*, I, part 2 (1899), 54–68.

Greg, W. W., 'Bibliographical and textual problems of the English miracle cycles', *The Library*, 3rd series, 5 (1914), 1–30, 168–205, 280–319, 365–99.

Gusick, Barbara I., 'Time and unredemption: perception of Christ's work in the Towneley *Lazarus*', *FCS*, 22 (1996), 19–41.

——, 'Death and resurrection in the Towneley *Lazarus*', in B. I. Gusick and E. DuBruck (eds), *Death and Dying in the Middle Ages* (New York: Peter Lang, 1999), pp. 331–54.

Hamelius, P., 'The character of Cain in the Towneley plays', *Journal of Comparative Literature*, 1 (1903), 324–44.

Happé, Peter, 'Review of Towneley plays at Wakefield', *RORD*, 23 (1980), 81–2.

——, 'Devils' languages in some Corpus Christi plays', *Theta*, 3 (1996), 43–61.

——, 'Cycle plays: the state of the art', *EMD*, 2 (1998), 63–84.

——, 'The English cycle plays: contexts and development', *EDAMR*, 20 (1998), 71–87.

——, 'Devils in the York cycle: language and dramatic technique', *RORD*, 37 (1998), 79–98.

——, *English Drama Before Shakespeare* (London: Longman, 1999).

——, 'Performing passion plays in France and England', *EMD*, 4 (2000), 57–75.

——, 'Subversion in *The Towneley Cycle*: strategies for evil', in M. Pincombe (ed.), *The Anatomy of Tudor Literature* (Aldershot: Ashgate, 2001), pp. 11–23.

——, 'Farcical elements in the English mystery cycles', in W. Hüsken and Konrad Schoell (eds), *Farce and Farcical Elements* (Amsterdam and New York: Rodopi, 2002), pp. 29–43.

——, 'Procession and the cycle drama in England and Europe: some dramatic possibilities', *EMD*, 6 (2002), 31–47.

——, 'Dramatic images of man in medieval drama and Shakespeare', in P. Dorval (ed.), *Shakespeare et le Moyen Age* (Paris: Société Française Shakespeare, 2002), pp. 71–93.

——, *Cyclic Form and the English Mystery Plays* (Amsterdam and New York: Rodopi, 2004).

——, '"Erazed in the Booke": the mystery cycles and reform', in Lloyd Kermode, Jason Scott-Warren and Martine van Elk (eds), *Tudor Drama before Shakespeare, 1485–1590: New Directions for Research, Criticism, and Pedagogy* (New York and Basingstoke: Palgrave, 2004), pp. 15–33.

——, 'The Towneley Cycle without the Wakefield Master', *RORD*, 45 (2006), 23–38.

——, 'Staging God in some last judgement plays', (forthcoming).

Harty, K. J., 'The unity and structure of the Charter Mystery Cycle', in Kevin J. Harty (ed.), *The Chester Mystery Cycle: A Casebook* (New York and London: Garland, 1993).

Hassall, W. O. (ed.), *The Holkham Bible Picture Book* (London: Dropmore Press, 1954).

Havely, N., 'The Towneley Cycle of Toronto: the audience as actor', *METh*, 7 (1985), 51–7.

Helterman, Jeffrey, *Symbolic Action in the Plays of the Wakefield Master* (Athens, GA.: University of Georgia Press, 1981).

Hirsch, J. C., 'Mak Tossed in a Blanket', *N&Q*, 226 (1981), 117–18.

Holford, M. L., 'Language and regional identity in the York Corpus Christi Cycle', *LSE*, 33 (2002), 171–96.

Horrox, R. (ed.), *Fifteenth-Century Attitudes: Perceptions of Society in Late Medieval England* (Cambridge: Cambridge University Press, 1994).

Howard-Hill, T. H., 'The evolution of the form of plays during the Renaissance', *Renaissance Quarterly*, 43 (1990), 112–45.

Hutton, Richard, *The Rise and Fall of Merry England: The Ritual Year, 1400–1700* (Oxford: Oxford University Press, 1994).

Jack, R. D. S., *Patterns of Divine Comedy: A Study of Medieval English Drama* (Cambridge: D. S. Brewer, 1989).

Jambeck, T., 'The canvas-tossing allusion in the *Secunda Pastorum*', *MP*, 76 (1978), 49–54.

James, Mervyn, 'Ritual body and social drama in the late medieval English town', *Past and Present*, 98 (1983), 3–29.

Jeffrey, David L., 'Pastoral care in the Wakefield shepherd plays', *American Benedictine Review*, 22 (1971), 208–21.

Jennings, Margaret, 'Tutivillus: the literary career of the recording demon', Texts and Studies, *SP*, 74 (1977).

Johnston, Alexandra F., 'Evil in the Towneley Cycle', *METh*, 11 (1989), 94–103.

——, 'Four York pageants performed in the streets of York', *RORD*, 31 (1992), 101–4.

——, 'The word made flesh: Augustinian elements in the York Cycle', in R. A. Taylor et al. (eds), *The Centre and its Compass: Studies in Medieval Literature in Honor of Professor John Layerle*, Studies in Medieval Culture, 33 (Kalamazoo: Medieval Institute Publications, 1993).

——, 'Acting Mary: the emotional realism of the mature Virgin in the N Town plays', in John A. Alford (ed.), *From Page to Performance* (East Lansing: Michigan State University Press, 1995), pp. 85–98.

——, '"At the still point of the turning world": Augustinian roots of medieval dramaturgy', *EMD*, 2 (1998), 1–19.

——, 'York Cycle 1998: what we learned', *ET*, 3 (2000), 199–203.

——, 'The *York Cycle* and the Libraries of York', in Caroline Barron and Jenny Stratford (eds), *The Church and Learning in Late Medieval Society: Essays in Honour of Barrie Dobson*, Harlaxton Medieval Studies XI (Donnington, 2002), pp. 335–70.

——, 'The city as patron: York', in Paul Whitfield White and Suzanne R. Westfall (eds), *Shakespeare and Theatrical Patronage in Early Modern England* (Cambridge: Cambridge University Press, 2002), pp. 150–75.

—— and Margaret Rogerson (eds), *REED: York* (Toronto: University of Toronto Press, 1979).

Jones, Malcolm, '"Slawpase fro the Myln-Wheele": seeing between the lines', in Twycross (ed.), *Festive Drama*, pp. 242–58.

Kendall, Ritchie D., *The Drama of Dissent: The Radical Poetics of Nonconformity, 1380–1590* (Chapel Hill: University of North Carolina Press, 1986).

King, Pamela M., 'Calendar and text: Christ's ministry in the York plays and the liturgy', *MÆ*, 67 (1998), 30–59.

——, 'Contemporary cultural models for the trial plays in the York Cycle', in Alan Hindley (ed.), *Drama and Community: People and Plays in Medieval Europe* (Turnhout: Brepols, 1999), pp. 200–16.

——, 'The York plays and the feast of Corpus Christi: a reconsideration', *METh*, 22 (2000), 13–32.

—— and Clifford Davidson (eds), *The Coventry Corpus Christi Plays* (Kalamazoo: The Medieval Institute, 2000).

Kinneavy, G. B., *A Concordance to the Towneley Plays* (New York and London: Garland, 1990).

Kobialla, M., 'Historic time, mythical time, and mimetic time: the impact of the humanistic philosophy of St Anselm on early medieval drama', *Medieval Perspectives*, 3.1 (1998).

Kolve, V. A., *The Play Called Corpus Christi* (London: Edward Arnold, 1966).

Kroll, Norma, 'The Towneley and Chester plays of the shepherds: the dynamic interweaving of power, conflict, and destiny', *SP*, 100 (2003), 315–45.

Laroque, François, *Shakespeare's Festive World* (Cambridge: Cambridge University Press, 1991).

Lepow, Lauren, *Enacting the Sacrament: Counter-Lollardry in the Towneley Cycle* (London and Toronto: Associated University Presses, 1990).

Lerud, Theodore K., *Social and Political Dimensions of the English Corpus Christi Drama* (New York and London: Garland, 1988).

Lloyd, Megan, 'Reflections of a York survivor: the York Cycle and its audience', *RORD*, 39 (2000), 223–35.

Lumiansky R. M., and David Mills, *The Chester Mystery Cycle: Essays and Documents* (Chapel Hill and London: University of North Carolina Press, 1983).

Lyle, M. C., *The Original Identity of the York and Towneley Plays* (Minneapolis: University of Minnesota, 1919).

MacCulloch, Diarmaid, *Reformation: Europe's House Divided, 1490–1700* (London: Penguin Books, 2004).

McDonald, Peter, 'The Towneley Cycle at Toronto', *METh*, 8 (1986), 51–60.

McIntosh, Angus, M. L. Samuels, and M. Benskin, *A Linguistic Atlas of Late Medieval English*, 4 vols (Aberdeen: Aberdeen University Press, 1986).

Mack, Maynard, 'The Second Shepherds play: a reconsideration', *PMLA*, 93 (1978) 78–85.

McKinnell, John, 'The medieval pageant wagons at York: their orientation and height', *ET*, 3 (2000), 79–99.

Manly, W. M., 'Shepherds and prophets: religious unity in the Towneley *Secunda Pastorum*', *PMLA*, 78 (1963), 151–5.

Marrow, J. H., *Passion Iconography in Northern European Art of the Late Middle Ages and Early Renaissance* (Courtrai: Van Ghemmert, 1979).

Marshall, L. E., ' "Sacral Parody" in the *Secunda Pastorum*', *Speculum*, 47 (1972), 720–36.

Marx, C. W., *The Devil's Right and the Redemption in the Literature of Medieval England* (Cambridge: D. S. Brewer, 1995).

Meredith, Peter, 'John Clerke's hand in the York Register', *LSE*, 12 (1981), 245–71.

——, 'The York millers' pageant and the Towneley *Processus Talentorum*', *METh*, 4 (1982), 104–14.

——, 'Original-staging productions of English medieval plays: ideals, evidence and practice', in *Popular Drama in Northern Europe in the Later Middle Ages*, ed. Flemming G. Andersen (Odense: Odense University Press, 1988), pp. 65–100.

——, 'Manuscript, scribe and performance: further looks at the N Town manuscript', in Felicity Riddy (ed.), *Regionalism in Late Medieval Manuscripts and Texts* (Cambridge: D. S. Brewer, 1991), pp. 109–28.

——, 'The Towneley Cycle', in Richard Beadle (ed.), *The Cambridge Companion to Medieval English Theatre* (Cambridge: Cambridge University Press, 1994), pp. 134–62.

Meyers, W. E., *A Figure Given: Typology in the Wakefield Plays* (Pittsburgh: Duquesne University Press, 1968).

Mills, David, 'Characterisation in the English mystery cycles', *METh*, 5 (1983), 5–17.

——, 'Medieval and modern views of drama', in A. C. Cawley, Marion Jones, Peter F. McDonald and David Mills (eds), *The Revels History of Drama in English: Volume I, Medieval Drama* (London and New York: Methuen, 1983), pp. 79–91.

——, 'Religious drama and civic ceremonial', in A. C. Cawley, Marion Jones, Peter F. McDonald and David Mills (eds), *The Revels History of Drama in English: Volume I, Medieval Drama* (London and New York: Methuen, 1983) pp. 152–206.

——, ' "The Towneley Plays" or "The Towneley Cycle"?', *LSE*, 17 (1986), 95–104.

——, *Recycling the Cycle: The City of Chester and its Whitsun Plays* (Toronto: University of Toronto Press, 1998).

Minnis, A. J., *Medieval Theory of Authorship: Scholastic Literary Attitudes in the Later Middle Ages*, second edition (Aldershot: Wildwood House, 1988).

Moore, S., S. B. Beech and H. Whitehall, *Middle English Dialect Characteristics and Dialect Boundaries* (Ann Arbor: University of Michigan Press, 1935).

Morey, J. H., 'Plow laws and sanctuary in medieval England and in the Wakefield *Mactatio Abel*', *SP*, 95 (1998), 41–55.

Morgan, M., ' "High Fraud": paradox and double-plot in the English cycle plays', *Speculum*, 39 (1964), 676–89.

Munson, William F., 'Typology and the Towneley *Isaac*', *RORD*, 11 (1968), 129–39.

——, 'Self, action, and sign in the Towneley and York plays on the baptism of Christ and in Ockhamist salvation theology', in H. Keiper, C. Bode and R. I. Utz (eds), *Nominalism and Literary Discourse* (Amsterdam: Rodopi, 1997), pp. 191–216.

Nelson, Alan H., ' "Sacred" and "Secular" currents in the Towneley play of *Noah*', *Drama Survey*, 3 (1964), 393–401.

——, *The Medieval English Stage: Corpus Christi Pageants and Plays* (Chicago and London: University of Chicago Press, 1974).

Neuss, Paula, 'God and embarrassment', in *Themes in Drama 5: Drama and Religion*, ed. James Redmond (Cambridge: Cambridge University Press, 1983), pp. 241–53.

Nissé, Ruth, 'Staged interpretations: civic rhetoric and Lollard politics in the York plays', *JMEMS*, 28 (1998), 427–52.

——, *Defining Acts: Drama and the Politics of Interpretation in Late Medieval England* (Notre Dame: University of Notre Dame Press, 2005).

Nitecki, K., 'The sacred elements of the secular feast in *Prima Pastorum*', *Medievalia*, 3 (1977), 229–37.

Normington, Katie, 'Giving voice to women: teaching feminist approaches to the mystery plays', *College Literature*, 28 (2001), 130–54.

——, 'Reviving the Royal National Theatre's *The Mysteries*', *RORD*, 40 (2001), 133–47.

——, *Gender and Medieval Drama* (Cambridge: D. S. Brewer, 2004).

—— 'The actor/audience contract in modern restagings of the mystery plays', *RORD*, 43 (2004), 29–37.

Oakden, J. P., *Alliterative Poetry in Middle English: The Dialectical and Metrical Survey* (Manchester: Manchester University Press, 1930).

O'Connell, Michael, *The Idolatrous Eye: Iconoclasm and Theatre in Early Modern England* (Oxford: Oxford University Press, 2000).

Onions, C. T., 'Middle English *Alod, Olod*', *MÆ*, 1.3 (1932), 206–8; 2.1 (1933), 73.

Ostovich, Helen (ed.), *The York Cycle Then and Now: Special Volume, ET*, 3 (Hamilton: McMaster University Press, 2000).

Owst, G. R., *Literature and Pulpit in Medieval England* (Cambridge: Cambridge University Press, 1933).

Palmer, Barbara D., ' "Towneley Plays" or "Wakefield Cycle" revisited', *CD*, 21 (1987–8), 318–48.

——, 'Corpus Christi cycles in Yorkshire: the surviving records', *CD*, 27 (1993), 218–31.

——, 'Early English northern entertainment: patterns and peculiarities', *RORD*, 34 (1995), 167–82.

——, 'Staging the Virgin's body: spectacular effects of annunciation and assumption', *EDAMR*, 21 (1999), 63–80.

——, 'Recycling "The Wakefield Cycle": the records', *RORD*, 41 (2002), 88–130.

——, D. Bevington, Garrett P. J. Epp, R. Blasting, D. Mills and P. Meredith, 'The York Cycle in performance: Toronto and York', *ET*, 1 (1998), 139–69.

Pantin, W. A., *The English Church in the Fourteenth Century* (Cambridge: Cambridge University Press, 1955).

Parker, Roscoe E., 'The reputation of Herod in early English literature', *Speculum*, 8 (1933), 59–67.

Parkes, M. B., 'The influence of the concepts of Ordinatio and Compilatio on the development of the book', in his *Scribes, Scripts and Readers: Studies in the Communication, Presentation and Dissemination of Medieval Texts* (London: Hambledon Press, 1991), pp. 25–69.

Parry, David, 'The York mystery cycle at Toronto', *METh*, 1 (1979), 19–31.

Paull, M., 'The figure of Mahomet in the Towneley Cycle', *CD*, 6 (1972–3), 187–204.

Paxson, J. J., 'The structure of anachronism in the middle English mystery plays', *Medievalia*, 18 (1995), 321–40.

——, L. J. Clopper and S. Tomasch (eds), *The Performance of Middle English Culture: Essays on Chaucer and the Drama in Honor of Martin Stevens* (Cambridge: D. S. Brewer, 1998).

Pearson, Lu Emily, 'Isolable lyrics of the mystery plays', *ELH*, 3 (1936), 228–52.

Pietropoli, Cecilia, 'The characterisation of evil in the Towneley plays', *METh*, 11 (1989), 85–93.

——, *Il teatro dei Miracoli e delle Moralità* (Naples: Liguori, 1996).

Potkay, Monica Bzezinsky, and Regula Meyer Evitt, *Minding the Body: Women and Literature in the Middle Ages* (New York: Twayne, 1997).

Prosser, Eleanor, *Drama and Religion in the English Mystery Plays* (Stanford: Stanford University Press, 1961).

Purdon, Liam O., *The Wakefield Master's Dramatic Art: A Drama of Spiritual Understanding* (Gainesville, FL: University of Florida Press, 2003).

Rastall, Richard, 'Music in the Cycle' in Lumiansky and Mills, *The Chester Mystery Cycle: Essays and Documents*, (Chapel Hill and London: University of North Carolina Press, 1983) pp. 111–64.

——, 'Music in the cycle plays', in Marianne G. Briscoe and John C. Coldewey (eds), *Contexts for Early English Drama*, pp. 192–218.

——, *The Heaven Singing: Music in Early English Religious Drama: 1* (Cambridge: D. S. Brewer, 1996).

Remly, L., '*Deus Caritas*: the Christian message of the *Secunda Pastorum*', *Neuphilologische Mitteilungen*, 72 (1971), 742–8.

Richardson, C., 'Medieval English and French shepherds plays', in Twycross (ed.), *Festive Drama*, pp. 259–69.

Ricke, Joseph M., 'Parody, performance, and the "Ultimate" meaning of Noah's shrew', *Medievalia*, 18 (1995), 263–81.

Robinson, John W., 'The late medieval cult of Jesus and the mystery plays', *PMLA*, 80 (1965), 508–14.

——, *Studies in Fifteenth-Century Stagecraft* (Kalamazoo: Medieval Institute Publications, 1991).

Rogerson, Margaret, 'The medieval plough team on stage: judicial process as satiric theme in the Wakefield *Mactatio Abel*', *CD*, 28 (1994), 182–200.

——, 'Raging in the streets of medieval York', *ET*, 3 (2000), 105–25.

——, '"Everybody got their brown dress": mystery plays for the millennium', *New Theatre Quarterly*, 17 (2001), 123–40.

Roney, L., 'The Wakefield *First* and *Second Shepherds Plays* as complements in psychology and parody', *Speculum*, 58 (1983), 715–20.

Rose, Martial, and Julia Hedgecoe, *Stories in Stone* (London: Herbert Press, 1997).

Ross, E. M., *The Grief of God: Images of the Suffering of Jesus in Late Medieval England* (Oxford: Oxford University Press, 1997).

Ross, L. J., 'A study of the language of the Wakefield group in Towneley', (Unpublished Ph.D. thesis, Chicago: University of Chicago, 1933).

—— , 'Symbol and structure in the *Secunda Pastorum*', in Jerome Taylor and Alan H. Nelson (eds), *Medieval English Drama: Essays Critical and Contextual* (Chicago and London: University of Chicago Press, 1972), pp. 177–211.

Runnalls, Graham A., *Les Mystères Français Imprimés* (Geneva: Droz, 1999).

Salter, Elizabeth, 'Ludolphus of Saxony and his English translators', *MÆ*, 33 (1964), 26–35.

—— , *Nicolas Love's "Myrrour of the Blessed Lyf of Jesu Christ"*, Analecta Cartusiana 10 (Salzburg: Institut für Engliche Sprache und Literatur, 1974).

Sawyer, Karen E., 'The work of the Wakefield Master in the Towneley mystery cycle', (Unpublished M. Phil. thesis, Oxford: University of Oxford, 1993).

—— , 'Saints in *The Second Shepherds' Play*', *EDAMR*, 24 (2001), 22–33.

Schell, Edgar T., 'The distinctions of the Towneley *Abraham*', *MLQ*, 41 (1980), 315–27.

—— , 'The limits of typology in the Wakefield Master's *Processus Noe*', *CD*, 25 (1991), 168–87.

Schmidt, G. D., '*Vides Festinare Pastores*: the medieval artistic vision of shepherding and the manipulation of cultural expectations in the *Secunda Pastorum*', *Neophilologus*, 76 (1992), 290–304.

Scoville, Chester N., *Saints and the Audience in Middle English Biblical Drama* (Toronto: University of Toronto Press, 2004).

Sheingorn, Pamela, 'The moment of resurrection in the Corpus Christi plays', *Medievale et Humanistica*, 11 (1982), 111–29.

Simpson, James, *Reform and Cultural Revolution*, Oxford English Literary History, Volume 2: 1350–1547 (Oxford: Oxford University Press, 2002).

Sinangolou, L., 'The Christ child as sacrifice: a medieval tradition and the Corpus Christi plays', *Speculum*, 48 (1973), 491–509.

Smith, J. H., 'Another allusion to costume in the work of the "Wakefield Master"', *PMLA*, 52 (1937), 901–2.

Smith, Lucy Toulmin, 'The date of some Wakefield borrowings from York', *PMLA*, 53 (1938), 595–600.

Smyser, H. M., and T. B. Stroup, 'Analogues to the Mak story', *Journal of American Folklore*, 47 (1934), 378–81.

Soule, L. W., 'Performing the mysteries: demystification, story-telling and over-acting like the devil', *EMD*, 1 (1997), 219–31.

Spector, Stephen, 'The composition and development of an eclectic manuscript: Cotton Vespasian D VIII', *LSE*, 9 (1997), 62–83.

Speirs, John, 'The mystery cycle: some Towneley Cycle plays', *Scrutiny*, 18 (1951–2), 86–117, 246–65.

Sponsler, C., 'The culture of the spectator: conformity and resistance to medieval performances', *Theatre Journal*, 44 (1992), 15–29.

—— , *Drama and Resistance: Bodies, Goods and Theatricality in Late Medieval England* (Minneapolis: University of Minnesota Press, 1997).

Stearns, M., 'Gyll as Mary and Eve: order and disorder in *Secunda Pastorum*', *FCS*, 15 (1989), 295–304.

Steinberg, Leo, *The Sexuality of Christ in Renaissance Art and in Modern Oblivion* (New York: Random, 1983).

Stevens, Martin, 'The accuracy of the Towneley scribe', *HLQ*, 22 (1958), 1–9.

——, Review of A. C. Cawley, *The Wakefield Pageants in the Towneley Cycle*, *Speculum*, 34 (1959), 453–5.

——, 'The composition of the Towneley *Talents* play: a linguistic examination', *JEGP*, 58 (1959), 423–33.

——, 'The dramatic setting of the Wakefield *Annunciation*', *PMLA*, 81 (1966), 99–119.

——, 'The staging of the Wakefield plays', *RORD*, 11 (1968), 115–28.

——, 'The missing parts of the Towneley Cycle', *Speculum*, 45 (1970), 254–65.

——, 'Illusion and reality in the medieval drama', *College English*, 32 (1971), 448–64.

——, 'The York Cycle: from procession to play', *LSE*, 6 (1972), 37–62; and 'Postscript', 113–15.

——, 'The manuscript of the Towneley plays: its history and editions', *PBSA*, 67 (1973), 231–44.

——, 'The theatre of the world: a study in medieval dramatic form', *Chaucer Review*, 7 (1973), 234–49.

——, 'Language as theme in the Wakefield plays', *Speculum*, 52 (1977), 100–17.

——, 'Did the Wakefield Master write a nine-line stanza?', *CD*, 15 (1981), 99–119.

——, *Four Middle English Mystery Cycles* (Princeton: Princeton University Press, 1987).

——, 'The Towneley plays manuscript: *Compilatio* and *Ordinatio*', *Text*, 5 (1991), 157–73.

——, 'Herod as carnival king in the medieval biblical drama', *Mediaevalia*, 18 (1995), 43–66.

—— and J. Poxson, 'The fool in the Wakefield plays', *Studies in Iconography*, 13 (1992), 48–79.

Storm, M., 'Uxor and Alison: Noah's wife in the flood plays and Chaucer's Wife of Bath', *MLQ*, 48 (1987), 303–19.

Sutherland, S., '"Not or I see more neede": the wife of Noah in the Chester, York and Towneley cycles', in W. R. Elton and W. B. Long (eds), *Shakespeare and the Dramatic Tradition* (Newark: University of Delaware Press, 1989), pp. 181–93.

Swanson, R. N., 'Passion and practice: the social and ecclesiastical implications of passion devotion in the late Middle Ages', in A. A. MacDonald, H. N. B. Ridderbos and R. M. Schlusemann (eds), *The Broken Body: Passion Devotion in Late Medieval Culture* (Groningen: Forsten, 1998), pp. 1–30.

Tasioulas, J. A., 'Between doctrine and domesticity: the portrayal of Mary in the N-Town plays', in Diane Watt (ed.), *Medieval Women in their Communities* (Cardiff: University of Wales Press, 1997), pp. 222–45.

Taylor, Jerome, 'The dramatic structure of the middle English Corpus Christi, or cycle, plays', in Taylor and Nelson (eds), *Medieval English Drama: Essays Critical and Contextual*, pp. 148–56.

—— and Alan H. Nelson (eds), *Medieval English Drama: Essays Critical and Contextual* (Chicago and London: University of Chicago Press, 1972).

Templeton, L., 'Cast them in canvas: carnival and the *Second Shepherds' Play*', *Medieval Perspectives*, 16 (2001), 151–64.

Thomas, Keith, *Religion and the Decline of Magic* (London: Weidenfeld and Nicholson, 1970).

Tilley, M. P., *A Dictionary of the Proverbs in England in the Sixteenth and Seventeenth Centuries* (Ann Arbor: University of Michigan Press, 1950).

Tolmie, Jane, 'Mrs Noah and didactic abuses', *ET*, 5 (2002), 11–35.

Travis, Peter W., 'The social body of the dramatic Christ in medieval England', in Albert H. Tricomi (ed.), *Early Drama to 1600, Acta XIII* (Binghamton: State University of New York, 1987), pp. 17–36.

——, 'The semiotics of Christ's body in the English cycles', in R. K. Emmerson (ed.), *Approaches to Teaching Medieval English Drama* (New York: Modern Language Association of America, 1990), pp. 67–78.

Trusler, Margaret, 'Some textual notes based on an examination of the Manuscript', *PQ*, 14 (1935), 301–6.

——, 'The language of the Wakefield playwright', *SP*, 33 (1936), 15–39.

Twycross, Meg, 'The Toronto passion play', *METh*, 3 (1981), 122–31.

—— (ed.), *Festive Drama* (Cambridge: D. S. Brewer, 1996).

——, 'Forget the 4.30a.m. start: recovering a palimpsest in the York *Ordo paginarum*', *METh*, 25 (2003), 98–152.

Velz, John W., 'Fox, Bull and Lion in the Towneley *Coliphizacio*', *EDAMR*, 14 (1991), 1–10.

Vinter, Donna Smith, 'Didactic characterisation – the Towneley *Abraham*', *CD*, 14 (1980), 117–36.

Walker, J. W., 'The burgess court, Wakefield: 1533, 1554, 1556, and 1579', *Yorkshire Archaeological Society Records Series*, lxxiv (1929), 16–32.

Wann, Louis, 'A new examination of the manuscript of the Towneley plays', *PMLA*, 43 (1928), 137–52.

Watt, Homer A., 'The dramatic unity of the *Secunda Pastorum*', in *Essays and Studies in Honor of Carleton Brown*, (New York: New York University Press, 1940), pp. 158–66.

Weimann, Robert, *Shakespeare and the Popular Tradition in the Theater*, ed. Robert Schwartz (Baltimore and London: Johns Hopkins University Press, 1978).

West, G. A., 'An analysis of the Towneley play *Lazarus*', *PQ*, 56 (1977), 320–8.

White, Eileen, 'Places to hear the play in York', *ET*, 3 (2000), 49–78.

Whitfield White, Paul, 'Reforming mysteries' end: a new look at Protestant intervention in English provincial drama', *JMEMS*, 19 (1999), 121–47.

Whiting, Bartlett J., 'An analogue of the Mak story', *Speculum*, 7 (1932), 552.

——, *Proverbs, Sentences and Proverbial Writings* (Cambridge, Mass.: Harvard University Press, 1968).

——, *Proverbs in the Earlier English Drama* (Cambridge, Mass.: Harvard University Press, 1938, repr. New York: Octagon, 1969).

Williams, Arnold, *The Characterization of Pilate in the Towneley Plays* (East Lansing: Michigan State College Press, 1950).

——, 'Typology and the Cycle plays: some criteria', *Speculum*, 43 (1968), 677–84.

Woolf, Rosemary, 'The effect of typology on the English medieval plays of Abraham and Isaac', *Speculum*, 32 (1957), 805–25.

——, *The English Religious Lyric in the Middle Ages* (Oxford: Clarendon Press, 1968).

——, *The English Mystery Plays* (London: Routledge, 1972).

Wright, J., *The English Dialect Dictionary*, 7 vols, (Oxford: Oxford University Press, 1923).

Young, Karl, *The Drama of the Medieval Church*, 2 vols, (Oxford: Clarendon Press, 1933).

Zimbardo, R. A., 'A generic approach to the first and second Shepherd plays', *FCS*, 13 (1988), 79–89.

# Index

York Cycle, links with Towneley Cycle
   7–8, 10, *24*, 25, 231; *Abel* 174;
   *Ascension* 169; Christ-centred
   episodes 212; dialect 36–9, *38*;
   *Doctors* 27, 51, 146; *Flight into
   Egypt* 31, 50; groups of characters
   131; *Harrowing* 26, 27, 166;
   *Judgement* 27–8, 170–1; *Magi* 179;
   minor correspondences 29–35;

*Offering of the Magi* 49; *Pharaoh*
   26; Pilate 193; *Remorse of Judas*
   55; *Resurrection* 28–9, 166;
   *Scourging* 74–5, 147, 150; soldiers
   and torturers 196; stage directions
   90–1, 242n3; tyrants' boasts 182;
   *see also* York Cycle
Young, Karl 178